Socratic Epistemology
Explorations of Knowledge-Seeking by Questioning

Socratic Epistemology challenges most current work in epistemology—which deals with the evaluation and justification of information already acquired—by discussing instead the more important problem of how knowledge is acquired in the first place.

Jaakko Hintikka's model of information-seeking is the old Socratic method of questioning, which has been generalized and brought up to date through the logical theory of questions and answers that he has developed. Hintikka argues that the quest by philosophers for a definition of knowledge is ill-conceived and that the entire notion of knowledge should be replaced by the concept of information. And he further offers an analysis of the different meanings of the concept of information and of their interrelations. The result is a new and illuminating approach to the field of epistemology.

Jaakko Hintikka is an internationally renowned philosopher known as the principal architect of game-theoretical semantics and of the interrogative approach to inquiry, and as one of the architects of distributive normal forms, possible-worlds semantics, tree methods, infinitely deep logics, and present-day-theory of inductive generalization. Now a professor of philosophy at Boston University, he is the author of more than thirty books and has received a number of honors, most recently the Rolf Schock Prize for Logic and Philosophy, for his pioneering contributions to logical analysis for modal concepts, in particular the concepts of knowledge and belief.

Socratic Epistemology

Explorations of Knowledge-Seeking by Questioning

JAAKKO HINTIKKA

Boston University

CAMBRIDGE
UNIVERSITY PRESS

CAMBRIDGE UNIVERSITY PRESS
Cambridge, New York, Melbourne, Madrid, Cape Town, Singapore, São Paulo, Delhi

Cambridge University Press
32 Avenue of the Americas, New York, NY 10013-2473, USA

www.cambridge.org
Information on this title: www.cambridge.org/9780521851015

First published 2007

Printed in the United States of America

A catalog record for this publication is available from the British Library.

Library of Congress Cataloging in Publication Data
Hintikka, Jaakko, 1929–
Socratic epistemology : explorations of knowledge-seeking by questioning /
Jaakko Hintikka.
p. cm.
Includes bibliographical references and index.
ISBN 978-0-521-85101-5 (hardback) – ISBN 978-0-521-61651-5 (pbk.)
1. Knowledge, Theory of. I. Title.
BD161.H536 2007
121–dc22 2006102664

ISBN 978-0-521-85101-5 hardback
ISBN 978-0-521-61651-5 paperback

Contents

Acknowledgments

I would like to thank the original publishers of Chapters 1, 2, 3, 4, 6, 7, 9, and 10 for kindly granting me permission to reprint my previously published essays.

Chapter 1 has not appeared in English before. It was originally published in French as "Une epistemologie sans connaisance et sans croyance" in the series of pamphlets *Journée de la philosophie*, No. 2, Jaakko Hintikka, "Une epistemologie," UNESCO, 2004.

Chapter 2 first appeared under the title "What Is Abduction? The Fundamental Problem of Contemporary Epistemology" in *Transactions of the Charles Peirce Society*, vol. 34 (1998), pp. 503–533. It is reprinted here with additions.

Chapter 3 first appeared in Vincent F. Hendricks et al., editors, *Knowledge Contributors*, Kluwer Academic Publishers, Dordrecht (2003), pp. 33–56. Copyright © 2003. Reprinted with kind permission of Springer Science+Business Media.

Chapter 4 is a revised version of the essay "Presuppositions of Questions, Presuppositions of Inquiry," forthcoming in *Proceedings of the 2001 IIP Annual Meeting*, Matti Sintonen, editor, Springer, Dordrecht. Reprinted with kind permission of Springer Science+Business Media.

Chapter 5 is new.

Chapter 6, written jointly with John Symons, first appeared under the title "Systems of Visual Identification in Neuroscience: Lessons from Epistemic Logic," in *Philosophy of Science*, vol. 70 (2003), pp. 89–104. John Symons is an assistant professor of philosophy at The University of Texas, El Paso.

Chapter 7 is new. Some of the material first appeared in Jaakko Hintikka and Ilpo Halonen, "Interpolation as Explanation," *Philosophy of Science*, vol. 66 (1999), pp. 779–805.

Chapter 8 is new.

Chapter 9 first appeared in *Synthese*, vol. 140 (2004), pp. 25–35. Copyright © 2004. Reprinted with kind permission of Springer Science+Business Media.

Chapter 10 first appeared in *Synthese*, vol. 145 (2005), pp. 169–175. Copyright © 2005. Reprinted with kind permission of Springer Science+Business Media.

In writing the different chapters of this book, and before that in thinking the thoughts that have gone into them, I have incurred more intellectual debts than I can recount here. The earliest is to Dr. Einari Merikallio, the headmaster of my high school, who was the most masterful practitioner of the Socratic method of questioning I have ever witnessed.

On a more mundane level, there is the old joke answer to the question: Who *really* did write the works of great scholars? The answer: Their secretaries, of course. In the case of this book, this answer is even more appropriate than in most other instances. The book would not have been possible without the industry, patience, judgment, and diplomacy of my secretary, Ms. Lynne Sullivan. My greatest and most direct debt is to her.

Ms. Sullivan's services were made possible by support from Boston University. I also appreciate whole-heartedly the patience and expertise of the editors of Cambridge University Press, and above all the decision of the Press to accept this book for publication.

Introduction

If Thomas Kuhn had not sworn to me a long time ago that he would never again use the p-word, I would have been tempted to introduce my viewpoint in this volume by saying that contemporary epistemology draws its inspiration from an incorrect paradigm that I am trying to overthrow. Or, since the individuation of paradigms is notoriously difficult, I might have said instead that our present-day theory of knowledge rests on a number of misguided and misguiding paradigms. One of them is in any case a defensive stance concerning the task of epistemology. This stance used to be expressed by speaking of contexts of discovery and contexts of justification. The former were thought of as being inaccessible to rational epistemological and logical analysis. For no rules can be given for genuine discoveries, it was alleged. Only contexts of justification can be subjects of epistemological theorizing. There cannot be any logic of discovery, as the sometime slogan epitomized this stance—or is it a paradigm? Admittedly, in the last few decades, sundry "friends of discovery" have cropped up in different parts of epistemology. (See, for example, Kleiner 1993.) However, the overwhelming bulk of serious systematic theorizing in epistemology pertains to the justification of the information we already have, not to the discovery of new knowledge. The recent theories of "belief revision"—that is, of how to modify our beliefs in view of new evidence—do not change this situation essentially, for they do not take into account how that new evidence has been obtained, nor do they tell us how still further evidence could be obtained.

The contrast between contexts of discovery and contexts of justification originated from the philosophy of science rather than from the traditional theory of knowledge. In the received epistemology, the same preoccupation with justification appears in the form of questions concerning the concept of knowledge, especially its definition, as well in the form of sundry theories of confirmation or other kinds of justification.

Furthermore, the same defensive, not to say insecure, attitude pervades the epistemology of the deductive sciences. It has even distorted the terminology of contemporary logic. For instance, what does a so-called rule of inference have to do with the actual drawing of inferences? If you are given twenty-one potential premises, do the "rules of inference" tell you which conclusions you should draw from them? What conclusions a rational person would draw? To what conclusions would "the laws of thought" lead you from these premises? Or, descriptively, what conclusions do people usually draw from them? The right answer is: None of the above. Logic texts' "rules of inference" only tell you which inferences you may draw from the given premises without making a mistake. They are not rules either in the descriptive sense or in the prescriptive sense. They are merely permissive. They are guidelines for avoiding fallacies. Recently, some philosophers have been talking about "virtue epistemology." But in practice, the virtues that most epistemologists admire in this day and age are in fact Victorian rather than Greek. They are not concerned with true epistemological virtue in the sense of epistemological excellence, but only with how not to commit logical sins, how, so to speak, to preserve one's logical or epistemological virtue. Logical excellence—virtue in the sense that is the first cousin of virtuosity—means being able to draw informative conclusions, not just safe ones.

One main thrust of the results presented in this volume is that this defensive picture of the prospects of epistemology is not only inaccurate but radically distorted. A logic of discovery is possible because it is already actual. There exists a logic of pure discovery, a logic that is not so-called by courtesy, but a logic that is little more than the good old deductive logic viewed strategically. In contrast, there does not exist, and there cannot exist, a fully self-contained theory of justification independent of theories of discovery. If this change of viewpoint is not a "paradigm shift" in the Kuhnian sense, it is hard to see what could be.

But paradigm shifts are not implemented simply by deciding to do so, by merely shaking the kaleidoscope, so to speak, even though some seem to think so. In actual science, they require a genuinely new theory or a new method. In the case of the present volume, the "new" method is in a sense as old as Western epistemology. I am construing knowledge acquisition as a process of questioning, not unlike the Socratic *elenchus*. I have been impressed by Socrates' method as strongly as was Plato, who turned it into a universal method of philosophical argumentation and philosophical training in the form of the questioning games practiced in his Academy. They were in turn systematized and theorized about by Aristotle, who thought of the questioning processes among other uses as the method of reaching the first premises of the different sciences. (See Hintikka 1996.)

In a sense, even the main formal difference between Plato's dialogical games and my interrogative ones had already been introduced by Aristotle. He was as competitive as the next Greek, and hence was keenly interested in winning his questioning games. Now any competent trial lawyer knows what the most important feature of successful cross-examination is: being able to predict witnesses' answers. Aristotle quickly discovered that certain answers were indeed perfectly predictable. In our terminology, they are the answers that are logically implied by the witness' earlier responses. By studying such predictable answers in their own right in relation to their antecedents, Aristotle became the founder of deductive logic. Since such predictable answers are independent of the answerer, they can be considered *ad argumentum*—that is to say, by reference to the structure of the argument only. They might even be provided by the questioner rather than by an actual answerer. Hence, in my interrogative model, logical inference steps are separated from interrogative steps and are thought of as being carried out by the inquirer. It is historically noteworthy, however, that Aristotle still thought of the entire epistemological process, including deductive inferences, as being performed in the form of question-answer dialogues. (For the interrogative approach to epistemology, see Hintikka 1999.)

The general applicability of the interrogative model admits of a kind of transcendental deduction. This argument is sketched in the essay "Abduction—Inference, Conjecture, or an Answer to a Question?" (Chapter 2 in this volume). The format of the argument is simple. Let us assume that each step in an inquiry allows for rational evaluation. If so, for each step that introduces new information into the argument, it must be specified where that novel information comes from. Furthermore, it must be known what other responses the same source of information might have provided, and if so, with what probabilities, what other "oracles" the inquirer could have consulted, what their responses might have been, and so on. But if all of this is known, we might as well consider the new information as a reply or an answer to a question addressed to a source of information—that is to a source of answers. It can also be argued that the role of questions in the interrogative model is closely similar to the role of abduction according to C. S. Peirce, even though abduction has been repeatedly and misleadingly considered as inference to the best explanation.

An important aspect of this general applicability of the interrogative model is its ability to handle uncertain answers–that is, answers that may be false. The model can be extended to this case simply by allowing the inquirer to tentatively disregard ("bracket") answers that are dubious. The decision as to when the inquirer should do so is understood as a strategic problem, not as a part of the definition of the questioning game. Of course, all the subsequent answers that depend on the bracketed one must then also be bracketed, together with their logical consequences. Equally obviously, further inquiry might lead the inquirer to reinstate ("unbracket") a previously bracketed answer. This means thinking of interrogative inquiry as a self-corrective process. It likewise means considering discovery and justification as aspects of one and the same process. This is certainly in keeping with scientific and epistemological practice. There is no reason to think that the interrogative model does not offer a framework also for the study of this self-correcting character of inquiry.

From this, it follows that much of the methodology of epistemology and of the methodology of science will be tantamount to the strategic principles of bracketing. From this, it is in turn seen that a study of uncertain answers is an enormously complicated enterprise, difficult to achieve an overview of. It nevertheless promises useful insights. A sense of this usefulness of the interrogative model in dealing with the problems of methodology and inference can perhaps be obtained by considering suitable special problems of independent interest. The two brief essays, "A Fallacious Fallacy" and "Omitting Data—Ethical or Strategic Problem" (Chapters 9 and 10), illustrate this purpose. The former deals with the so-called conjunctive fallacy. This allegedly mistaken but apparently hardwired mode of human probabilistic reasoning is a prize specimen in the famous theory of cognitive fallacies proposed by Amos Tversky and Daniel Kahneman. The interrogative viewpoint helps to show that this would-be fallacy is in reality not fallacious at all, but instead reveals a subtle problem in the Bayesian approach to probabilistic reasoning. This result cries out for more discussion than can be devoted to the problem of cognitive fallacies here. Are the other Tversky and Kahneman "fallacies" perhaps equally dubious?

Omitting observational or experimental data is often considered a serious breach of the ethics of science. In the second brief essay just mentioned, it is pointed out, as is indeed fairly obvious from the interrogative point of view, that such a view is utterly simplistic. Even though data are sometimes omitted for fraudulent purposes, there is per se nothing ethically or methodologically wrong about omitting data. Such a procedure can even be required by optimal strategies of reasoning, depending on circumstances.

But if the basic idea of the interrogative approach to inquiry is this simple and this old, it might seem unlikely that any new insights could be reached by its means. Surely its interest has been exhausted long ago, one might expect to find. The interrogative approach has in fact been used repeatedly in the course of the history of Western philosophy, for instance in the form of the medieval *obligationes* games and in the guise of the "Logic of questions and answers" in which R. G. Collingwood saw the gist of the historical method. However, Collingwood's phrase (taken over later by Hans-Georg Gadamer) indirectly shows why the *elenchus* idea has not generated full-fledged epistemological theories. Collingwood's "logic" cannot be so-called by the standards of contemporary logical theory. In the absence of a satisfactory grasp of the logical behavior of questions and answers, the idea of "inquiry as inquiry" could not serve as a basis of successful epistemological theorizing. Such a grasp has only been reached in the last several years. Admittedly, there have been much earlier attempts at a logic of questions and answers, also known as "erotetic logic." But they did not provide satisfactory accounts of the most important questions concerning questions, such as the questions about the relation of a question to its conclusive (desired, intended) answers, about the logical form of different kinds of questions, about their presuppositions, and so on. One might be tempted to blame these relative failures to a neglect of the epistemic character of questions. For in some fairly obvious sense, a direct question is nothing more and nothing less than a request for information, a request by the questioner to be put into a certain epistemic state. Indeed, the specification of this epistemic state, known as the desideratum of the question in question, is the central notion in much of the theory of questions and answers, largely because it captures much of the essentially (discursive) notions of question and answer in terms of ordinary epistemic logic.

But the time was not yet ripe for an interrogative theory of inquiry. As is pointed out in "Second-Generation Epistemic Logic and its General Significance" (Chapter 3), initially modern epistemic logic was not up to the task of providing a general theory of questions and answers. It provided an excellent account of the presuppositions and conclusiveness conditions of simple *wh*-questions (*who, what, where*, etc.) and propositional questions, but not of more complicated questions, for instance of experimental questions concerning the dependence of a variable on another. However, I discovered that they could reach the desired generality by indicating explicitly that a logical operator (or some other kind of notion) was independent of another one. Technically considered, it was game-theoretical semantics that first offered to logicians and logical analysts a tool for handling this crucial notion of independence in the form of informational independence. These developments form the plot of Chapter 3.

The interrogative model helps to extend the basic concepts and insights concerning questions to inquiry in general. Some of these insights are examined in the essay "Presuppositions and Other Limitations of Inquiry" (Chapter 4). They even turn out to throw light on the earlier history of questioning methods, including Socrates' ironic claim to ignorance and Collingwood's alleged notion of ultimate presupposition.

Even more radical conclusions ensue from an analysis of the "presuppositions of answers," which are known as conclusiveness conditions on answers. They can be said to define the relation of a question to its conclusive answers. They are dealt with in the essay "The place of the *a priori* in epistemology" (Chapter 5). It quickly turns out that the conclusiveness conditions on answers to purely empirical questions have conceptual and hence *a priori* components. Roughly speaking, the questioner must know, or must be brought to know, what it is that the given reply refers to. For a paradigmatic example, nature's response to an experimental question concerning the dependence of a variable on another can be thought of as a function-in-extension—in other words, as something like a curve on graph paper. But such a reply truly answers the dependence question only if the experimental inquirer comes to know what the function is that governs the dependence between variables—in other (mathematical) words, which function the curve represents. Without such knowledge, the experimental question has not been fully answered. But this collateral knowledge is not empirical, but mathematical. Hence, *a priori* mathematical knowledge is an indispensable ingredient even of a purely experimental science. Among other consequences, this result should close for good the spurious issue of the (in)dispensability of mathematics in science.

Since experimental questions are a typical vehicle of inductive inquiry, the entire problem of induction assumes a new complexion. Inductive reasoning has not just one aim, but two. It aims not only at the "empirical generalization" codified in a function-in-extension or in a curve, however accurate, but also at the mathematical identification of this curve. In practice, these two aims are pursued in tandem. Their interplay is not dealt with in traditional accounts of induction, even though its role is very real. For instance, if the mathematical form of the dependence-codifying function is known, an inductive inference reduces to the task of estimating the parameters characterizing the function in question. This explains the prevalence of such estimation in actual scientific inquiry.

In another kind of case, the task of identifying the mathematical function in question has already been accomplished within the limits of observational accuracy for several intervals of argument values. Their induction becomes the task of combining several partial generalizations (and reconciling them as special cases of a wider generalization). This kind of induction turns out to have been the dominating sense of *inductio* and *epagoge* in earlier discussions, including the use of such terms by Aristotle and by Newton. (See Hintikka 1993.)

Thus, conclusiveness conditions are seen to play a pivotal role in the epistemology of questioning. They are also a key to the logic of knowledge. They express *wh*-knowledge (knowing *who, what, where*, etc.) as distinguished from knowing *that*, and show how the former construction can be expressed in terms of the latter. However, from this expressibility it does not follow that the truth conditions of expressions such as knowing *who* also reduce to those governing knowing *that*. They do not. The underlying reason is that the measuring of quantifiers depends on the criteria of identification between different epistemically relevant scenarios (possible worlds, possible occasions of use) as distinguished from criteria of reference. For this reason, we have to distinguish an identification system from a reference system in the full semantics of any one language, be it a formal language or our actual working language— called by Tarski "colloquial language." I have argued for the vital importance of this distinction in numerous essays, some of which are reprinted in Hintikka (1999).

The unavoidability of this distinction is highlighted by the intriguing fact that in our actual logico-linguistic practice, we are using two different identification systems in a partnership with one and the same reference system all the time. This dichotomy means a dichotomy between two kinds of quantifiers, public and perspectival ones.

This dichotomy and its expressions in formal and natural languages have been explained in my earlier papers. However, what has not been fully spelled out is the even more intriguing fact that the two identification systems are manifested neuroscientifically as two cognitive systems. This insight is spelled out and discussed in the essay (written jointly with John Symons, Chapter 6 of this volume) entitled "Systems of Visual Identification and Neuroscience: Lessons from Epistemic Logic" in the case of visual cognition. These two systems are sometimes known as the *what* system and the *where* system. It is known from neuroscience that they are different not only functionally but anatomically. They are implemented in two different areas of the brain with different pathways leading to them from the eye. Symons and I point out the conceptual distinction that manifests itself as the difference between the two cognitive systems and the consequences of this insight for neuroscience.

This opens up an unexpected and unexpectedly concrete field for logical and epistemological analysis. An epistemologist can tell, for instance, what was conceptually speaking wrong with Oliver Sacks's "Man Who Mistook His Wife for a Hat." (Sacks 1985.) Such possibilities of conceptual clarification are not restricted to systems of visual cognition and their disturbances, but occur *mutatis mutandis* in the phenomena of memory, and might very well be offered also by such phenomena as dyslexia and autism.

The most important aspects of epistemology illuminated by the interrogative model are likely to be the strategic ones. Considering inquiry as a question-answer sequence enables us to theorize about entire processes of inquiry, including strategies and tactics of questioning, not only about what to do in some one given situation. Aristotle already had a keen eye on the tactics of questioning. The strategic viewpoint can be dramatized by considering interrogative inquiry as a game. However, an explicit use of game-theoretical concepts and conceptualizations is not necessary for most of the philosophical conclusions, even though it can be most instructive for the purpose of conceptual analysis.

In fact, in many goal-directed processes, including the strategic games considered in the mathematical theory of games, one can distinguish the definitory rules of the game from its strategic rules or strategic principles. The former define a game, by specifying what is permissible in it—for example, what are the legitimate moves of chess. Such rules do not by themselves tell a player anything about what he or she (or it, if the player is a computer) should do in order to play well, to increase one's chances of reaching the goal. Such advice is what the strategic rules of a game provide to a player. We can thus express the earlier point concerning the merely permissive character of the so-called rules of inference of logic by saying that such rules are merely definitory, serving to specify what is permitted in the "game" of deduction.

Another point that can be made here is that even though one can distinguish in interrogative games definitory rules governing deductive "moves" from definitory rules governing question-answer steps, in the strategic rules of such games one cannot likewise consider deductive rules and interrogative rules apart from each other.

As has been to some extent spelled out in my earlier work (largely collected in Hintikka 1999), the strategic viewpoint necessitates radical changes in philosophers' ideas of what the task of epistemology is and how it can be achieved. For one thing, it is the strategic viewpoint that enables us to uncover the logic of discovery mentioned earlier. It turns out that in the case of pure discovery—that is, in the case where all answers are known to be true—the choice of the optimal question to be asked is essentially the same as the choice of the optimal premise to draw an inference from in a purely deductive situation. Thus, Sherlock Holmes was right: Strategically speaking, all good reasoning consists of "deductions," if only in the case of pure discovery.

But we can say more than that contexts of discovery can be theorized about epistemologically and logically, notwithstanding the misguided traditional paradigm. It is contexts of justification that cannot be studied alone, independently of the task of discovery. For discovery and justification have to be accomplished both through the same process of inquiry as inquiry. Hence the strategies of this process have to serve both purposes. There are no separate strategies of justification in isolation from strategies of discovery. For instance, reaching the truth early, even by means of a risky line of thought, may subsequently open previously unavailable avenues of justification.

Some other repercussions affect more directly the nitty-gritty detailed work of epistemologists. Typically inquiry is thought of by them in terms of particular steps of the epistemological process. For instance, the justification of the results of empirical inquiry is assumed to depend on the justifiability of the several steps that have led to that conclusion—for example, in terms of what "warrants" there are to back each of them up. Now, whatever else we may learn from game theory, it is that a player's performance can be judged absolutely only in terms of his or her (or its, if the player is a team, a computer, or nature) entire strategies. (The term "strategy" should here be taken in the strong sense used in game theory, roughly amounting to a completely determined strategy.) As a game theorist would put it, utilities can in the first place be associated with strategies, not with individual moves.

From this it follows that no epistemological theory can tell the whole story that deals only with rules for particular moves or with the epistemic evaluation of a single cognitive situation. Such a theory may yield us truths and nothing but truths, but it does not tell the whole truth. This limitation obviously applies, among other conceptualizations, to the rules of inductive inference, to the rules of belief revision, and to all theories of inferential "warrants." But it applies even more centrally to most of the epistemological discussion concerning the concept of knowledge. For the typical question concerning it in traditional epistemology is whether a given body of evidence justifies bestowing on a certain belief the honorific title "knowledge." While such a question perhaps makes sense, its place in a realistic theory of knowledge and knowledge acquisition is marginal, and the question itself, glorified by philosophers as a question concerning the definition of knowledge, may not be answerable in general terms.

The overall picture of the structure of the epistemological enterprise at which we thus arrive is outlined in the central essay, "Epistemology without Knowledge and without Belief" (Chapter 1). If we review the questioning process through which we obtain our knowledge and justify it and inventory the concepts employed in the process, we find all the notions of a logic of questions and answers, the notions of ordinary deductive logic, and something like the notions of acceptance and rejection in the form of rules of bracketing and unbracketing. We also find an notion roughly tantamount to the concept of information. What we do not find are philosophers' concepts of knowledge and belief. Hence the problems of knowledge acquisition can be examined, and must be examined, without using the two concepts. This is perhaps not surprising, for if knowledge is going to be the end product of interrogative inquiry, it cannot be one of the means of reaching this goal. The role of the concept of knowledge deals with the evaluation of stages that our interrogative inquiry has reached. But if so, it is not likely that such an evaluation can be carried out independently of the subject matter at hand. And if so, the quest of a general definition of knowledge, supposedly the main task of epistemologists, is a wild goose chase. It can also be argued that belief should not be thought of as a naturalistic state, either, but likewise as a term related to the evaluation of the results of inquiry.

Admittedly, the logic of questions and answers that plays a crucial role in interrogative inquiry involves an intensional epistemic notion. But this concept is not the philosophers' concept of knowledge, but something that could perhaps most happily be called information. Unfortunately, Quine's misguided rejection of the analytic versus synthetic distinction has discouraged philosophers from examining the notion of information, even though this term is current as an epithet of our entire age. As a result, it has been purloined by various specialists, from communication theorists to theorists of computational complexity. In the essay "Who Has Kidnapped the Concept of Information?" (Chapter 8), an attempt is made to find some method in this madness. Among the main results reported in that essay, there is a distinction between two kinds of information—depth information and surface information—the behavioral indistinguishability of the two (this is the true element in Quine's views), the depth tautologicity of logical truths, the inevitable presence of factual assumptions in any measure of either kind of information, and the possibility of interpreting complexity theorists' notion of information as a variant of surface information. The consequences of these results require further analysis (and synthesis).

A strategic viewpoint also relates the interrogative approach to epistemology to the theory of explanation. (See Halonen and Hintikka 2005.) A convenient reference point in this direction is offered by the covering law explanation. In the simplest terms, according to this theory to explain an *explanandum* E is to deduce it from a suitable theory or generalization T. But neither what is true nor what is false in this covering law view has been fully spelled out in the earlier discussion. In the essay "Logical Explanations" (Chapter 7), it is spelled out, as the covering law theorists never did, in what way a deduction of E from T can explain their connection. It is also argued that procedurally and substantially, explaining does not consist of a deduction of E from T but of the finding of the ad hoc facts A from which E follows in conjunction with T.

As a bonus, we obtain in this way also an explicit analysis of *how possible* explanations. Such explanations turn out to have an important function in the overall strategies of inquiry in that they can be used to investigate which answers perhaps an inquirer should perhaps bracket—namely, by examining how the different answers could possibly be false.

Thus, epistemic logic turns out to be able to put several different aspects of the epistemological enterprise to a new light. This it does by making possible a viable theory of questions and answers, which in turn enables us to develop a theory of information acquisition by questioning.

References

Halonen, Ilpo, and Jaakko Hintikka, 2005, "Toward a Theory of the Process of Explanation," *Synthese*, vol. 143, pp. 5–61

Hintikka, Jaakko, 1999, *Inquiry as Inquiry: A Logic of Scientific Discovery*, Kluwer Academic, Dordrecht.

Hintikka, Jaakko, 1996, "On the Development of Aristotle's Ideas of Scientific Method and the Structure of Science," in William Wians, editor, *Aristotle's Philosophical Development: Problems and Prospects*, Rowman and Littlefield, Lanham, Maryland, pp. 83–104.

Hintikka, Jaakko, 1993, "The Concept of Induction in the Light of the Interrogative Approach to Inquiry," in John Earman, editor, *Inference, Explanation, and Other Frustrations*, University of California Press, Berkeley, pp. 23–43.

Kleiner, S. A., 1993, *The Logic of Discovery: A Theory of the Rationality of Scientific Research*, Synthese Library, Kluwer Academic, Dordrecht.

Sacks, Oliver, 1985, *The Man Who Mistook His Wife for a Hat and Other Clinical Tales*, HarperCollins, New York.

Epistemology without Knowledge and without Belief

1. Knowledge and Decision-Making

He did not think this study would become well-known

Epistemology seems to enjoy an unexpectedly glamorous reputation in these days. A few years ago, William Safire wrote a popular novel called *The Sleeper Spy*. It depicts a distinctly post-Cold War world in which it is no longer easy to tell the good guys—including the good spies—from the bad ones. To emphasize this sea change, Safire tells us that his Russian protagonist has not been trained in the military or in the police, as he would have been in the old days, but as an epistemologist.

But is this with-it image deserved? Would the theory of knowledge that contemporary academic epistemologists cultivate be of any help to a sleeper spy? This question prompts a critical survey of the state of the art or, rather, the state of the theory of knowledge. I submit that the up-to-date image is not accurate and that most of the current epistemological literature deals with unproductive and antiquated questions. This failure is reflected in the concepts that are employed by contemporary epistemologists. *He saying contemporary is not effective and outdated*

What are those concepts? It is usually thought and said that the most central concepts of epistemology are knowledge and belief. The prominence of these two notions is reflected in the existing literature on epistemology. A large chunk of it consists in discussions of how the concept of knowledge is to be defined or is not to be defined. Are those discussions on the target? An adequate analysis of such concepts as knowledge and belief, whether it is calculated to lead us to a formal definition or not, should start from the role that they play in real life. Now in real life we are both producers and consumers of knowledge. We acquire knowledge in whatever ways we do so, and we then put it to use in our actions and decision-making. I will here start from the latter role, which takes us to the question: What is the role that the notion of knowledge plays in that decision-making?

To take a simple example, let us suppose that I am getting ready to face a new day in the morning. How, then, does it affect my actions if I know that it will

He is asking if their current discussions get to the point of explaining the fundamentals of epistemology

not rain today? You will not be surprised if I say that what it means is that I am
entitled to behave as if it will not rain—for instance to leave my umbrella home.
However, you may be surprised if I claim that most of the important features
of the logical behavior of the notion of knowledge can be teased out of such
simple examples. Yet this is the case. My modest example can be generalized.
The role of knowledge in decision-making is to rule out certain possibilities. In
order to use my knowledge, I must know which possibilities it rules out. In other
words, any one scenario must therefore be either incompatible or compatible
with what I know, for I am either entitled or not entitled to disregard it. Thus
the totality of incompatible scenarios determines what I know and what I do
not know, and vice versa. In principle, all that there is to logic of knowledge
is this dichotomy between epistemically impossible and epistemically possible
scenarios.

It is also clear how this dichotomy serves the purposes of decision-making,
just as it does in my mini-example of deciding whether or not to take an
umbrella with me. But the connection with overt behavior is indirect, for what
the dichotomy merely demarcates are the limits of what I am *entitled to* disregard. And being entitled to do something does not always mean that I do it. It
does not always show up in the overt ways one actually or even potentially acts.
For other considerations may very well enter into my decision-making. Maybe
I just want to sport an umbrella even though I know that it need not serve its
function of shielding myself from rain. Maybe I am an epistemological *akrates*
and act against what I know. The connection is nevertheless real, even though
it is a subtle one. There is a link between my knowledge and my decisions, but
it is, so to speak, a *de jure* connection and not a *de facto* connection. I think that
this is a part of what John Austin (1961(a)) was getting at when he compared
"I know" with "I promise." To know something does not mean simply to have
evidence of a superior degree for it, nor does it mean to have a superior kind
of confidence in it. If my first names were George Edward, I might use the
open-question argument to defend these distinctions. By saying "I promise,"
I entitle you to expect that I fulfill my promise. By saying "I know," I claim
that I am entitled to disregard those possibilities that do not agree with what
I know. There is an evaluative element involved in the concept of knowledge
that does not reduce to the observable facts of the case. Hence, it is already
seen to be unlikely that you could define what it means to know by reference
to matters of fact, such as the evidence that the putative knower possesses or
the state of the knower's mind.

This evaluative element is due to the role of knowledge in guiding our
life in that it plays a role in the justification of our decisions. This role determines in the last analysis the logic and in some sense the meaning of knowledge. A Wittgensteinean might put this point by saying that decision-making
is one of the language-games that constitute the logical home of the concept of
knowledge. You can remove knowledge from the contexts of decision-making,
but you cannot remove a relation to decision-making from the concept of

knowledge. For this reason, it is among other things misguided in a fundamental way to try to separate epistemic possibility from actual (natural) possibility. Of course, the two are different notions, but the notion of epistemic possibility has conceptual links to the kind of possibility that we have to heed in our decision-making. For one thing, the set of scenarios involved in the two notions must be the same.

But the main point here is not that there is an evaluative component to the notion of knowledge. The basic insight is that there is a link between the concept of knowledge and human action. The evaluative element is merely a complicating factor in the equation. The existence of a link between the two is not peculiar to the notion of knowledge. There is a link, albeit of a different kind, also in the case of belief. In fact, the conceptual connection is even more obvious in the case of belief. Behavioral scientists have studied extensively decision principles where belief constitutes one component, as, for instance, in the principle of maximizing expected utility. It usually comes in the form of degrees of belief. (They are often identified with probabilities.) Typically, utilities constitute another component. Whether or not such explicit decision principles capture the precise links between belief and behavior, they illustrate the existence of the link and yield clues to its nature.

Indeed, from a systematic point of view, the relative roles assigned to knowledge and to belief in recent epistemology and recent decision theory cannot but appear paradoxical. Belief is in such studies generally thought of as a direct determinant of our decisions, whereas knowledge is related to action only indirectly, if at all. Yet common sense tells us that one of the main reasons for looking for more knowledge is to put us in a better position in our decision-making, whereas philosophers often consider belief—especially when it is contrasted with knowledge—as being initially undetermined by our factual information and therefore being a much worse guide to decision-making. Probability is sometimes said to be a guide to life, but surely knowledge is a better one. Or, if we cannot use black-or-white concepts here, shouldn't rational decision-making be guided by degrees of knowledge rather than degrees of mere belief?

The same point can perhaps be made by noting that in many studies of decision-making, a rational agent is supposed to base his or her decisions on the agent's beliefs (plus, of course, utilities) and then by asking: Would it not be even more rational for the agent to base his or her decisions on what the agent *knows*?

In order for a rational agent to act on his or her belief, this belief clearly must be backed up by some evidence. Otherwise, current decision theory makes little sense. The difference is that the criteria of what entities are to act are different in the case of belief from what they are in the case of knowledge. If I act on a belief, that belief must satisfy my personal requirements for that role. They may vary from person to person. In contrast, the criteria of knowing are impersonal and not dependent on the agent in question. In order to define knowledge as distinguished from beliefs, we would have to spell out those impersonal criteria. This is obviously an extremely difficult task at best.

Another fact that complicates the connection between knowledge and behavior—that is, between what I know and what I do—is that in principle, this link is holistic. What matters to my decisions in the last analysis is the connection between the totality of my knowledge. There is not always any hard-and-fast connection between particular items of knowledge and my behavior. In principle, the connection is via my entire store of knowledge. This is reflected by the fact emphasized earlier that the dichotomy that determines the logic of knowledge is a distinction between scenarios that are ruled out by the *totality* of what I know and scenarios that are compatible with the *totality* of my knowledge and that I therefore must be prepared for. The same feature of the concept of knowledge also shows up in the requirement of total evidence that is needed in Bayesian inference and which has prompted discussion and criticism there. (See, e.g., Earman 1992.)

To spell out the criteria of the justification involved in the applications of the concept of knowledge is to define what knowledge is as distinguished from other propositional attitudes. Characterizing these conditions is obviously a complicated task. I will return to these criteria later in this chapter.

2. The Logic of Knowledge and Information

Meanwhile, another dimension of the concept of knowledge is brought out by homely examples of the kind I am indulging in. By this time it should be clear—I hope—that it is extremely hard to specify the kind of entitlement or justification that knowing something amounts to. This difficulty is perhaps sufficiently attested to by the inconclusiveness of the extensive discussions about how to define knowledge that one can find in the literature. (See, e.g., Shope 1983.) But another aspect of this notion is in principle as clear as anything one can hope to find in philosophical analysis (or synthesis). It may be difficult to tell whether a certain propositional attitude amounts to knowledge, belief, opinion or whatnot, but there is typically no difficulty in spelling out the *content* of any one of these attitudes on some particular occasion. Here, the lesson drawn from my rain-and-umbrella example is applicable. It was seen that what someone knows specifies, and is specified by, the class of possible scenarios that are compatible with what he or she knows. And such classes of scenarios or of "possible worlds" can be captured linguistically as the classes of scenarios (alias possible worlds) in which a certain sentence is true. Indeed, for Montague (1974, p. 153) such classes of possible worlds (or, strictly speaking, the characteristic functions of these classes, in the sense of functions from possible worlds to truth-values) *are* propositions. In this way, the content of a propositional attitude can normally be captured verbally. For another instance, for Husserl (1983, sec. 124), the task would be to capture the noematic *Sinn* of an act, which he says can in principle always be accomplished linguistically—that is, in Husserl's terminology, through *Bedeutungen.*

Let us now call the members of the class of scenarios admitted by someone's knowledge that someone's epistemic alternatives. That I know that it will not rain today means that none of the scenarios under which the wet stuff falls down are among my epistemic alternatives, and likewise for all *knowing that* statements. What the concept of knowledge involves in a purely logical perspective is thus a dichotomy of the space of all possible scenarios into those that are compatible with what I know and those that are incompatible with my knowledge. What was just seen is that this dichotomy is directly conditioned by the role of the notion of knowledge in real life. Now this very dichotomy is virtually all we need in developing an explicit logic of knowledge, better known as epistemic logic. This conceptual parentage is reflected by the usual notation of epistemic logic. In it, the epistemic operator K_a ("a knows that") receives its meaning from the dichotomy between excluded and admitted scenarios, while the sentence within its scope specifies the content of the item of knowledge in question.

Basing epistemic logic on such a dichotomy has been the guiding idea of my work in epistemic logic right from the beginning. I have seen this idea being credited to David Lewis, but I have not seen any uses of it that predate my work.

But here we seem to run into a serious problem in interpreting epistemic logic from the vantage point of a dichotomy of excluded and admitted scenarios. Such an interpretation might seem to exclude "quantifying in"—that is to say, to exclude applications of the knowledge operator to open formulas for them, it would not make any sense to speak of scenarios in which the content of one's knowledge is true or false. Such "quantifying in" is apparently indispensable for the purpose of analyzing the all-important *wh*-constructions with *knows*. For instance, "John *knows* who murdered Roger Ackroyd" apparently must be expressed by

$$(\exists x)K_{John}(x \text{ murdered Roger Ackroyd}) \tag{1}$$

as distinguished from

$$K_{John}(\exists x)(x \text{ murdered Roger Ackroyd}) \tag{2}$$

which says that John knows that someone murdered the victim and hence can serve as the presupposition of the question, "Who murdered Roger Ackroyd?"

But in (1), the notion of knowledge apparently cannot be interpreted by reference to a distinction between admitted and excluded scenarios. The reason is that the knowledge operator in (1) is prefixed to an open formula. Such an open formula cannot be said to be true or false in a given scenario, for its truth depends on the value of the variable x. Hence it cannot implement the required dichotomy.

In order for our epistemic discourse to express the *wh*-constructions, the knowledge operator must apparently be allowed to occur also internally, prefixed to open formulas rather than sentences (formulas without free variables). This prompts a serious interpretational problem. Indeed we can see here the reason for the deep theoretical interest of the problem of "quantifying in," which otherwise might strike one as being merely the logicians' technical problem. Fortunately, this apparent problem can be solved by means of suitable analysis of the relations between different logical operators (see Section 3).

An epistemic logic of this kind can obviously be developed within the framework of possible worlds semantics. (For a sketch of how this can be done, see Hintikka 2003(b).) In fact, the truth condition for *knows that* is little more than a translation of what was just said: "b knows that S" is true in a world W if and only if S is true in all the epistemic b-alternatives to W. These alternatives are all the scenarios or "worlds" compatible with everything b knows in W. In certain important ways, this truth condition for knowledge statements is clearer than its counterpart in the ordinary (alethic) modal semantics, in that in epistemic logic the interpretation of the alternativeness relation (alias accessibility relation) is much clearer than in the logic of physical or metaphysical modalities.

Here we have already reached a major conclusion. Epistemic logic presupposes essentially only the dichotomy between epistemically possible and epistemically excluded scenarios. How this dichotomy is drawn is a question pertaining to the definition of knowledge. However, we do not need to know this definition in doing epistemic logic. Thus the logic and the semantics of knowledge can be understood independently of any explicit definition of knowledge. Hence it should not be surprising to see that a similar semantics and a similar logic can be developed for other epistemic notions—for instance, belief, information, memory, and even perception. This is an instance of a general law holding for propositional attitudes. This law says that the content of a propositional attitude can be specified independently of differences between different attitudes. This law has been widely recognized, even if it has not always been formulated as a separate assumption. For instance, in Husserl (1983, e.g., sec.133) it takes the form of separating the noematic *Sinn* from the thetic component of a noema. As a consequence, the respective logics of different epistemic notions do not differ much from each other. In particular, they do not differ at all in those aspects of their logic that depend merely on the dichotomical character of their semantics. These aspects include prominently the laws that hold for quantifiers and identity, especially the modifications that are needed in epistemic contexts in the laws of the substitutivity of identity and existential generalization.

The fact that different epistemic notions, such as knowledge, belief, and information, share the same dichotomic logic should not be surprising in the light of what has been said. The reason is that they can all serve the same purpose of guiding our decisions, albeit in different ways. Hence the same line of thought can be applied to them as was applied earlier to the concept of knowledge, ending up with the conclusion that their logic is a dichotomic logic not unlike the logic that governs the notion of knowledge. The common ingredient in all these different logics is then the true epistemic logic. But it turns out to be a logic of information rather than a logic of knowledge.

This distinction between what pertains to the mere dichotomy between admitted and excluded scenarios and what pertains to the criteria relied on in this dichotomy is not a novelty. It is at bottom only a restatement in structural terms of familiar contrast, which in the hands of different thinkers has received apparently different formulations. The dichotomy defines the content of a propositional attitude, while the criteria of drawing it determine which propositional attitude we are dealing with. Hence we are naturally led to the project of developing a generic logic of contents of attitudes, independent of the differences between different attitudes.

This generic logic of epistemology can be thought of as the logic of information. Indeed, what the content of a propositional attitude amounts to can be thought of as a certain item of information. In attributing different attitudes to agents, different things are said about this information—for instance, that it is known, believed, remembered, and so on. This fits in well with the fact that the same content can be known by one person, believed by another, remembered by a third one, and so on. This idea that one and the same objective content may be the target of different people's different attitudes is part of what Frege (see, e.g., 1984) was highlighting by his notion of *the thought*. Thus it might even be happier to talk about the logic of information than about epistemic logic. John Austin (1961(b)) once excused his use of the term "performative" by saying that even though it is a foreign word and an ugly word that perhaps does not mean very much, it has one good thing about it: It is not a deep word. It seems to me that epistemology would be in much better shape if instead of the deep word "knowledge," philosophers cultivated more the ugly foreign word "information," even though it perhaps does not capture philosophers' profound sense of knowing. In any case, in the generic logic of epistemology here envisaged, philosophers' strong sense of knowledge plays no role.

3. Information Acquisition as a Questioning Procedure

But what about the other context in which we encounter knowledge in real life—the context of knowledge acquisition? As was noted, what the concept of knowledge amounts to is revealed by two questions: What is it that we are searching for in the process of knowledge acquisition? What purpose can the product of such an inquiry serve? The second question has now been discussed. It remains to examine the crucial first question. Surely the first order of business of any genuine theory of knowledge—the most important task both theoretically and practically—is how new acquired, not merely how previously obtained information can be evaluated. A theory of information (knowledge) acquisition is both philosophically and humanly much more important than a theory of whether or not already achieved information amounts to knowledge. Discovery is more important than the defense of what you already know. In epistemology, as in warfare, offense frequently is the best defense.

This point can be illustrated in a variety of ways. For instance, a thinker who does not acquire any information cannot even be a skeptic, for he or she would not have anything to be skeptical about. And a skeptic's doubts must be grounded on some grasp as to how that information is obtained, unless these doubts are totally irrational. Epistemology cannot start from the experience of wonder or doubt. It should start from recognition of where the item of information that we are wondering about or doubting came from in the first place. Any rational justification or rational distinction of such wonder or doubt must be based on its ancestry.

Fortunately we now have available to us a framework in which to discuss the logic and epistemology of knowledge acquisition or, rather, if I have the terminological courage of my epistemological convictions, information acquisition. The framework is what is referred to as the interrogative model of inquiry or interrogative approach to inquiry. (See Hintikka 1999.) Its basic idea is the same as that of the oldest explicit form of reasoning in philosophy, the Socratic method of questioning or *elenchus*. In it, all new information enters into an argument or a line of reasoning in the form of answers to questions that the inquirer addresses to a suitable source of information.

It might at first seem implausible that this approach might yield a viable theory of ampliative reasoning in general, for several different reasons. Fortunately all these objections can be overcome. First, it might not seem likely that this model can be developed into a form explicit and detailed enough to allow for precise conclusions. This objection would have been eminently appropriate as recently as a decade or two ago. For it is only in the last several years that there has existed a general and explicit logical theory of all the relevant kinds of questions. This logic of questions and answers is the backbone of the interrogative model. This theory has not yet been presented in a monographic or textbook form, but its basic ideas are explained in recent and forthcoming papers of mine. (See, e.g., Hintikka 2003(a).) This logic of questions and answers is an extension and application of epistemic logic (logic of knowledge). It has been made possible by a quiet revolution in epistemic logic. One of the main problems in representing questions is to specify which ingredients of the aimed-at information are the questioned elements—that is to say, are supposed to be made known by the answer. It turns out that their specification can sometimes be accomplished only by means of the independence indicators whose logic is only now being explored, even though it cannot be done in the earlier "first-generation" epistemic logic. The details of the new "second-generation" epistemic logic that makes use of the notion of independence need not concern us here. It may nevertheless be noted that this new logic solves the problem of "quantifying in" in that in it, the epistemic operator K always occurs sentence-intitially. There is no problem of quantifying in, one might say here, only quantifying (binding variables) independently of an epistemic operator.

Another main requirement that can be addressed to the interrogative approach—and indeed to the theory of any goal-directed activity—is that it must do justice to the strategic aspects of inquiry. Among other things, it ought to be possible to distinguish the definitory rules of the activity in question from its strategic rules. The former spell out what is possible at each stage of the process. The latter express what actions are better and worse for the purpose of reaching the goals of the activity. This requirement can be handled most naturally by doing what Plato already did to the Socratic *elenchus* and by construing knowledge-seeking by questioning as a game that pits the questioner against the answerer. Then the study of the strategies of knowledge acquisition becomes another application of the mathematical theory of games, which perhaps ought to be called "strategy theory" rather than "game theory" in the first place. The distinction between the definitory rules—usually called simply the rules of the game—and strategic principles is built right into the structure of such games.

The greatest obstacle to generality might seem to be the apparently restricted range of applicability of the interrogative model. Some of the resistance to this approach, which I have referred to as the idea of "inquiry as inquiry," can be dispelled by pointing out that questions and answers can be understood in a wide sense, and have to be so understood if the generality claim is to be acceptable. Sources of answers to explicit or implicit questions have to include not only human witnesses and other informants or databases in a computer, but observation and experimentation as well as memory and tacit knowledge. One of the leading ideas of the interrogative approach is that all information used in an argument must be brought in as an answer to a question. In claiming such generality for the interrogative model, I can appeal to such precedents as Collingwood's (1940) and Gadamer's (1975) "logic of questions and answers," even though what they called logic really was not. My claims of generality on behalf of the interrogative approach are not even as sweeping as Collingwood's thesis that every proposition may be considered as an answer to a question. Likewise in construing experiments as questions to nature, I can cite Kant and Bacon.

4. Interrogation and Justification

But the context of knowledge acquisition is vital even if the aim of your game is justification and not discovery. Suppose that a scientist has a reason to think that one of his or her conclusions is not beyond doubt. What is he or she to do? Will the scientist try to mine his or her data so as to extract from them grounds for a decision? Sometimes, perhaps, but in an overwhelming majority of actual scientific situations, the scientist will ask what further information one should in such circumstances try to obtain in order to confirm or disconfirm the suspect proposition—for instance, what experiments it would be advisable to perform or what kinds of observation one should try to make in order to throw light on the subject matter. Unfortunately such contexts—or should I say, such language-games—of verification by means of new information have not received much attention from recent philosophers. They have been preoccupied with the justification of already acquired knowledge rather than with the strategies of reaching new knowledge.

Thus we must extend the scope of the interrogative model in such a way that it enables us to cope with justification and not just pure discovery. What we need is a rule or rules that authorize the rejection—which is tentative and may be only temporary—of some of the answers that an inquirer receives. The *terminus technicus* for such rejection is *bracketing*. The possibility of bracketing widens the scope of epistemological and logical methods tremendously. After this generalization has been carried out, the logic of interrogative inquiry can serve many of the same purposes as the different variants of non-monotonic reasoning, and serve them without the tacit assumptions that often make nonmonotonic reasoning epistemologically restricted or even philosophically dubious. A telling example is offered by what is known as circumscriptive reasoning. (See McCarthy 1990.) It relies on the assumption that the premises present the reasoner with all the relevant information, so that the reasoner can assume that they are made true in the intended models in the simplest possible way. This is an assumption that in fact can often be made, but it is not always available on other occasions. As every puzzle fan knows, often a key to the clever reasoning needed to solve a puzzle lies precisely in being able to imagine circumstances in which the normal expectations evoked by the specification of the puzzle are not realized. Suppose a puzzle goes as follows: "Evelyn survived George by more than eighty years, even though she was born many decades before him. How come?" The explanation is easy if you disregard the presumption that "George" is a man's name and "Evelyn" a woman's. Evelyn Waugh in fact survived George Eliot by eighty-six years. Here the solution of the puzzle depends entirely on going beyond the *prima facie* information provided by the putative—in other words, on violating the presuppositions of a circumscriptive inference. Reasoning by circumscription is enthymemic reasoning. It involves tacit premises that may be false.

Thus by introducing the idea of bracketing, we can dispense with all modes of ampliative reasoning. The only rules besides rules of logical inference are the rules for questioning and the rule allowing bracketing. This may at first look like a cheap trick serving merely to sweep all the difficulties of epistemic justification under the rug of bracketing. In reality, what is involved is an important insight. What is involved is not a denial of the difficulties of justification, but an insight into their nature as problems. Once a distinction is made between strategic and definitory rules, it is realized that the definitory rules can only be permissive, telling what one may do in order to reach knowledge and to justify it. The problem of justification is a strategic problem. It pertains to what one ought to do in order to make sure that the results of one's inquiry are secure. This is to be done by the double process of disregarding dubious results and confirming the survivors through further inquiry. The only new permissive rule needed for the purpose is the rule that allows bracketing.

Thus the question as to which answers to bracket is always at bottom a strategic problem. It is therefore futile in principle to try to capture the justificatory process by means of definitory rules of this or that kind. To attempt to do so is a fallacy that in the last analysis vitiates all the usual "logics" of ampliative reasoning. This mistake is committed not only by non-monotonic logics but also by inductive logic and by the current theories of belief revision. Ampliative logics can be of considerable practical interest and value, but in the ultimate epistemological perspective, they are but types of enthymemic reasoning, relying on tacit premises quite as much as circumscriptive reasoning. An epistemologist's primary task here is not to study the technicalities of such modes of reasoning, fascinating though they are in their own right. It is to uncover the tacit premises on which such euthymemic reasoning is in reality predicated.

Allowing bracketing is among other things important because it makes it possible to conceive of interrogative inquiry as a model also of the confirmation of hypotheses and other propositions in the teeth of evidence. The interrogative model can thus also serve as a general model of the justification of hypotheses. It should in fact be obvious that the processes of discovery and justification cannot be sharply separated from each other in the practice or in the theory of science. Normally, a new discovery in science is justified by the very same process—for instance, by the same experiments—by means of which it was made, or could have been made And this double duty service of questioning is not due only to the practical exigencies of "normal science." It has a firm conceptual basis. This basis is the fact that information (unlike many Federal appropriations) does not come to an inquirer earmarked for a special purpose—for instance, for the purpose of discovery rather than justification. The inquirer may ask a question for this or that proximate purpose in mind, but there is nothing in the answer that rules out its being used for other purposes as well.

And such an answer can only be evaluated in terms of its service for both causes. This is because from game theory we know that in the last analysis, game-like goal-directed processes can be evaluated only in terms of their strategies, not in terms of what one can say of particular moves—for instance, what kinds of "warrants" they might have. As a sports-minded logician might explain the point, evaluating a player's skills in a strategic game is in principle like judging a figure-skating performance rather than keeping score in a football game. In less playful terms, one can in generally associate utilities (payoffs) only with strategies, not with particular moves. But since discovery and justification are aspects of the same process, they have to be evaluated in terms of the different possible strategies that are calculated to serve both purposes.

When we realize this strategic inseparability of the two processes, we can in fact gain a better understanding of certain otherwise puzzling features of epistemic enterprise. For instance, we can now see why it sometimes is appropriate to jump to a conclusion on the basis of relatively thin evidence. The reason is that finding what the truth is can help us mightily in our next order of business of finding evidence for that very truth. Sherlock Holmes has abductively "inferred" that the stablemaster has stolen the famous racing horse "Silver Blaze" (see the Conan Doyle story with this title) in order to lame it partially. He still has to confirm this conclusion, however, and in that process he is guided by the very content of that abductive conclusion—for instance, in directing his attention to the possibility that the stablemaster had practiced his laming operation on the innocent sheep grazing nearby. He puts a question to the shepherd as to whether anything had been amiss with them of late. "Well, sir, not of much account, but three of them have gone lame, sir." Without having already hit on the truth, Holmes could not have thought of asking this particular question.

If you disregard the strategic angle, the frequent practice of such "jumps to a conclusion" by scientists may easily lead one to believe that scientific discovery is not subject to epistemological rules. The result will then be the hypothetico-deductive model of scientific reasoning, which is hence seen to rest on a fallacious dismissal of the strategic angle.

Thus we reach a result that is neatly contrary to what were once prevalent views. It used to be held that discovery cannot be subject to explicit epistemological theory, whereas justification can. We have found out that not only can discovery be approached epistemologically, but that justification cannot in the long run be done justice to by a theory that does not also cover discovery.

A critical reader might initially have been wondering why contexts of verification and of other forms of justification do not constitute a third logical home of the notion of knowledge, besides the contexts of decision-making and information-acquisition. The answer is that processes of justification can only be considered as aspects of processes of information-acquisition.

5. The Generality of the Interrogative Model

The most general argument for the generality of the interrogative approach relies only on the assumption that the inquirer's line of thought can be rationally evaluated. What is needed for such an evaluation? If no new information is introduced into an argument by a certain step, then the outcome of that step is a logical consequence of earlier statements reached in the argument. Hence we are dealing with a logical inference step that has to be evaluated by the criteria of logical validity. It follows that interrogative steps are the ones in which new information enters into the argument. In order to evaluate the step, we must know what the source of this information is, for the reliability of the information may depend on its source. We must also know what else might have resulted from the inquirer's approaching this particular source in this particular way and with what probabilities. If so, what the inquirer did can be thought of as a question addressed to that source of information. Likewise, we must know what other sources of information the inquirer could have consulted and what the different results might have been. This amounts to knowing what other sources of answers the inquirer might have consulted. But if all of this is known, we might as well consider what the inquirer did as a step in interrogative inquiry.

In an earlier work (Hintikka 1998), I have likened such tacit interrogative steps to Peircean abductions, which Peirce insists are inferences even though they have interrogative and conjectural aspects.

The interrogative model can be thought of as having also another kind of generality—namely, generality with respect to the different kinds of questions. Earlier epistemic logic was incapable of handling questions more complicated than simple *wh*-questions. In particular, it could not specify the logical form of questions in which the questioned ingredient was apparently within the scope of a universal quantifier, which in turn was in the scope of a *knows that* operator. This defect was eliminated by means of the independence indicator (slash) /. (See Hintikka 2003(b).) What characterizes the questioned ingredient is its independence of the epistemic operator, and such independence is perfectly compatible with its being dependent on a universal quantifier, which is in turn dependent on the universal quantifier. In symbols we can now write, for instance, $K(\forall x)(\exists y/K)$ without having to face the impossible task of capturing the threefold dependence structure by means of scopes—that is, by ordering K, $(\forall x)$, and $(\exists y)$ linearly so as to capture their dependence relations.

In this way, we can treat all *wh*-questions and all propositional questions (involving questions where the two kinds of question ingredients are intermingled). The question ingredient of propositional questions turns out to be of the form $(\vee/K)$ and the question ingredient of *wh*-questions of the form $(\exists x/K)$. We can also close a major gap in our argument so far. The connection between knowledge and decision-making discussed in Section 1 is apparently subject to the serious objection mentioned in Section 2. It helps to understand a knowledge operator K only when it occurs clause-initially, prefixed to a closed sentence. For it is only such sentences, not all and sundry formulas, that express a proposition that can serve as a justification of an action. Occurrences of K inside a sentence prefixed to an open formula cannot be interpreted in the same way. Now we can restrict K to a sentence-initial position, which eliminates this objection. This also helps to fulfill the promise made in Section 2 of constructing a general logic for the epistemic operator. Here we are witnessing a major triumph of second-generation epistemic logic, which relies on the notion of independence. It solves once and for all the problem of "quantifying in." It turns out that we do not at bottom *quantify into* a context governed by the epistemic operator K. What we in effect do is to *quantify independently* of this operator.

Why-questions and *how*-questions require a special treatment, which nevertheless is not hard to do. (See, e.g., Hintikka and Halonen 1995.)

The most persuasive argument for the interrogative model nevertheless comes from the applications of the interrogative viewpoint to different problems in epistemology. An important role in such applications is played by the presuppositions of questions and by the presuppositions of answers, better known as their conclusiveness conditions. Examples of such application are offered in Chapters 4 and 5 of this volume.

6. The Place of Knowledge in Inquiry

It would take me too far afield here to essay a full-fledged description of the interrogative model. It is nevertheless easy to make an inventory of the concepts that are employed in it. In an explicit model, question-answer steps are interspersed with logical inference steps. Hence the concepts of ordinary deductive logic are needed. As long as the inquirer can trust all the answers, the concepts that are needed are the presuppositions of a question, the conclusiveness condition of an answer (which might be called the "presupposition" of the answer), and the notion of information. To describe an interrogative argument with uncertain answers (responses), we need the notion of tentative rejection of an answer, also known as *bracketing*, and hence also the converse operation of unbracketing, plus ultimately also the notion of probability needed to judge the conditions of bracketing and unbracketing.

What is remarkable about this inventory is that it does not include the concept of knowledge. One can construct a full epistemological theory of inquiry as inquiry without ever using the k-word. This observation is made especially significant by the generality of the interrogative model. As was indicated, not only is it by means of an interrogative argument that all new information can be thought of as having been discovered, it is by the same questioning method that its credibility must be established in principle.

What this means is that by constructing a theory of interrogative inquiry we apparently can build up a complete theory of epistemology without using the concept of knowledge. We do not need the notion of knowledge in our theory of knowledge—or so it seems. We do not need it either in the theory of discovery or in the theory of justification.

This conclusion might seem to be too strange to be halfway plausible. It is not, but it needs explanations to be seen in the right perspective.

It might perhaps seem that the concept of knowledge is smuggled into interrogative argumentation by the epistemic logic that has to be used in it. This objection is in fact a shrewd one. I said earlier that the logic of questions and answers, which is the backbone of the interrogative model, is part of the logic of knowledge. And this need to resort to epistemic notions is grounded deeply in the facts of the case. It might at first seem that in an interrogative inquiry, no epistemic notions are needed. The presuppositions of questions, questions themselves, and replies to them can apparently be formulated without using epistemic notions.

However, this first impression turns out to be misleading. The structure of and the rules governing it cannot be specified without using some suitable epistemic logic. For one thing, many of the properties of questions and answers are best explained by reference to what is known as the desideratum of a question. This desideratum specifies the epistemic state that the questioner wants to be brought about (in the normal use of questions). For instance, the desideratum of "Who murdered Roger Ackroyd?" is "I know who murdered Roger Ackroyd." But the desideratum with its *prima facie* knowledge operator is not only a part of a theory of question-answer sequences, it is a vital ingredient of the very interrogative process.

In particular, it is needed to solve Meno's problem (Plato 1924) applied to interrogative inquiry. In the initial formulation of the rules for interrogative inquiry, it is apparently required that we must know not only the initial premises of inquiry but also their ultimate conclusion. This seems to mean that we can use interrogative inquiry only to explain conclusions we have already reached but not to solve problems—in other words, answer questions by means of questions. But in trying to answer a question by means of interrogative inquiry, we apparently do not know what the ultimate conclusion is. We are instead looking for it. How, then, can we use interrogative inquiry for the purpose of answering questions? The answer is that we must formulate the logic of inquiry in terms of what the inquirer knows (in the sense of being informed about) at each stage. Then we can solve Meno's problem merely by using the desideratum of the overall question as the ultimate conclusion. But then we seem to need the notion of knowledge with vengeance.

What is true is that a viable theory of questions and answers will inevitably involve an intensional operator, and in particular an epistemic operator in a wide sense of the word. However, the epistemic attitude this operator expresses is not knowledge in any reasonable sense of the word, not just not in the philosopher's solemn sense. Here, the results reached in Section 2 are applicable. Before an interrogative inquiry has reached its aim—that is, knowledge—we are dealing with information that has not yet hardened into knowledge. It was seen earlier that the logic of such unfinished epistemological business is indeed a kind of epistemic logic, but a logic of information rather than of knowledge.

This point is worth elaborating. Indeed the real refutation of the accusation of having smuggled the concept of knowledge into interrogative inquiry in the form of the epistemic operator used in questions and answers lies in pointing out the behavior of this operator in epistemic inquiry. It may sound natural to say that after having received what is known as a conclusive answer to a question, the inquirer now knows it. But the notion of knowledge employed here is a far cry from the notion of knowledge that philosophers have tried to define. It looks much more like the ugly foreign notion of information. It does not even carry the implication of truth, for the answer might very well have to be bracketed later in the same inquiry. By the same token, it does not even presuppose any kind of stable belief in what is "known." Instead of saying that after having received a conclusive answer, the inquirer knows it, it would be more accurate to say that he or she has been informed about it. Here the advantages of the less deep notion of information are amply in evidence. Unlike knowledge, information need not be true. If an item of information offered to me turns out to be false, I can borrow a line from *Casablanca* and ruefully say, "I was misinformed." The epistemic operator needed in the logic of questions and answers is therefore not a knowledge operator in the usual sense of the term. My emphasis on this point is a penance, for I now realize that my statements in the past might have conveyed to my readers a different impression. What is involved in the semantics of questions and answers is the logic of information, not the logic of knowledge. This role of the notion of information in interrogative inquiry is indeed crucial, but it does not involve epistemologists' usual concept of knowledge at all.

This point is so important as to be worth spelling out even more fully. Each answer presents the inquirer with a certain item of information, and the distinction between question-answer steps and logical inferences steps hinges on the question of whether this information must be old or whether it can be new information. But it is important to realize that such information does not amount to knowledge. In an ongoing interrogative inquiry, there are no propositions concerning which question is ever raised, whether they are known or not. There may be a provisional presumption that, barring further evidence, the answers that an inquirer receives are true, but there is not even a whiff of a presumption that they are known. Conversely, when an answer is bracketed, it does not mean that it is definitively declared not to be known, for further answers may lead the inquirer to unbracket it. In sum, it is true in the strictest possible sense that the concept of knowledge in anything like philosophers' sense is not used in the course of interrogative inquiry.

These observations show the place of knowledge in the world of actual inquiry, and it also shows the only context in which questions about the definition of knowledge can legitimately be asked. The notion of knowledge may or may not be a discussion-stopper, but it is certainly an inquiry-stopper.

It might be suspected that this is due to the particular way the interrogative model is set up. Such a suspicion is unfounded, however. The absence of the concept of knowledge from ampliative inquiry is grounded in the very nature of the concept of knowledge. Questions of knowledge do not play any role in the questioning process itself, only in evaluating its results. For what role was it seen to play in human life? It was seen as what justifies us to act in a certain way. The concept of knowledge is therefore related to interrogative inquiry by asking: When has an interrogative inquiry reached far enough to justify the inquirer's acting on the basis of the conclusions it has so far reached? Or, to align this question with the locutions used earlier, when has the inquiry entitled the inquirer to dismiss the scenarios that are incompatible with the propositions accepted in the inquiry at the time? This is a genuine question, and it might seem to bring the concept of knowledge to the center of the theory of interrogative inquiry.

In a sense it does that. But this sense does not bring the notion of knowledge back as a concept that can possibly figure in the definitory rules of inquiry. It brings knowledge back to the sphere of strategic aspects of inquiry. The question as to whether a conclusion of inquiry has been justified strongly enough for it to qualify as knowledge is on a par with the question as to whether or not a step in an inquiry (typically an answer to a question) should perhaps be bracketed (however tentatively). Both are strategic questions. It is hopeless to try to model knowledge acquisition in a way that turns these decisions into questions of definitory correctness.

Any context-free definition of knowledge would amount to a definitory rule in the game of inquiry—namely, a definitory rule for stopping an inquiry. And once one realizes that this is what a definition of knowledge would have to do in the light of the conception of inquiry as inquiry, one realizes that the pursuit of such a definition is a wild goose chase.

It is important to realize that this conclusion does not only apply to attempted definitions of knowledge that refer only to the epistemic situation that has been reached at the putative end stage of the "game" of inquiry. In other words, it does not apply only to the state of an inquirer's evidence at the end of an inquiry. It also applies to definitions in which the entire history of inquiry so far is taken into account.

This conclusion is worth spelling out more fully. What the conclusion says is that no matter how we measure the credence of the output of interrogative inquiry, there is no reason to believe that an answer to the question as to when an inquirer is justified to act on his or her presumed knowledge depends only on the process of inquiry through which the inquirer's information has been obtained independently of the subject matter of the inquiry. In an old terminology, the criteria of justification cannot be purely *ad argumentum*, but must also be *ad hoc*. Neither the amount of information nor the amount of justification that authorizes an agent to stop his or her inquiry and act on its results can always be specified independently of the subject matter—for instance, independently of the seriousness of the consequences of being wrong about the particular question at hand. And if the justification depends on the subject matter, then so does the concept of knowledge, because of the roots of our concept of knowledge in action.

But since the notion of knowledge was seen to be tied to the justification of acting on the basis of what one knows, the concept of knowledge depends on the subject matter and not only on the epistemological situation. Accordingly, no general definition of knowledge in purely epistemological terms is possible.

This point is not a relativistic one as far as the possibility of *a priori* epistemology is concerned. If anything, the divorce of knowledge from inquiry underlines the objectivity of inquiry and its independence of the value aspects of the subject matter. The fashionable recent emphasis on the alleged value-ladenness of science is misleading in that it is typically predicated on forgetting or overlooking that the question as to when the results of scientific inquiry authorize acting on them is different from questions concerning the methodology of scientific inquiry itself. The dependence of the criteria of knowledge on subject matter ought to be a platitude. It is one thing for Einstein to claim that he knew that the special theory of relativity was true notwithstanding *prima facie* contrary experimental evidence, and another thing for a medical researcher to be in a position to claim to know that a new vaccine is safe enough to be administered to sixty million people. But some relativists mistakenly take this platitude to be a deep truth about scientific methodology and its dependence on subject matter. This is a mistake in the light of the fact that the allegedly value-laden concept of knowledge does not play any role in the actual process of inquiry.

Here, a comparison with such decision principles as the maximization of expected utility is instructive. What an inquiry can provide is only the expectations (probabilities). But they do not alone determine the decision, which depends also on the decider's utilities. Hence the criteria of knowing cannot be defined by any topic-neutral general epistemology alone. But this dependence does not mean that the probabilities used—misleadingly called "subjective" probabilities—should in rational decision-making depend on one's utilities. Decision-making based on such probability estimates would be paradigmatically irrational.

The influence of subject matter on the notion of knowledge does not imply that the interrogative process through which putative knowledge has been obtained is irrelevant for the evaluation of its status. Here lies, in fact, a promising field of work for applied epistemologists. Material for such work is available in, among many other places, different kinds of studies of risk-taking. Even though considerations of strategies do not help us to formulate a topic-neutral definition of knowledge, in such a topic-sensitive epistemology they are bound to play a crucial role. This is a consequence of the general fact that in game-like processes, only strategies, not individual moves, can in the last analysis be evaluated.

7. Comparisons with Other Epistemologists

Relativizing our humanly relevant concept of knowledge to some particular subject matter also provides a strategy of answering a philosophical skeptic. If knowledge claims depend for their very meaning on the criteria governing some particular walk of human action, then so also must reasonable doubts. It is only unspecific "philosophical" doubts that do not have built into their own logic standards that show how they can be surmounted.

One philosopher who would have agreed with my thesis concerning the dependence of the criteria of knowledge on the subject matter, and who in fact supplied reasons for it, is Ludwig Wittgenstein. In Hintikka forthcoming, I have shown that according to Wittgenstein's mature views, the concept of knowledge cannot be used in what I have called "primary language-games." These language-games are for Wittgenstein the direct links between language and reality. In them, we cannot, in Wittgenstein's metaphor, drive a wedge between language and what it expresses. Such a primary language-game does not operate by means of criteria, but by means of spontaneous responses. If I try to say in such a primary language-game "I know that I am in pain," all that I can express is the same as "I am in pain." And in a primary language-game, to utter "I am in pain" is but a form of pain-behavior.

In Wittgenstein's view, epistemic concepts can be used only in what I have called "secondary language-games." These secondary language-games pre-suppose primary ones. They do not operate through spontaneous responses, verbal or behavioral, and hence they must involve criteria. For this reason, epistemic vocabulary can be used in them. But those criteria are different in different secondary games. Hence the force of epistemic terms depends on the particular secondary game in which they are being used. Saying this is very nearly nothing but Ludwigspeak for saying that the criteria of knowing depend on the subject matter.

Other epistemologists have not been unaware, either, of connections between the justifiability of knowledge claims and the subject matter involved. (See, e.g., DeRose 1995; Cohen 1998; Williams 2001, ch. 14; Bonjour 2002, pp. 267–271.) They seem to have ascribed the dependence in question to the context of inquiry rather than to its subject matter, however. Unless and until the notion of context used here is clarified, I remain doubtful of such claims of context-dependence. For instance, criteria of knowing that a vaccine is safe depend on the life-or-death character of the subject matter, but they pre-sumably should not depend on the context, which may be an administrative decision to initiate compulsory vaccination or a pharmaceutical company's promise to produce the requisite vaccine. However, if the notion of context is interpreted in such a way that it includes first and foremost the subject matter of inquiry, contextualist epistemology might very well converge with the views expressed here. In this work, contextualism is not examined further, however.

Moreover, contextual epistemologists seem to have assimilated the insight into the context-dependence of knowledge to another insight—namely, to the insight that every epistemological inquiry concerns some particular model, a "system" as physicists would call it, which typically is not an entire world. (See here Hintikka 2003(a).) All epistemological inquiry is therefore contextual in this sense of being relative to a model (scenario or "possible world"). But this does not make epistemology itself contextual or relative as a scientific theory is made contextual or relative by the fact that it is inevitably applied to reality system by system. Hence the impact of the line of thought pursued here is diametrically opposed to the most common form of contextualism. This form of contextualism aims at the rejection of global epistemological questions. (See Bonjour 2002, p. 267). For us, global epistemological questions concern in the first place the nature of interrogative inquiry, and they are in no sense context-dependent or even dependent on the subject matter.

8. The Folly of Trying to Define Knowledge

The concept of knowledge thus belongs to applied epistemology, not to general epistemology. The criteria of knowledge concern the conditions on which the results of epistemological inquiry can be relied as a basis of action. It follows that it is an exercise in futility to try to define knowledge in any general episte-mological theory. Such a definition could never help Safire's sleeper spy. But my point is not only about what is not useful in practice. The extensive discus-sions about how to define knowledge are not only useless for applications, they are theoretically misguided. Here the true relations of the concepts knowledge and truth to definability are almost precisely opposite to what they have been taken to be recently. Tarski (1956) proved certain results concerning the unde-finability of truth. Philosophers and other thinkers have taken Tarski's results at their apparent face value, without realizing how restrictive the assumptions are on which these impossibility results are predicated. (See Hintikka 2002.) They have even let Tarski's results discourage them to the extent of giving up attempts to define truth. Tarski notwithstanding, a truth predicate can be formulated for sufficiently rich languages in a philosophically relevant sense in the same language. In contrast, no major philosopher has to the best of my knowledge openly maintained it to be a folly to try to define knowledge. Yet if someone has done so, that philosopher would have been much closer to truth than a philosopher who argues that it is foolish to try to define truth. (See Davidson 1996.)

9. Belief as a Product of Inquiry

The notion of knowledge belongs to applied epistemology because it is con-nected conceptually with the notions of acting and decision-making. The par-ticular connection is not crucial. But if it does not matter, similar conclusions must hold also for those other epistemic concepts that are connected concep-tually with behavior, especially with decision-making. The concept of belief is a case in point. And conclusions similar to the ones that have been reached here concerning the notion of knowledge can in fact be drawn concerning the notion of belief. If you are inspired by this line of thought to review the structure of interrogative inquiry with a view to finding a role for the notion of belief there, you will not find such a role. Receiving an answer and incorporating it into one's interrogative inquiry is not the same as adopting a new belief. Acceptance is not the same thing as belief-formation. (For a discussion of their relationship, see Cohen 1992.) For one thing, at no stage of an interrogative inquiry are there any indications whether or not the inquirer is prepared to act on the truth of the propositions that the inquirer has at that stage accepted (and not bracketed). Hence the entire theory of knowledge acquisition can—and must—be developed without using the notion of belief. This notion does not play any role in an interrogative inquiry, only in the evaluation of its putative end-point. If one thinks about it, the notion of belief does not play much of a role in the methodology of science. What I am suggesting is that is should not play any more of a role in general epistemology either.

There is thus a certain partial epistemological parallelism between belief and knowledge. This parallelism has not been appreciated by epistemologists. Ever since Plato, the two notions are habitually contrasted to each other. This contrast is nevertheless seriously misleading, as far the epistemology of belief is concerned.

It seems to me that the same point is unwittingly attested to by all the decision theorists who are using beliefs as an ingredient in rational decision-making. Such a use would be pointless unless there were some previous reasons to think that the beliefs in question can rationally be expected to be true. And such reasons must somehow come from the inquirer's previous experience, if one is a good empiricist.

Belief, too, is connected with criteria as to when I am ready to act on a certain item of information I have received. But whereas the criteria of knowing are impersonal (even though they can be relative to the subject matter), the criteria of belief can be personal and dependent on an even wider selection of the aspects of the subject matter. In claiming to know, I am making a commitment to others, but in forming a belief, I am usually responsible only to myself.

There are also intermediate cases. For instance, a scientist's beliefs *qua* scientist are subject to the standards of acceptance in his or her scientific community. The crucial point is that those beliefs are, in the case of a scientist, formed as a result of an inquiry, rather than, so to speak, as a response to the question, "What do you think about it?" One may very well catch a physicist asking whether he or she should believe a certain hypothesis in the light of available evidence. But one is even likelier to find a scientific inquirer asking what new information he or she should try to acquire—for instance, what experiments to carry out—in order to be in a position to entertain a certain belief.

In general, the same things can thus be said of belief and its standards as were said earlier of knowledge. Belief statements, like knowledge statements, express entitlement of a certain sort. In neither case does an agent have to avail himself or herself of such entitlement. Beliefs need not manifest themselves in overt behavior any more than knowledge. Hence, decision theorists' frequent assumption that an agent's beliefs (or degrees of belief) together with utilities determine his, her, or its behavior is in need of scrutiny. Above all, beliefs, too, must be thought of as being formed by means of inquiry.

What I take to be a related point has been expressed by Timothy Williamson by pointing out that a "reason is needed for thinking that beliefs tend to be true." (Quoted from the abstract of his contribution to the conference on "Modalism and Mentalism in Modern Epistemology," Copenhagen, January 29–31, 2004.) The relationship is mediated by the fact that, if I am right, interrogative inquiry is, in the last analysis, the only way of arriving at true beliefs.

The conclusions reached here have repercussions for the entire research strategies that should be pursued in epistemology. For instance, there is a major school of thought that conceives of inquiry as a series of belief revisions. But is this at all realistic as a description of what good reasoners actually do? Georges Simenon's Inspector Maigret is sometimes asked what he believes about the case he is investigating. His typical answer is: "I don't believe anything." And this does not mean, contrary to what one might first suspect, that Maigret wants only to know and not to believe and that he has not yet reached that state of knowledge. No—in one story he says, "The moment for believing or not believing hasn't come yet." (Georges Simenon, *Maigret and the Pickpocket*, Harcourt Brace Jovanovich, San Diego, 1985.) It is not that Maigret has not carried his investigation far enough to be in a position to know something. He has not reached for enough to form a belief. (The merc possibility of using the locution "belief formation" is instructive.) In serious inquiry, belief too is a matter whether an inquiry has reached far enough.

Belief, too, concerns the question of when to stop an inquiry. That is the place of this concept in the framework of the interrogative approach. The difference between belief and knowledge does not lie merely in the degree of justification the believer has reached. It does not mean that there is an evaluative component in knowledge but not in belief. The difference lies in the kind of evaluation involved. It is much more like the difference between satisfying an agent's own freely chosen standards of epistemic confidence and satisfying certain impersonal standards that are appropriate to the subject matter.

In linguists' terminology, knowing is an achievement verb. In a way, although not in a literal sense, believing is in the context of interrogative inquiry likewise an achievement notion. What should be studied in epistemology is belief-formation and not only belief change. The notion of belief cannot serve the role as a determinant of human action that is assigned to it in decision theory if it is not influenced by what the agent knows. But such influence is usually not studied in decision theory.

One corollary to the results we have reached concerns philosophers' research strategies. What we can see now is that the interrogative model is not only a rational reconstruction of knowledge acquisition, it can also be used as a model of belief formation. The insight that belief, too, is typically a product of inquiry lends some renewed interest to the "true belief" type of attempted definitions of knowledge. What they perhaps succeed in capturing is admittedly not philosophers' strong sense of knowledge. But there may be other uses (senses?) of the words *knowledge* and *knowing* that can be approached by means of such characterizations.

Philosophers tend to downplay the role of certainty, especially of experienced certainty, in explicating the notion of knowledge. There is nevertheless a third-person use of knowledge attributions in which the meaning of knowing is very close to true conviction reached through inquiry. In such cases, the inquirer has convinced himself or herself by means of inquiry of the truth of some proposition or other even when, by some standards, the inquirer has not yet reached sufficient justification.

A typical context is when an investigator has reached a correct conclusion—for instance, identified the perpetrator—through inquiry and has become convinced of this conclusion even though his or her reasons would not satisfy the standards of evidence in a court of law. It is interesting to note that in such a usage, the true conclusion must have been reached through a viable strategy. A mere guess would not amount to knowledge even in such cases. (Notice that one could not attribute knowledge in this sense to an automaton or to a database.) This observation may be related to Frank Ramsey's (1978) attempt to characterize knowledge as true belief obtained through a reliable method. This sense of knowing seems to be much closer to colloquial usage than the one philosophers have in vain been trying to define.

10. Repercussions for Other Approaches

From the point of view we have reached, we can also see some serious problems about the Bayesian approach to inquiry. (See, e.g., Earman 1992.) This approach deals with belief change rather than belief-formation. Insofar as we can find any slot for belief-formation within the Bayesian framework from the point of view of any simple application of, it is pushed back to the selection of priors. In other words, it is made entirely *a priori*, at least locally. This is by itself difficult to implement in the case of theory-formation (belief-formation) in science. Is it, for instance, realistic to assume that a scientist can associate an *a priori* probability with each and every possible law of nature? And these doubts are reinforced by general conceptual considerations. Assignments of priors amount to assumptions concerning the world. What is more, prior probabilities pertain to the entire system (model, "world") that the inquirer is investigating bit by bit. How can the inquirer choose such priors on the basis of his or her limited knowledge of the world? These difficulties might not be crucial if there existed a Bayesian theory of belief-change that included a study of changes of priors. Even though such changes have been studied, it seems to me that their theory has not been developed far enough in the Bayesian framework to cover all possibilities.

All sorts of difficult questions face us here. For instance, in order to use Bayesian inference, we need to know the prior probabilities. It seems to be thought generally that this does not amount to asking very much. This may be true in situations in which the primary data is reasonably reliable, as in typical scientific contexts. However, if our evidence is likely to be relatively unreliable, the situation may be different—for instance, when we are dealing with testimony as our basic form of evidence. I may easily end up asking: Do I really have enough information to make the guess concerning the world that was seem to be involved in the choice of the priors?

For one thing, even though the matter is highly controversial, fascinating evidence to this effect comes from the theory of so-called cognitive fallacies studied by mathematical psychologists such as Amos Tversky and Daniel Kahneman. (See, e.g., Kahneman et al., 1982; Piatelli-Palmerini 1994.) These alleged fallacies include the conjunction fallacy and the base-rate fallacy. As I have suggested in Chapter 9 of this volume (and in Hintikka 2004), at least in certain "crucial experiment" cases, the alleged mistakes are not fallacious at all, but rather point to certain subtle but very real ways in which one's prior probabilities can (and must) be changed in the light of new evidence. They do not show that certain fallacious ways of thinking are hardwired into human beings. Rather, what they show is that Bayesians have so far failed to master certain subtle modes of ampliative reasoning. Tversky's and Kahneman's Nobel Prize notwithstanding, epistemologists should take a long critical look at the entire theory of cognitive fallacies.

Here I can only give indications of how to view the cognitive fallacies conundrum. Very briefly, in the kind of situation that is at issue in the alleged conjunctive fallacy, the prior probabilities that one in effect relies on include the degrees of probability (credibility) assigned to the reports one receives. But that credibility can not only be affected by suitable new evidence, it can be affected by the very report itself. If the report shows that the reporter is likely to know more about the subject matter than another one, it is not fallacious to assign a higher prior probability to his or her report, even though it is a conjunction of a less credible report and further information.

In the case of an alleged base-rate fallacy, there is no conceivable mistake present if the intended sample space consists simply of the different possible courses of events concerning the crucial event—for example, a traffic accident. Base rates enter into the picture only when a wider class of courses of events is considered—for example, all possible courses of events that might have led to the accident. This means considering a larger sample space. Either sample space can of course be considered entirely consistently, depending on one's purposes. A fallacy would inevitably be committed only if the only legitimate application of our language and our epistemological methods was to the entire world—in this case, the larger sample space. But such an exclusive preference of the larger sample space is but an instance of the one-world assumption, which I have criticized elsewhere. (See Hintikka 2003(a).)

11. Whither Epistemology?

The moral of the insights we have thus reached is not merely to avoid certain words in our epistemological theorizing. It calls for rethinking our overall research strategies in epistemology. And the spirit in which we should do so is perhaps illustrated by the first epistemologist in the Western philosophical tradition. Socrates did not claim that he knew anything. In the manner of a practitioner of my interrogative method, what he did was to ask questions. I suspect that it is only in Plato's dialogues that he was looking for a definition of knowledge. And Plato put this question (and other questions of definition) into Socrates's mouth because Plato shared the widespread Greek assumption that the definition of X gives us the "blueprint" that enables us to bring about X. (See Hintikka 1974, ch. 1–2.) This applies both to the generic search for knowledge and to the quest of particular items of knowledge. Thus, insofar as Plato contemplated knowledge-seeking (information-seeking) by questioning in our sense, he would have had to say that we must know what we are looking for there and that it is this knowledge alone that can guide our search. (No wonder he was worried about Meno's problem.) By the same token, all search for knowledge would have had to be guided by our knowledge of what knowledge is.

Hence it is seen that Plato had in one important respect the same focus as we: the quest for knowledge rather than the justification of beliefs. The definition of knowledge was thought of by Plato as a means for this quest. If so, the pursuit of the definition of knowledge would indeed have been the alpha and omega of epistemology. But we do not think in that way. The training that Safire's spymaster is supposed to have received did not aim exclusively at learning the definition of knowledge. For us, the fact that knowledge can be considered the end product of inquiry shows on the contrary that it cannot play any role in the process of inquiry. Hence the wild goose chase of the definition of knowledge only shows that too many contemporary epistemologists are still bewitched by Plato's assumptions. This is one of the reasons why at the beginning of this chapter, I called contemporary academic epistemology antiquated. Maybe it is time for its practitioners to take up some more up-to-date problems.

References

Austin, John, 1961(a) (original 1946), "Other Minds," in *Philosophical Papers*, Clarendon Press, Oxford, especially pp. 67–68.

Austin, John, 1961(b), "Performative Utterances," in *Philosophical Papers*, Clarendon Press, Oxford, ch. 10, especially p. 220.

Bonjour, Laurence, 2002, *Epistemology: Classical Problems and Contemporary Responses*, Rowman & Littlefield, Lanham, Maryland.

Cohen, L. Jonathan, 1992, *Essay on Belief and Acceptance*, Clarendon Press, Oxford.

Cohen, Stewart, 1998, "Contextual Solutions to Epistemological Problems," *Australasian Journal of Philosophy*, vol. 76, pp. 289–306.

Collingwood, R. G., 1940, *An Essay on Metaphysics*, Clarendon Press, Oxford, especially ch. I, sec. 5.

Davidson, Donald, 1996, "The Folly of Trying to Define Truth," *Journal of Philosophy*, vol. 93, pp. 263–278.

DeRose, Keith, 1995, "Solving the Skeptical Problem," *Philosophical Review*, vol. 104, pp. 1–52.

Earman, John, 1992, *Bayes or Bust? A Critical Examination of Bayesian Confirmation Theory*, MIT Press, Cambridge.

Frege, Gottlob, 1984 (original 1918–19), "Thoughts," in *Collected Papers*, Basil Blackwell, Oxford.

Gadamer, Hans-Georg, 1975 (original 1960), *Truth and Method*, Continuum, New York, especially the section "Logic of Questions and Answers," pp. 333–341.

Hintikka, Jaakko, forthcoming, "Wittgenstein on knowledge and skepticism."

Hintikka, Jaakko, 2004, "A fallacious fallacy?" *Synthese* vol. 140, pp. 25–35. And as Chapter 9 in this volume.

Hintikka, Jaakko, 2003 (a), "A Distinction Too Few or Too Many: A Vindication of the Analytic vs. Synthetic Distinction," in *Constructivism and Practice: Toward a Historical Epistemology*, Carol C. Gould, editor, Rowman & Littlefield, Lanham, Maryland, 47–74.

Hintikka, Jaakko, 2003(b), "A Second-Generation Epistemic Logic and Its General Significance," in Vincent F. Hendricks et al., editors, *Knowledge Contributors*, Kluwer Academic, Dordrecht, pp. 33–56. And as Chapter 3 in this volume.

Hintikka, Jaakko, 2002, "Post-Tarskian Truth," *Synthese*, vol. 126, pp. 17–36.

Hintikka, Jaakko, 1999, *Inquiry as Inquiry: A Logic of Scientific Discovery*, Kluwer Academic, Dordrecht.

Hintikka, Jaakko, 1998, "What Is Abduction? The Fundamental Problem of Contemporary Epistemology," *Transactions of the Charles Peirce Society*, vol. 34, pp. 503–533. A revised version, "Abduction—Inference, Conjecture, or an Answer to a Question," appears as Chapter 2 in this volume.

Hintikka, Jaakko, 1974, *Knowledge and the Known*, Reidel, Dordrecht.

Hintikka, Jaakko, and Ilpo Halonen, 1995, "Semantics and Pragmatics for Why-Questions," *Journal of Philosophy*, vol. 92, pp. 636–657.

Husserl, Edmund, 1983 (original 1913), *Ideas Pertaining to a Pure Phenomenology. First Book*, Martinus Nijhoff, The Hague.

Kahneman, D., P. Slovic, and A. Tversky, editors, 1982, *Judgment under Uncertainty: Heuristics and Biases*, Cambridge University Press, Cambridge.

Kant, Immanuel, 1787, *Kritik der reinen Vernunft*, second edition (see preface, p. xiii).

McCarthy, John 1990, "Circumscription—a Form of Non-Monotonic Reasoning," *Artificial Intelligence*, vol. 13, pp. 27–39 and 171–172.

Montague, Richard, 1974, *Formal Philosophy*, Yale University Press, New Haven.

Piatelli-Palmarini, Massimo, 1994, *Inevitable Illusions*, John Wiley & Sons, New York.

Plato, 1924, *Meno, Plato: with an English Translation*, Loeb Classical Library, vol. IV, Harvard University Press, Cambridge.

Ramsey, Frank, 1978 (original 1929), "Knowledge," in *Foundations: Essays in Philosophy, Logic, Mathematics, and Economics*, Routledge & Kegan Paul, London, pp. 126–127.

Safire, William, 1995, *The Sleeper Spy*, Random House, New York.

Shope, Robert K., 1983, *The Analysis of Knowing: A Decade of Research*, Princeton University Press, Princeton.

Tarski, Alfred, 1956 (original 1935), "The Concept of Truth in Formalized Languages," in *Logic, Semantics, Metamathematics*, Clarendon Press, Oxford, pp. 152–278.

Williams, Michael, 2001, *Problems of Knowledge: A Critical Introduction to Epistemology*, Oxford University Press, Oxford.

Notes

Sea change: profound, notable transformation (Shakespearean)

dejure: lawful

defacto: pragmatic

propositional attitude: believing rooting for

epistemic logic: logic of knowledge

Bedeutung: meaning, sense: significance (pl. for Bedeutungen)

Semantic: study of linguistics and how language changes its structures (etymology-syn)

2

Abduction—Inference, Conjecture, or an Answer
to a Question?

಄ⴰ

It is sometimes said that the highest philosophical gift is to invent important new philosophical problems. If so, Peirce is a major star in the firmament of philosophy. By thrusting the notion of abduction to the forefront of philosophers' consciousness, he created a problem that—I will argue—is the central one in contemporary epistemology.

Now, what is the notion of abduction, what is new about it, and why is it a problem? Peirce's notion and some of the problems it raises have recently been summed up by Tomis Kapitan (1997, pp. 477–478) in four theses:

Inferential Thesis. Abduction is, or includes, an inferential process or processes (5.188–189, 7.202).

Thesis of Purpose. The purpose of "scientific" abduction is both (1) to generate new hypotheses and (2) to select hypotheses for further examination (6.525); hence, a central aim of scientific abduction is to "recommend a course of action" (MS 637:5).

Comprehension Thesis. Scientific abduction includes all the operations whereby theories are engendered (5.590).

Autonomy Thesis. Abduction is, or embodies, reasoning that is distinct from, and irreducible to, either deduction or induction (5.146).

In his earlier work, Peirce identified abduction with Aristotelian *epagoge* and interpreted it as an inverse of a syllogism. According to Kapitan (1997, p. 480), "Peirce's 1878 model of reasoning by "hypothesis" from result and rule to case (2.623) is familiar:

All As that are B are C.	(rule)	
This A is C.	(result)	(F1)
Therefore, the A is B.	(case)	

In working on this chapter, I have greatly benefited from comments and suggestions by Risto Hilpinen.

Abduction differs from deduction, which moves from rule and case to result, and from induction, which goes from case and result to rule, and it is this tidy contrast in terms of syllogistic permutations that very likely led Peirce to trichotomize inference in the first place." But such an inference does not necessarily yield even probabilistic support for its conclusion. Hence it is extremely puzzling as to why the early Peirce should have claimed that abduction in this sense is an inference (See Inferential Thesis.)

Moreover, the inverse syllogism model cannot be seriously claimed to be the only way in which new hypotheses and theories are engendered in science. (See Comprehension Thesis.) This model is a special case of the idea, to be discussed later, that abduction is an inference to the best explanation. Peirce's early schema of abduction presupposes, if he is to claim universality for it, that all the best explanations are syllogistic. We know better than that, and Peirce came to know better, too.

But his later sense of abduction does not seem to fare much better. For one thing, it is still extremely difficult to see why abduction, whatever it is or may be, can be not only a rational operation but even a logical inference, in any sense of logical inference.

This puzzle can be said to be created by the combination of the different theses that Peirce defended and that were listed at the beginning of the chapter. Abduction is ampliative, according to the theses of Purpose and Comprehension. Hence it cannot be deductive, for valid deduction is tautological in the sense of not yielding any new information, such as new hypotheses. Hence abduction is not necessarily truth-preserving. Furthermore, it is contrasted by Peirce with induction, which according to him is the process of testing new hypotheses provided by abduction. For this reason, abduction cannot very well provide even probabilistic support for its output. In other (more general) words, all the factors that might affect the reliability of abductive hypothesis formation belong to the inductive phase of inquiry, not to the abductive one. In what sense can abduction then be an inference?

This puzzle about what abduction really is is deepened by Peirce's explicit acknowledgement of the presence of a conjectural element in abduction. It even seems that our abductive hypothesis-forming power is nothing but a mysterious power of guessing right. Indeed, Peirce himself writes as follows:

In very many questions, the situation before us is this: We shall do better to abandon the whole attempt to learn the truth, however urgent may be our need of ascertaining it, unless we can trust to the human mind's having such a power of guessing right that before very many hypotheses shall have been tried, intelligent guessing may be expected to lead us to the one which will support all tests, leaving the vast majority of possible hypotheses unexamined. Of course, it will be understood that in the testing process itself there need be no such assumption to mysterious guessing-powers. It is only in selecting the hypothesis to be tested that we are to be guided by that assumption. MS no. 315 entitled "Pragmatism and the Logic of Abduction," dated May 14, 1903.

Elsewhere, Peirce speaks of a *method* of making good conjectures instead of a power of doing so. Sometimes he also uses the word *habit* in this context. I will return to these formulations later.

The conjectural element in Peirce's notion of abduction is precisely the kind of reason that has led other philosophers of science to embrace a hypothetico-deductive model of science. (Needless to say, we might equally well speak here of a hypothetico-deductive model of knowledge acquisition in general.) For nothing seems to be less rational and less subject to rules than guessing. Thus, Peirce's idea of abductive inference as the source of all new hypotheses stands in a stark contrast to any hypothetico-deductive theory of science.

Here one can begin to see what I have in mind by calling the problem of abduction the basic question of contemporary epistemology. The most general problem to which both the hypothetico-deductive approach and the idea of abduction are attempted solutions is: What is ampliative reasoning like? Purely logical (in the sense of deductive) reasoning is not ampliative. It does not give one any really new information. Yet all our science and indeed our whole life depends on ampliative reasoning. But what is that reasoning really like? When we speak of the reasonings of the likes of Sherlock Holmes or Nero Wolfe as "deductions" accomplished by means of "logic," we do not mean philosophers' deductive logic, which is not ampliative. But what are they, then? The hypothetico-deductive approach tries to brush them all under the carpet of "contexts of discovery," which allegedly cannot be dealt with by means of logical, epistemological, or other rational means. Such a way of thinking might be congenial to the cultists of the irrational, but it is deeply dissatisfying in that it leaves unexamined an important part of the cognitive lives of all of us and hence is deeply un-Socratic.

The identification of the problem of Peircean abduction with the problem of the nature of ampliative inference is largely justified by Peirce's Comprehension Thesis (see the beginning of this chapter).

Before essaying my own answer, it is in order to deal with a widespread alternative interpretation of abduction. According to this interpretation, abduction is an inference to the best explanation.

This idea has a great deal of initial plausibility. In fact, abductive inference is often, perhaps typically, related to explanation. Peirce already emphasized that the new hypothesis that abduction yields should explain the available data. (See, e.g. "Pragmatism as the Logic of Abduction," pp. 15–16 in Peirce's numbering; Kapitan 1997, pp. 480–481.) Others have later strengthened the role of explanation in the definition of abduction and identified abduction with what is known as "inference to the best explanation."

This view is seriously simplified at best. Part of the difficulty can be seen by asking, first, what explanation is or, perhaps more pertinently, what explaining is. Most people who speak of "inferences to best explanation" seem to imagine that they know what explanation is. In reality, the nature of explanation is scarcely any clearer than the nature of abduction. I have argued elsewhere that explaining a certain explanandum E is to derive it from an assumed background theory T plus a number of contingent truths A that are relative to E and that have to be found in order for an attempt to explain E is to succeed. An explainer's job description is thus twofold: on the one hand to find the auxiliary facts A and on the other hand to deduce the explanandum from them together with the background theory T. This entire process, including both the search for A and the derivation of E from T and A, can be thought of as an interrogative inquiry in the sense that the contingent data A can be conceptualized as nature's answers to the inquirer's questions. Certain further conditions may have to be satisfied by T and A in relation to E.

The pertinent features of explanation thus include the fact that the theory T is not in any literal sense a generalization from the different explananda E_1, E_2, that it can help to explain, for in each case, E_i is implied by T only in conjunction with the *ad hoc* data (nature's answers) A_i, which may be different for different values of i—that is for different explananda.

What follows from these observations for the interpretation of abduction as inference to the best explanation? The first pertinent question here is: explanation of what facts? The merits of a theory or hypothesis include its ability to explain new, previously unknown facts. But these facts will be, if they are genuinely new ones, unknown at the time of the abduction, and even more so must the auxiliary data that help to explain them be unknown. Hence these future, so far unknown, explananda cannot be among the premises of an abductive inference. For Peirce makes it clear that according to his lights, abduction is like any inference in that it leads to new knowledge on the basis of what is already known. Moreover, an inference is a conscious operation, wherefore this earlier knowledge must be explicit at the time of the inference. Hence the unknown explananda cannot be what "an inference to the best explanation" is calculated to explain, for they are not in the conscious control of the reasoner at the time of the inference.

This observation is worth elaborating on. Quite often, scientists frequently become aware of interesting phenomena explainable by means of a theory of interesting phenomena only through the theory itself, once it has been discovered. This happens, for instance, when a theory predicts the existence of an entity, such as a certain kind of sub-atomic particle, which then is subsequently discovered. The theory admittedly explains the existence of the particle, but the theory can scarcely be said to have been arrived at by means of inference to such explanations. The same goes for the existence of new phenomena. For an amusing example—Einstein was aware of the possibility of Brownian motion and thinking about the laws governing it before he even knew that Dr. Brown actually had observed such a motion. (See, e.g., Fölsing, 1997, pp. 128–131.) If Dr. Brown had not so observed, Brownian motion would have been observed in connection with the testing of Einstein's explanation. In such a case, a scientist's reasoning looks less like an inference from certain explananda to a hypothesis that explains them than an inference from an abductive hypothesis to the existence of a new phenomenon it turns out to explain.

Einstein's discoveries provide still further examples. Needless (perhaps) to say, the discovery of the general theory of relativity was not an inference to the best explanation of the perihelion movement of the planet Mercury and of the curvature of light rays in a gravitational field during a solar eclipse, even though they were the first two new phenomena explainable by the general theory.

Hence the explananda relevant to the idea of an "inference to the best explanation" must be data known to the scientist drawing an abductive inference at the time of the inference. Otherwise, the idea of abduction as an inference does not make much sense. But even when the explananda E and the background theory T are known to the scientist, he or she may not be aware of the explanation that T can yield of E—for instance, because he or she is unaware of the derivation of E from T and A. For instance, in the discovery of the outer planets, the conclusion of the crucial abductive inference is naturally taken to be the existence of a new planet. But the mere existence assumption does not explain the apparent irregularities in the motions of known planets that are the starting point of the discoverer's line of thought. In order to reach an explanation, the orbit of the new planet has to be established and its influence on the known planets calculated. But these tasks were not accomplished when the initial existence assumption was proposed.

Hence, since the abductive reasoner does not always have at his or her disposal explanations even of the known data, the abductive inference cannot be a step to the known data to a hypothesis or theory that best explains them.

Moreover, many of the most important types of scientific reasoning cannot be described as inferences to the best explanation in the first place. For instance, when a controlled experiment produces a dependence law telling us how the observed variable depends on the controlled one, the law does not *explain* the result of the experiment. It is the *result* of the experiment, nature's answer to the experimental investigator's question. Thus the claim that inference to the best explanation is the only or merely a typical way of forming new hypotheses in science is simply false. An experimental formation of new laws has an excellent claim of being the typical way of forming new laws in experimental sciences.

For another instance or group of instances, many of the scientific inferences that presumably should be thought of as abductive are not generalizations from particular cases or explanations of such particular cases. They may, for instance, be successful syntheses of two earlier laws or theories that might even have seemed to be irreconcilable. In such cases, the wider new theory unifying the earlier ones does not always "explain" the earlier ones in any natural sense of the word. It reconciles them with each other. (See Hintikka, 1993(a).)

An instructive example is offered by the special theory of relativity. The old-fashioned philosophical view would have sought to interpret Einstein's theory as an attempt to explain certain "anomalies" left unaccounted for by the earlier views. And an explanandum apparently serving this role was in fact available in the form of the famous Michelson-Morley experiment. Einstein's theory did in fact, in the light of hindsight, explain why a terrestrial observer appears to be stationary with respect to the ether. Alas, historical scholarship has revealed that the Michelson-Morley experiment played no role in Einstein's actual line of thought that led him to the special theory of relativity. (See Holton, 1969; Fölsing, 1997, pp. 217–219.)

The most instructive way of looking at Einstein's discovery is to see it as a way of reconciling Maxwell's electromagnetic theory with Newtonian mechanics. This is reflected in the very title of Einstein's famous paper "Zur Elektrodynamik bewegter Körper." But it would be ridiculous to say that Einstein's theory "explains" Maxwell's theory any more than it "explains" Newton's laws of motion.

Hence the first and crucial step to a scientific hypothesis or theory that abduction is supposed to be cannot be thought of as an inference to the best explanation.

Defenders of abduction interpreted as "inference to the best explanation" sometimes try to support their idea by appealing to examples from the history of science. Thus John R. Josephson (Josephson & Josephson, 1994, pp. 7–8) writes: "Abductions are common in scientific reasoning on large and small scales. The persuasiveness of Newton's theory of gravitation was enhanced by its ability to explain not only the motions of the planets, but also the occurrence of the tides." Such appeals to history are superficial, and on a closer examination easily turn against the appealer. In the cases referred to by Josephson, Newton most definitely does not present his discoveries as results of abduction (or equivalent). Abduction is described by Peirce and by others as a hypothesis-forming operation. Newton blandly denies that he is "feigning hypotheses." At times, Newton goes so far as to say that according to him, laws are "deduced" from phenomena.

The interpretation of abduction as an inference to the best explanation is also in conflict with what Peirce says in so many words. In the passage quoted earlier from 6.525 (Thesis of Purpose), he says that in abduction, one hypothesis may be preferred over others if the preference is *not* based on previous knowledge. But the whole idea of inference to the best explanation is that the choice is determined by the facts that are to be explained—that the outcome is the best explanation of these particular data.

Some defenders of the idea of inference to the best explanation have even tried to subsume enumerative induction under such a procedure (e.g., Harman 1968). This was in effect Peirce's early perspective on abduction, but it was not Peirce's mature view. On the one hand, induction for Peirce is essentially a procedure of testing and confirming hypotheses arrived at by abduction. On the other hand abduction was for Peirce the only way of introducing new hypotheses into inquiry. (See Comprehension Thesis) Yet nobody has in his wildest dreams suggested that all out new general knowledge is first arrived at by enumerative induction.

There are still other ways of seeing the limitations of the idea of "inference to the best explanation." One of them is probabilistic. From a probabilistic point of view, this idea amounts to using only the likelihood in the search of new hypotheses. Even though this might have satisfied Sir Ronald Fisher, it means leaving other kinds of relevant information unused. (For a defense of the importance of likelihoods, see Edwards 1992.)

Before venturing my own solution to the problem of abduction, I will first call attention to a dimension of this problem that has not yet come up. This dimension is present in Peirce, albeit not fully articulated. One context in which it can be seen is Peirce's notion of inference. It has already been seen that it is not quite what we are used to. As Peirce himself puts it,

I call all such inference by the peculiar name, *abduction*, because its legitimacy depends upon altogether different principles from those of other kinds of inference. "Hume on Miracles," CP 6.524-525, 1901.

What are those "altogether different principles?" Peirce's views on inference have been summarized as follows (Kapitan, 1997, p. 479):

(1) Inference is a conscious, voluntary act over which the reasoner exercises control (5.109, 2.144).
(2) The aim of inference is to discover (acquire, attain) new knowledge from a consideration that which is already known (MS 628: 4).
(3) One who infers a conclusion *C* from a premise *P* accepts *C as a result* of both accepting *P* and approving a general *method* of reasoning according to which if any *P*-like proposition is true, so is the correlated *C*-like proposition (7.536, 2.444, 5.130, 2.773, 4.53–55, 7.459, L232:56).
(4) An inference can be either *valid* or *invalid* depending on whether it follows a method of reasoning it professes to and that method is conductive to satisfying the aim of reasoning—namely, the acquisition of truth (2.153, 2.780, 7.444, MS 692: 5).

The most interesting aspect of Peirce's notion of inference is (4). Usually the validity and the other merits of an inference are judged in terms of the relation of the premise or premises to the conclusion—for instance, whether the truth of the premises guarantees the truth of the conclusion or perhaps whether it makes the conclusion probable to a certain degree. The term "rule of inference" is usually restricted to cover only such inferences as can be justified in terms of the premise-conclusion relation either because the step from the premises to the conclusion is truth-preserving or because the premises make the conclusion probable to a certain degree. Peirce is making a much more important break with this traditional idea than he himself seems to realize. He is going beyond rules of inference that depend on the premise-conclusion relation alone and is considering also rules or principles of inference "of an altogether different kind." These rules or principles are justified by the fact that they exemplify a method that is conducive to the acquisition of new knowledge.

Hence there are two different kinds of rules (principles) that can justify an inference. Peirce does not seem to distinguish these two kinds of rules or principles from each other systematically. It would have been most helpful, however, if he had done so. I have called the former kind of rules *definitory rules* and assimilated them to the rules that define a strategic game like chess—or deduction or scientific inquiry, for that matter. Such definitory rules are merely permissive. They tell us what moves one may make in given circumstances, but they do not tell anything about which moves are good, bad, or indifferent. Such advice is codified in what I have called *strategic rules* (or principles). From the general theory of games, we know that such rules cannot be formulated in move-by-move terms—for instance, in terms of the relationship of premises to a conclusion—but only in terms of complete strategies. (A game theorist would express this point by saying that in general, utilities can absolutely speaking be associated only with entire strategies, not with particular moves.)

Now we can see that Peirce's vantage point contained at one and the same time a brilliant insight and a serious limitation. The insight was into the importance of strategic rules. For what Peirce's statement quoted earlier amounts to is that the validity of an abductive inference is to be judged by strategic principles rather than by definitory (move-by-move) rules. This is what makes an abductive inference depend for its legitimacy "upon altogether different principles from those of other kinds of inference." What these "different principles" were in Peirce's mind can be gathered from his various statements. One typical expression of the difference is Peirce's distinction between the validity and the strength of an argument.

... it is only in Deduction that there is no difference between a *valid* argument and a *strong* one. ("Pragmatism as the Logic of Abduction," p. 17)

Thus an argument can be logical but weak. Such statements leave little doubt that the kind of validity Peirce had in mind was essentially strategic.

There was nevertheless a limitation that handicapped Peirce's thinking in his failure to appreciate fully the difference between definitory and strategic rules. Whenever he tries to explain the kind of validity that does not go with strength, he becomes hesitant and resorts to examples. He never gives a general characterization of the difference between what I have called definitory and strategic rules. These two kinds of rules do not deal with different kinds of inference. They are different kinds of rules governing the same kinds of inferential steps. Peirce recognizes the difference between the ways in which definitory and strategic rules are legitimized or validated. Definitory rules of inquiry are validated insofar as they confer truth or high probability on the conclusion of each particular application of theirs. In contrast, strategic rules of inquiry are justified by their propensity to lead the inquirer to new truths when consistently pursued as a general policy. It is worth emphasizing that this propensity to lead to new knowledge must not be assimilated to an inference rule's ability to confer truth or high probability on its conclusion in each particular case. The former propensity can, for instance, be manifested when a rule application opens up new future possibilities of knowledge acquisition even when it does not itself provide the inquirer with any new truths or even new hypotheses. Peirce seems to have realized fairly clearly what a strategic justification of a rule application consists in. Indeed, he seems to see the justification not only of abductive but also inductive steps as strategic.

Induction is reasoning which professes to pursue such a method that, being persistent in, each special application of it ... must at least indefinitely approximate to the truth about the subject in hand, *in the long run*. [Emphasis added.] *Abduction* is reasoning, which professes to be such, that in the case there is any ascertainable truth concerning the matter in hand, the general method of this reasoning though not necessarily each special application of it must *eventually* [emphasis added] approximate the truth. (Eisele, ed., *The New Elements of Mathematics*, vol. 4, p. 37)

What Peirce does not realize is that one and the same step of reasoning, including deductive reasoning, can normally be considered both as an application of a definitory rule and as an application of a strategic rule—in fact, several alternative strategic rules that differ in their consequences for other particular cases. It is admittedly the case that deduction differs from abduction in the kind of justification of particular steps. As Peirce puts it:

Deduction is reasoning which proposes to pursue such a method that if the premises are true the conclusion will in every case be true. (loc. cit.)

But this does not obliterate the fact that we can in deduction, too, distinguish definitory and strategic rules from each other. Furthermore, if abduction is to obey formal laws like any other inference, as Peirce believes, it must likewise be subject to definitory (formal) rules. In brief, what Peirce does not realize is that there is a definitory versus strategic distinction that cuts across his trichotomy, deduction-abduction-induction.

The same shortcoming can also be described by saying that even though Peirce recognized the vital importance of strategic rules in inquiry, he did not possess the general concept of strategy in the abstract sense which was first spelled out clearly by von Neumann (1928; see also von Neumann and Morgenstern, 1944). He had to try to make other concepts do the job of the notion of strategy. How he did that requires a separate investigation. I believe that such an investigation might yield interesting insights into Peirce's ways of thinking and into the concepts he employed. For instance, it seems to me that the concept of habit was one of the notions he used to serve some of the same purposes as the notion of strategy introduced by later thinkers. This would, among other things, help to understand why Peirce's concept of habit differs from its customary namesake in being a conscious operation of the human mind. I suspect, in other words, that inside each Peircean habit there lurks (at least in the area of epistemology) a strategic rule trying to get out.

In the light of hindsight, Peirce's failure to command the general concept of strategy can in any case be seen to manifest itself in other parts of his thought. For instance, as Risto Hilpinen first pointed out, Peirce put forward completely explicitly what is known as the game-theoretical interpretation of quantifiers. This is no mean feat, for this "interpretation" is in my judgment the only one that does justice to the actual logic of these crucial logical notions. Yet Peirce never incorporated the game-theoretical idea into his logical theory or otherwise put it to major uses. Why? The answer in my view is that on the game-theoretical interpretation, the truth of quantificational sentences can only be conceptualized in terms of the strategies that the verifier has available. These strategies have their technical incarnation in the form of what is known as Skolem functions. Alas, they were introduced only in the 1920s, as was the general game-theoretical notion of strategy. (See Hintikka, 1988.)

Another idea of Peirce's that can perhaps be interpreted as an indication of a need of some notion such as strategy is his requirement that the aim of scientific abduction is to "recommend a course of action." For such recommendation can scarcely mean a preference for one particular action in one particular kind of situation, but presumably means a policy recommendation. Alas, again Peirce does not seem to have developed this idea further.

The distinction between definitory rules and strategic rules reveals an ambiguity in Peirce's characterization of the criteria of the validity of an inference. When is a method or rule "conductive to the acquisition of truth"? A definitory rule is valid when the truth of its premise or premises guarantees the truth (or at least the high probability) of its conclusion. But a strategic rule need not do so in order to further the aims of inquiry. It suffices for it to lead to truth in the long run. The answer to a strategically correct question might not provide any information that would by itself serve the ultimate end of the inquiry in question, yet might be instrumental in finding out the truth—for instance, by providing the inquirer with the presupposition of a question that the inquirer could not have asked without it and that will directly further the cause of the inquiry.

Applied to Peirce, this seems to reveal an inconsistency in his position. On the one hand, he seems to say that all inferences have to be judged strategically, in that it is the propensity of the method they instantiate to lead to truth that is the criterion of their validity. On the other hand, he suggests that it is a peculiarity of abductive inferences that they are so judged, in that their legitimacy is judged by altogether different principles from the other kinds of inference. For presumably those "altogether different" principles are the strategic ones.

Thus, recognizing that Peirce was considering abduction from an implicitly strategic vantage point does not solve all the problems concerning this notion. First and foremost, the distinction between definitory and strategic rules fails to help us discover any separate class of inferences that might be called abductive. Any move in any strategic game can be considered both from a definitory and from a strategic vantage point. One can raise two different questions about it. First, was it according to Hoyle?[1] Second, did it make it easier for the player who made it to win? These questions can concern the very same move in the very same game, which can be a "game" of inquiry. The former concerns the status of the move from a definitory vantage point, the latter from a strategic one.

Peirce's unspoken emphasis on the strategic viewpoint helps us to understand why he thought of abduction as a rational procedure and not as mere guessing. But it does not help us to identify a class of rules or even a class of steps in a line of thought that can be classified as abductive. Even less so does it help to explain why such steps could be assimilated by Peirce to inferences in the same sense as deductive inferences.

However, the idea of a strategic principle provides us with an Archimedean point by means of which we can identify the nature of abductive and, in general, ampliative inference. This Archimedean point is the requirement that any given ampliative step in a rational argument be capable of being judged strategically. In an argument or line of rational thought, the information that a fresh step codifies either is contained in the earlier propositions in that line of reasoning, or else is (partly or wholly) new. In the former case, the step in question is a deductive one and should be studied in deductive logic. In the latter case, the step is ampliative. And if Peirce is right, it must be abductive, at least if the output is a significant new hypothesis.

What has to be known before such an ampliative step of reasoning can be rationally evaluated? This means: before the concept of strategy can be applied to it. What is it that a reasoner must be conscious of and have under his or her control in an abductive inference?

Recall that an ampliative step of reasoning brings new information to the argument. Hence the following must clearly be the case:

(1) It has to be known who or what was the source of the new information. Otherwise the reliability of the answer cannot be gauged, for this reliability obviously depends on the source.

(2) In order for the inquirer's action to be rational, he or she must have intentionally chosen that particular oracle (source of information). As Peirce says, it has to be a conscious, voluntary act. The inquirer's performance hence cannot be evaluated rationally unless it is known what other sources of information were available to the inquirer. In other (more general) words, it has to be specified what the other moves are that were available to the inquirer.

---

[1] Translated from English into American, "Was it made in accordance with the definitory rules of the game?" (see, e.g., Hubert Phillips, *The Penguin Hoyle*, 1958).

(3) The inquirer cannot have known before the abductive step what the information is that the oracle provided him or her with, for otherwise the information would not have been new. However, the inquirer's move in turning to this particular oracle in this particular way would not have been fully in his or her conscious control, and as a result could not be rationally evaluated unless the inquirer knows which other items of information could have resulted from his or her decision to consult this particular source of information.

(4) Furthermore, by the same token, the inquirer must have known what results a consultation of each of the other different available oracles might have yielded.

But if (1)–(4) are satisfied, the new information might as well be thought of as an answer by the oracle to a question put to it (him, her) by the inquirer.

For instance, if the oracle consulted could have responded by the information specified by A_1 or A_2 or ... instead of A_0 (the actual answer), then the inquirer's action might as well be construed as asking the question:

Is it the case that A_0 or A_1 or A_2 or ...?

Thus all the new information flowing into a fully rational argument might as well be understood as answers to the inquirer's questions.

This, then, is my solution to the problem of abduction, which has meanwhile been generalized so as to become the problem concerning the nature of ampliative inference in general. Abductive "inferences" must be construed as answers to the inquirer's explicit or (usually) tacit question put to some definite source of answers (information).

This answer is not put forward as a total novelty. In spirit, and in some cases in letter, the picture of rational inquiry that embodies my answer is remarkably close to the questioning method (*elenchus*) of the Platonic Socrates. The same method constitutes (I have argued) the methodology of the early (and even of the mature) Aristotle. Much later, Collingwood (1944) and Gadamer (1975) likewise recommended what they call the logic of question and answer as the crucial method of inquiry.

My solution to the abduction problem is not merely an abstract theoretical thesis. It has direct implications for the way epistemology and, in general, philosophy of science is to be studied. The key to them is a general theory of questions and answers. This theory can be developed in great detail and with a great deal of precision. For instance, the theory of scientific explanation will amount to a study of the logic of *why*-questions. And since the logical theory of questions and answers is obviously dependent on the logic of knowledge (epistemic logic), which should more aptly be called the logic of information, the basis of all epistemology should be epistemic logic, suitably developed.

This solution prompts a number of further observations. One of them is that it was in part anticipated by Peirce. In fact, Peirce himself puts forward the interpretation of abduction as an interrogative step:

The first starting of a hypothesis and the entertaining of it, whether *as a simple interrogation* [emphasis added] or with any degree of confidence, is an inferential step which I propose to call *abduction*. (6.525)

Peirce continues:

This will include a preference for any one hypothesis over others which would equally explain the facts, as long as this preference is not based upon any previous knowledge bearing upon the truth of the hypotheses, nor on any testing of any of the hypotheses, after having admitted them on probation. I call such an inference by the peculiar name, abduction, because its legitimacy depends on altogether different principles from those of other kinds of inference.

Elsewhere, he writes:

It is to be remarked that, in pure abduction, it can never be justifiable to accept the hypothesis otherwise than as an *interrogation*. [Emphasis added.] But as long as that condition is observed, no positive falsity is to be feared. (Peirce, in Buchler, 1940, p. 154)

This passage is useful in that it refutes the interpretation offered by Isaac Levi of Peirce's notion of abduction as merely delineating a class of possible answers. Levi writes (1991, p. 71):

The task of constructing potential answers to a question is the task of abduction in the sense of Peirce." ... The "conclusions" of abductions are conjectures that are potential answers to questions. Deduction elaborates on the implications of assumptions already taken for granted or of conjectures when they are taken, for the sake of argument, to be true. Induction weeds out for rejection some conjectures, leaving the survivors for further consideration. (Ibid. p. 77)

This is not quite the whole story, for Peirce's words in 6.525 (see previous paragraph) show that for him in abduction, one possible conjecture may be preferred over others. However, from a strategic viewpoint, Levi may be right, in that the choice of the set of alternative answers amounts to the choice of the question to be asked. And it is that choice that is crucial strategically.

So why did Peirce not simply identify an abductive inference with a question-answer step in an interrogative inquiry? A fully confirmed answer to such a question is impossible to give. Nevertheless, Peirce's keen insights into the strategic aspects of inquiry, combined with his failure to separate the definitory and strategic aspects of inquiry from each other, suggest an instructive hypothesis. (Or perhaps I should say instead, suggests an instructive abductive question.) What can one say in general about the best choices of questions to be asked in inquiry for the purpose of finding new truths? How can one choose between different possible questions that can be asked? It will be seen later that the choice is determined by the same principles as the choice of the optimal deductive inference in the same circumstances. This was enough for Peirce to assimilate abductive questions to inferences, especially as he maintained that inferences are in general validated by their strategic propensities. But in an obvious sense, inferences cannot be identified with question-answer steps *simpliciter*, for that would mean assimilating them to each other also definitorily. Hence it was natural—albeit incorrect in the literal definitory sense—for Peirce to consider abductions a special class of inferences. Of course, definitorily speaking, there is a world of difference between raising one question rather than others and proposing a conjectured answer to it. But if someone like Peirce focuses his attention on the strategic questions, he might very well look away from these definitory differences.

Sometimes Peirce nevertheless relates interrogation to the "inductive" testing of hypotheses rather than to the formation of hypotheses; see, for example, Eisele, editor, *Historical Perspectives*, vol. II, p. 899.

This is *prima facie* different from what I have suggested. Yet it may not be impossible to reconcile with what I have argued. What I insist on is that the abductive part of inquiry be conceptualized as inquiry in the sense of interrogation; I do not maintain the converse. Hence I am not denying that what Peirce calls the inductive component of inquiry also involves interrogation. On the contrary, it fits very well with the idea that interrogative inquiry, like Peircean inquiry, is a self-correcting operation.

The systematic implications of my answer to the question that figures in the title of this chapter have been codified in what I have called the "interrogative model" of inquiry. The line of thought presented in this chapter helps to show why this name is too modest in that all ampliative reasoning can be thought of as involving a question–answer sequence. Among other things, the nature of explanations can be studied by considering them as answers to why-questions.

I will not expound this interrogative approach to epistemology here. It has been made possible by the important advances in epistemic logic reported in Hintikka (2003). A survey of some of the basic results of this approach is presented in Hintikka, Halonen, and Mutanen (1998). Instead, I will use the results of that theory to show how my answer to the abduction problems helps to put into a perspective the different things that Peirce says about induction. Thus, Peirce's views serve as a useful framework by reference to which I can explain some of the main features of the interrogative approach to inquiry.

Among the features of Peirce's views that can be understood and largely justified in terms of this framework:

(i) Abduction is an inference or, as I prefer to put it, is like an inference.
(ii) Abduction is the only way of introducing new hypotheses or, as I prefer to put it, new information into an argument.
(iii) Abductive steps in an inquiry have to be judged on the basis of strategic principles rather than definitory ones.

(iv) Abduction is different from induction. Induction is not a form of ampliative inference (introduction of new hypotheses), let alone the only form.

(v) We can now also understand the conjectural element in Peircean abduction.

I can discuss these points only selectively here. In its general features, the interrogative logic of epistemology ("epistemo-logic") is strongly reminiscent of Peirce's ideas. Consider, as an example, item (iv). In the interrogative model, there are three different kinds of steps—deductive and interrogative steps plus self-critical steps in which one of the earlier answers (or initial premises) is (at least tentatively) rejected ("bracketed"). Naturally, allowing such bracketing steps must be accompanied by allowing their mirror images, unbracketing steps. This is strongly reminiscent of Peirce's trichotomy—deduction, abduction, and induction. In particular, we can from this vantage point see why Peirce describes the inductive stage of inquiry as involving the testing of hypotheses rather than a series of inductive inferences. In the interrogative model, the critical stage consists in bracketing and unbracketing earlier answers, which are precisely the outcomes (Peirce's "hypotheses") of what, on my interpretation, are abductive steps of inquiry.

The most interesting of the five points just listed is the first one. As far as the status of abduction as a special form of inference is concerned, the basic conclusion here is: No, there is no such form of inference (in any natural sense of inference) as abduction. Abduction should be conceptualized as a question–answer step, not as an inference in any literal sense of the word. Peirce was entirely right in separating abduction both from deduction and from induction.

But this is not the end of the story. We are still left with an intriguing mystery to solve. If we approach this puzzle from the vantage point of Peirce interpretation, it can be formulated by asking: If abduction is so radically different from both of the usually recognized modes of inference, deduction, and induction, why on earth did Peirce call it inference? Systematically speaking, essentially the same question can be put by asking: If abduction is an inference, there must be rules for such inferences. What are these rules like? Peirce himself acknowledges that all inference takes place according to a certain method. (See earlier.) What is this method? It was seen that according to Peirce, an abductive method must be justified by strategic principles. What principles?

Many philosophers would probably bracket abductive inference with inductive inference. Some would even think of all ampliative inference as being, at bottom, inductive. In this matter, however, Peirce is one hundred percent right in denying the role of naked induction in forming new hypotheses. All the sharpest analysts from Hume on have pointed out that the justification of inductive arguments depends on the regularity of the courses of events in our universe. Such regularity assumptions are factual ones and can in principle be disproved by experience. Hence they can be known only *a posteriori*. And if they are spelled out and made explicit, we do not any longer need any specifically inductive rules of inference. Deductive ones do the trick perfectly well.

I have argued that the same conclusion can be drawn, appearances notwithstanding, from Carnap's heroic, and in the last analysis, self-defeating attempt to develop an *a priori* logic of induction. (See Hintikka 1993(b).) What is perhaps more timely to emphasize in this day and age is that, various currently fashionable modes of ampliative reasoning are in the same boat with inductive inference, including sundry non-monotonic and circumscriptive inferences. Accordingly, no modes of ampliative reasoning other than interrogative moves are included in our interrogative model of knowledge acquisition, just as in Peirce's trichotomy.

Hence the only remaining similarity that could even mistakenly motivate Peirce's calling abduction an inference must be between abduction and deduction. But my interrogative interpretation of abduction seems to destroy totally any such assimilation. For what could be more dissimilar than a deduction, which merely reshuffles and spells out previous information, and an interrogative step, in which the answer to a question brings in fresh information.

Yet this dissimilarity is only skin deep or, more accurately speaking, only definition deep. Here the logic of questions and answers mentioned earlier performs a major service for epistemological analysis (and synthesis). One thing that it brings out is the need to recognize the role of presuppositions in interrogative inquiry. Before the inquirer is in a position to ask, say, a *who*-question ("Who did it?"), he or she must establish its presupposition ("Someone did it"). Hence, on paper, as a transition from one proposition to another, an interrogative step looks rather similar to a deductive step. The latter takes the inquirer from a premise or premises to a conclusion, while the former takes the inquirer from the presupposition of a question to its answer.

Moreover, the very same sentence can serve as the presupposition of a question and as the premise of a deductive step. For instance, an existential sentence of the form

$$(\exists x)S[x] \tag{1}$$

can serve either as the presupposition of the question

$$\text{What (who, when, where, ...), say } x, \text{ is such that } S[x]? \tag{2}$$

or as the premise of an existential instantiation that introduces a "John Doe"-like "dummy name" of an "arbitrary individual," say β. In the former case, the output of the relevant step is a sentence of the form

$$S[b] \tag{3}$$

where b is a singular term—for instance, a proper name. In the latter case, the output is of the form

$$S[\beta] \tag{4}$$

Here, (4) differs from (3) only by having a dummy name, whereas in (3) there was a real name.

This analogy has not yet caught the eye of theorists, for the very good reason that it has not in the past been extended to all types of questions. It can be so extended, however, as I have shown in Hintikka 2003, Chapter 3 of this volume. (The only qualification needed here is that *why*- and *how*-questions have a different logic and therefore have to be dealt with separately; see Hintikka and Halonen, 1995.)

It seems to me that Peirce had an intuitive understanding of this type of similarity between abductive and deductive inferences. One of his main reasons for calling abductive steps "inferences" is that they have a "perfectly definite logical form," to quote "Pragmatism as the Logic of Abduction" (p. 15). Because of this definite logical form, an abductive inference cannot yield "quite new conceptions" (op. cit. p. 16), even though it (and it alone) can introduce new "hypotheses."

These similarities between questions (abductive steps) and logical inferences (deductive steps) are purely formal, however. An epistemological assimilation of the two to each other on the mere basis of such formal similarities would be irresponsible.

The crucial insight here is that behind these formal similarities there lies a remarkable strategic similarity. How do questions of strategy enter into the concrete situations of an interrogative or deductive reasoner? In either case, at any one given stage of inquiry, the reasoner has a number of propositions (sentences) available to be used as presuppositions or as premises. In either case, the proximate strategic question is: Which sentence or sentences should I use as the premise or as the premises of a deductive inference? It can be shown that the most sensitive strategic question in deduction is: Which sentence should I use first as the premise of an existential instantiation or its generalization, functional instantiation? If the inquirer is reasoning empirically (interrogatively), the next strategic question is: Which one of the available sentences should I use as the presupposition of a *wh*-question? These candidate sentences are the very same ones that could be used as premises of existential instantiations, suitably generalized.

Neither question admits in general of a mechanical answer, in the sense that there is in neither case any recursive function that always specifies an optimal choice. However, insofar as we are dealing with pure discovery in the sense that for all answers taken to be reliable, there is a remarkable connection between the two choices. Even if there is no mechanical way of making the optimal choice in either case, it can be shown that *the best choice is the same in both cases*. The strategically best question that can be asked has as its presupposition the optimal premise of an existential instantiation in the same circumstances. In this sense, the strategic principles of abductive reasoning, interpreted as I have done, are the same as the strategic principles governing deduction.

This result not only explains why somebody like Peirce should call abductive steps of reasoning inferences; it vindicates such a practice (aside from purely terminological questions). Even though interrogative and deductive steps are definitorily different in a radical way, they are strategically speaking governed by the same principles, at least insofar as we can look away from the critical and evaluative aspect of inquiry that Peirce called inductive.

Thus the interrogative interpretation of abduction, or more generally speaking the construal of all ampliative reasoning as interrogative, while in a sense vindicating Peirce's tripartite analysis of reasoning into deductive, abductive, and inductive inferences, at the same time but in a different sense reveals fundamental connections between the three.

These connections can be spelled out further in a different direction. It might seem that the critical and evaluative aspect of inquiry that Peirce called inductive still remains essentially different from the deductive and abductive aspects. A common way of thinking equates all ampliative inferences with inductive ones. Peirce was right in challenging this dichotomy. Rightly understood, the ampliative versus non-ampliative contrast becomes a distinction between interrogative (ampliative) and deductive steps of argument. As in Peirce, we also need over and above these two also the kind of reasoning that is involved in testing the propositions obtained as answers to questions. I do not think that it is instructive to call such reasoning inductive, but this is a merely terminological matter.

From the vantage point of the interrogative approach, Peirce's terminology can be claimed merely to follow ordinary usage when he calls an interrogatively interpreted abductive step an inference. The reasoning of the likes of Sherlock Holmes or Nero Wolfe is not deductive, nor does it conform to any known forms "inductive inference." The "deductions" of great detectives are in fact best thought of as question–answer sequences interspersed with deductive inferences (I have argued). Yet people routinely call them "deductions" or "inferences" accomplished by means of "logic" and "analysis." They now turn out to be right strategically speaking, though not literally (definitorily) speaking. From the strategic vantage point, we can say thus that any seriously asked question involves a tacit conjecture or guess.

We can also put into perspective Peirce's idea that there is a conjectural element in abductive inference. (See item (v) earlier.) From the strategic viewpoint, the crucial question about abductive questions is: Which one to ask first? So far, I have given only a conditional answer—namely, that the choice of the best question is determined by the same principles as the choice of the optimal deductive inference in the same circumstances. But how are these coordinated choices made? Probably the only general answer, which unfortunately does not yield any directly applicable recipes, is to say that the choice of the right questions depends on one's ability to anticipate their answers. Strategically, there is little difference between selecting a question to ask in preference to others and guessing what its answer will be—and guessing how it compares with the expected answers to other questions that could be asked. And even in the case of deductive rules, the secret of a good strategist is to be able to anticipate where the inferences lead. This is especially clear when one is using what are known as *tableau* methods. There, an attempted derivation of G from F is construed as an attempt to construct a model in which F is true but G is false. One's success in doing so typically lies in being able to steer the construction to an obviously impossible configuration. And this ability to anticipate where the successive construction steps would guide the logician.

Likewise, in interrogative inquiry, the crucial consideration is to anticipate the epistemic situation brought about by the answer—which in practice typically amounts to anticipating the answer. And such anticipation is hard to characterize in any terms other than guessing.

What is especially interesting—and especially reminiscent of Peirce—is that such an element of guessing in abductive questioning is completely compatible with the strategic analogy between deduction and interrogation that inspired Peirce to call abduction an inference.

Another, perhaps less interesting, way of reconciling the interrogative approach to inquiry with the idea of abduction as a method of guessing is based on the variety of different possible sources of answers. Such "informants" must include not only testimony, observation, and experiments, but the inquirer's memory and background knowledge. But what can an inquirer do when all such sources fail to provide an answer to a question? Obviously the best the inquirer can do is make an informed guess. For the purposes of a general theory of inquiry, what Peirce calls "intelligent guessing" must therefore be recognized as one of the many possible "oracles," alias sources of answers. Peirce may very well have been more realistic than I have so far been in emphasizing the importance of this particular "oracle" in actual human inquiry. Perhaps by recognizing this importance we can make the interrogation model coincide with Peirce's ideas of abduction and its role in inquiry.

This interplay of deduction, questioning, and conjecture has not been discussed very much by epistemologists, but it is old hat for puzzle fans. If one opens a typical book of what are known as "lateral thinking puzzles," one finds, besides an initial list of puzzles and a concluding section containing their solutions, an intermediate third section telling what questions should be asked to solve the problem. Of course, the questions do not necessitate the right answers, which means that the intended answer is in a sense conjectural. But if the puzzle is a good one, the natural answer is obvious once the right question has been asked. Here is an example (Sloane and MacHale, 1996, p. 32):

A man walked into a bar and asked the barman for a glass of water. They had never met before. The barman pulled a gun from under the counter and pointed it at the man. The man said "Thank you" and walked out. Why should that be so?

One of the questions that could be asked here is: What was it that the man needed and that could be satisfied as well by a glass of water and by having a gun pointed at him? (If you still don't get the solution, look for help in the footnote.)[2]

One more apparent contradiction in what I have said deserves a comment. Acknowledging the element of guessing in abduction does not gainsay its character as inference subject to precise (strategic) rules. This would not be the first case where an apparently purely psychological phenomenon turns out to have an objective, rule-governed rationale. The first striking explanation of this kind was the von Neumann explanation of the apparently irrational trick of bluffing in games like poker as being nothing more and nothing less than the use of a mixed strategy. Here, too, guessing the right answer to different questions is a little more than the phenomenological side of the same coin as the choice (or creation) of an optimal strategy.

These examples should be enough to convince the reader that my interrogative construal of Peircean abduction vindicates strikingly well what he says of abduction.

There is one more aspect of Peirce's views (and statements) that can serve to highlight the epistemological situation. It is the notion of hypothesis. Abduction is characterized by Peirce as the universal process of forming new hypotheses. I might appear to have departed from Peirce's intentions when I presented abduction as the universal method of introducing new information into a rational argument. The answer as that by information I do not mean necessarily true information. On the contrary, its being new information implies that it is not implied by what is already known (or at least accepted). In this sense, abduction, as here construed, always has a hypothetical element.

But there is even more than that to the hypothetical character of the conclusion of an abductive inference. This character, aptly emphasized by Peirce, illustrates one of the most important things about the justification of abductive inferences. According to Peirce, this justification lies in the abductive rule's being conducive to the acquisition of truth. Many contemporary philosophers will assimilate this kind of justification to what is called a reliabilist one. Such reliabilist views are said to go back to Frank Ramsey, who said that "a belief was knowledge if it is (1) true, (2) certain, (3) *obtained by a reliable process*" (emphasis added). Unfortunately for reliabilists, such characterizations are subject to the ambiguity that was pointed out earlier. By a reliable process one can mean either a process in which each step is conducive to acquiring and/or maintaining truth or closeness to truth, or one that as a whole is apt to lead the inquirer to truth. Unfortunately, most reliabilists unerringly choose the wrong interpretation—namely, the first one. As was pointed out earlier, the true justification of a rule of abductive inference is a strategic one. And such a strategic justification does not provide a warrant for any one particular step in the process. Such a particular step may not in any obvious way aid and abet the overall aim of the inquiry. For instance, such a step might provide neither

---

[2] When was the last time you had a hiccup?

any new information relevant to the aim of the inquiry nor any new confirmation for what has already been established, and yet might serve crucially the inquiry—for instance, by opening up the possibility of a question whose answer does so.

Furthermore, notwithstanding the views of reliabilists, the idea of a nonstrategic justification that they choose is not only mistaken but in the last analysis incoherent. From the theory of strategic processes misleadingly labeled game theory, it is known that what can be valuated (assigned "utilities" to) are in principle only strategies, not particular moves. Hence a theory of epistemic processes that operates with "warrants" for particular belief changes or other things that can be said of particular moves in our "games" of inquiry is inevitably going to be unsatisfactory in the long run.

One of the many things that Peirce's use of the term "hypothesis" can serve to highlight is precisely the strategic character of any justification of abduction. Being strategic, such justification does not *per se* lend any reliability to the outcome of some particular abductive inference. This outcome has the status of a hypothesis. Whatever reliability it may possess has to be established by the inductive component of inquiry.

Once again, it remains to be established precisely how clear Peirce himself was about this matter. I believe that he understood the point clearly enough, but was prevented from speaking out because he did not have an explicit notion of strategy at his disposal. This is why he did not fully explain what the "altogether different kind" of justification is that abductive rules can claim. In any case, Peirce disavows in so many words his own early identification of abduction as a species of probable inference. (See Kapitan, 1997, p. 493, note 1.)

References

Peirce is cited from the usual editions (Collected Papers, Writings, Eisele, Buchler, etc.). I have also used the following Peirce MSS, copies of which were kindly made available to me by the Peirce Edition Project:

"On the Logic of Drawing History from Ancient Documents, especially from Testimonies" (MS 690). This is a thick typescript that Peirce first handwrote in October and November 1901; it was typed by the secretary of his friend Francis Lathrop in early December 1901.

The seventh Harvard lecture of 1903, left untitled by Peirce (MS 315). In Essential Peirce 2, it will be titled "Pragmatism as the Logic of Abduction."

"An Essay toward Improving our Reasoning in Security & in Uberty" (MS 682). This is one of several essays that Peirce wrote at the end of his life on the topic of the fruitfulness of arguments. "Uberty" is Peirce's team for fruitfulness.

Eight pages (numbered 4 to 11 by Peirce, pp. 1–3 are missing) from MS683, an untitled manuscript that might have borne the same title as the previous document. It, too, bears upon the topic of uberty, and should also be dated September–October 1913.

Collingwood, R. G., 1946, *The Idea of History*, Oxford University Press. Oxford.

Edwards, A. W. F., 1992, *Likelihood (expanded edition)*, Johns Hopkins University Press, Baltimore.

Fölsing, Albrecht, 1997, *Albert Einstein: A Biography*, Viking, New York.

Freeman, Eugene, editor, 1983, *The Relevance of Charles Peirce*, The Hegeler Institute, La Salle, Illinois.

Gadamer, Hans Georg, 1975 (original 1960), *Truth and Method*, Continuum Publishing, New York.

Harman, G., 1968, "Enumerative Induction As Inference to the Best Explanation," *Journal of Philosophy*, vol. 65, pp. 529–533.

Harman, G., 1965, "Inference to the Best Explanation," *Philosophical Review*, vol. 74, pp. 88–95.

Hilpinen, Risto, 1983, "On C. S. Peirce's Theory of the Proposition," in Freeman, editor (1983), pp. 264–270.

Hintikka, Jaakko, 2003, "A Second Generation Epistemic Logic and Its General Significance," in *Knowledge Contributors*, Synthese Library, *322*, Vincent F. Hendricks, Klaus Frovin Jørgensen, and Stig Andur Pedersen, editors, Kluwer Academic Publishers, Dordrecht, 33–56.

Hintikka, Jaakko, 1993(a), "The Concept of Induction in the Light of the Interrogative Approach to Inquiry," in John Earman, editor, *Inference, Explanation, and Other Frustrations*, University of California Press, Berkeley and Los Angeles, pp. 23–43. Reprinted in Hintikka, 1999, *Inquiry as Inquiry*, Kluwer Academic, Dordrecht, pp. 161–181.

Hintikka, Jaakko, 1993(b), "On Proper (Popper?) and Improper Uses of Information in Epistemology," *Theoria,* vol. 59, pp. 158–165.

Hintikka, Jaakko, 1988, "On the Development of the Model-Theoretical Viewpoint in Logical Theory," *Synthese,* vol. 77, pp. 1–36.

Hintikka, Jaakko, and Ilpo Halonen, 1995, "Semantics and Pragmatics for Why-Questions," *Journal of Philosophy*, vol. 92, pp. 636–657. (Reprinted in Hintikka, 1999, *Inquiry as Inquiry*, Kluwer Academic, Dordrecht, pp. 183–204.

Hintikka, Jaakko, Ilpo Halonen, and Arto Mutanen, 1998, "Interrogative Logic as a General Theory of Reasoning," in R. Johnson and J. Woods, editors, *Handbook of Applied Logic*, Kluwer Academic, Dordrecht. Reprinted in Hintikka, 1999, *Inquiry as Inquiry*, Kluwer Academic, Dordrecht, pp. 47–90.

Holton, Gerald, 1969, "Einstein, Michelson and the 'Crucial' Experiment," *Isis,* vol. 60, pp. 133–197.

Houser, Nathan, Don D. Roberts, and James Van Evra, 1997, *Studies in the Logic of Charles Sanders Peirce*, Indiana University Press, Bloomington and Indianapolis.

Josephson, John R., and Susan G. Josephson, editors, 1994, *Abductive Inference: Computation, Philosophy, Technology*, Cambridge University Press, New York.

Kapitan, Tomis, 1997, "Peirce and the Structure of Abductive Inference," in *Houser* et al. (1997), pp. 477–496.

Levi, Isaac, 1991, *The Fixation of Belief and Its Undoing*, Cambridge University Press, New York.

Sloane, Paul, and Des MacHale, 1996, *The Lateral Logician, Quality* Paperback Book Club, New York.

Tursman, Richard, 1987, *Peirce's Theory of Scientific Discovery*, Indiana University Press, Bloomington and Indianapolis.

von Neumann, John, 1928, "Zur Theorie der Gesellschaftsspiele," *Mathematische Annalen,* vol. 100, pp. 295–320.

von Neumann, John, and O. Morgenstern, 1944, *Theory of Games and Economic Behavior*, Princeton University Press, Princeton.

3

A Second-Generation Epistemic Logic
and Its General Significance

1. The *prima facie* Conundrum of Epistemic Logic

Epistemic logic was already practiced in the Middle Ages. (See Boh 1993; Knuuttila 1993.) It was thrust to the awareness of contemporary philosophers by von Wright in his *An Essay in Modal Logic* (1951, see chapter 4). In this chapter, I will consider epistemic logic primarily in relation to its epistemological applications. Surely any satisfactory epistemic logic ought to be able to prove its mettle as an epistemo-logic, to coin a phrase. From this perspective, the half-century-long career of epistemic logic presents us with something of a paradox. Epistemic logic was created by philosophers for philosophical purposes. It is one of the core areas in what is (misleadingly) known as philosophical logic. Yet its most promising philosophical suggestions were put forward relatively late, and even then they received but lukewarm attention on the part of philosophers. These potential philosophical applications are in my judgment incomparably more interesting and significant than the technicalities of epistemic logic that routinely receive the lion's share of attention in books and papers on epistemic logic. In typical surveys of epistemic logic (see Lenzen 1978 and 1980), little attention is paid to the epistemological perspectives opened by epistemic logic.

There are several partial explanations of this paradoxical state of affairs. Reasoning about knowledge has become an important subject in such branches of computer science as AI and database theory. Epistemic logic has been harnessed to the service of such studies, which has encouraged work on the more computation-oriented, and hence more technical, aspects of the subject. Furthermore, since epistemic logic provides a refutation of Kripke's so-called New Theory of Reference (see Hintikka and Sandu 1995), the uncritical acceptance of this "theory" has discouraged serious interest in epistemic logic.

Even more generally, in spite of a nearly unanimous professed rejection of formalistic philosophy of logic and mathematics by contemporary philosophers, their argumentative practice exhibits a formalist bias. They tend to feel safest in discussing the formal behavior of different notions. When they venture on the uncharted seas of interpretational questions, their ideas are far too often arbitrary and myopic. A simple example may illustrate what I am saying. I understand perfectly what kind of reasoning the logicians have in mind when they speak of reasoning in terms of "arbitrary individuals," but the notion of such an individual has by itself no explanatory value. I have never seen, heard, smelled, touched, or kissed an arbitrary individual. Reifying logicians' jargon into such chancy entities seems to me entirely, well, arbitrary.

Nevertheless, it seem to me that there are—or perhaps I should say there were—valid reasons for philosophers' suspicion of the promised philosophical applications of epistemic logic. In this chapter, I propose to outline, first, what the promises were, second, why they did not at first pan out, and, third, how those reasons for disregarding the philosophical implications of epistemic logic can be removed by means of important new ideas that can be said to have launched a new generation of epistemic logics.

But, first, what was the old first-generation epistemic logic like? Syntactically, all that we need is to add to a suitable many-sorted but otherwise ordinary first-order language epistemic operators of the form K_a, to correspond roughly to the English expression *a knows that*. Often the identity of the knower does not matter. Then we can drop the knower indicator and read K as *it is known that*. This notation may not be entirely self-explanatory. For one thing, it hides the fact that the knower indicator a is semantically speaking outside the scope of the epistemic operator. Further clarifications are made in the following when we proceed.

Many of the basic properties of epistemic logic emerge already in application in which we have only one epistemic operator.

But what is the semantics of such an epistemic language? In order to answer this question, it is useful to raise the question of the pragmatic role of our notion of knowledge. Why do we have this notion in our conceptual repertoire? Suppose I am some morning considering how to prepare for the trials and tribulations of the impending day. Should I carry my raincoat and my umbrella? Should I don a suit in order to impress my boss? Then I learn from the weather forecast that the day will be sunny and warm and from my trusted secretary that my boss will be out of town. How does this enhanced knowledge affect my behavior? I do not have to tell you. I leave my raincoat and umbrella at home and instead of the uncomfortable suit don a comfortable blazer. What has happened? What has happened that I have been able, because of my newly acquired knowledge, to leave out certain possibilities as to what might happen during the day out of my planning and other considerations.

This shows the general conceptual role of the notion of knowledge. In order to speak of what a certain person a knows and does not know, we have to assume a class ("space") of possibilities. These possibilities will be called "scenarios." Philosophers typically call them "possible worlds." This usage is a symptom of intellectual megalomania. In most applications "possible worlds" are not literally worlds in the sense of universes but merely "small worlds,"—that is, so many applications of the language in question, typically applications to some relatively small nook and corner of our four-dimensional world. Such a space of scenarios is essentially the same as what probability theorists mean by "sample space." It might be called the "epistemic space." Depending on the application, the elements of that space can be states of affairs or sequences of events. What the concept of knowledge accomplishes in any case is a dichotomy (relative to the knower) of the elements of the epistemic space into those that are ruled out by a's knowledge and those that are compatible with everything he or she (or it, if we are dealing with a computer) knows in a given scenario. Its abstract semantical manifestation is relation $R(a, w_1, w_2)$ between a knower a in the scenario w_1 and those scenarios w_2 that are compatible with everything a knows in w_1. It is then true that a knows in w_1 that S if and only if it is true that S in all the scenarios w* such that $R(a, w_1, w^*)$. These scenarios w* are called the epistemic a-alternatives to w_1 or, more loosely, a's knowledge-worlds in w_1.

Thus the epistemic operator K_a is a kind of quantifier—a universal quantifier ranging over a's knowledge-worlds. Much of the logic and semantics of epistemic notions can be considered as implications of this simple insight.

This pragmatic motivation of epistemic logic calls for several comments. For one thing, in order to be considered seriously for the purposes of acting (or of being acted on), the possibilities that I have called scenarios must be in some sense real (concrete) possibilities. Hence it is not realistic (pace the likes of Chalmers) to introduce a separate dimension of epistemic possibilities different from real or metaphysical ones.

Furthermore, what has been said does not separate the notion of knowledge from those of information or even true belief. All of them have a similar role in guiding our actions. All of them induce similar dichotomies of the epistemic space, and all of them therefore have a similar logic. One difference is that in the case of knowledge, the rejection of excluded scenarios must be justified. However, much of the logic of knowledge is independent of the precise nature of this justification. For this reason, it will not be discussed here.

Another difference is that it is usually required that whatever is known must be true. This requirement is not discussed here either—it is impossible to implement in many real-life applications of epistemic notions. For this reason, it might in fact be more appropriate to speak of the "logic of information" than of the "logic of knowledge." Unfortunately the term "information" has other misleading overtones. But fortunately this issue does not affect what will be done in this chapter.

Another problem area that I will not deal with fully in this chapter is the behavior of identity. One reason why it would need a longer discussion is that the received approaches are seriously off the mark. The source of the problem is the fact that in epistemic and other intensional contexts, we have to consider individuals as potential members of several scenarios. This is true in particular

of individuals considered as values of bound variables. Hence we must have—
or, rather, there must be implicit in the semantics of our language—criteria of
identity for denizens of different scenarios. They are sometimes called "criteria of cross-identification." How are we to deal with them? Many philosophers
and linguists have approached this problem by means of the notion or reference. This is especially true of Kripke and his acolytes. Kripke postulates a
special kind of direct or rigid reference to explain the identity in question.
This "new theory of reference" nevertheless offers us merely a good analogue
of Karl Krauss's dictum about psychoanalysis. The so-called new theory of
reference embodies the very problem it is supposed to be a solution to. What
a system of reference does is provide criteria that tell us what the references
of our expressions are in each of the different possible scenarios that we might
want to approach by means of our language. Hence, almost by definition,
such a system does not tell anything about the identities of individuals (or
of objects of a higher type) in different scenarios. For this purpose, we need
another system—or rather, there is another system embedded in our working
conceptual system—governing such identities. This system might be called the
"identification system." It turns out to be largely independent of the reference
system. Hence, what is wrong about the new theory of reference in the first
place is that it is a theory of reference.

Epistemic logic plays an interesting role here in that it provides specific
examples of the failure of the "new theory of reference." For in whatever way
the reference of (say) a singular term is determined, it always makes sense to
ask, "Does b know what a is?" The answer cannot turn on the grammatical or
logical category of "a" used earlier. It is always a factual question.

Of course, a full treatment would here involve discussing the alleged mechanisms of creating direct reference that Kripke and others have proposed
(Kripke 1972). Suffice it here merely to put Kripke's idea of dubbing into a
historical perspective. Kripke's idea is but a dramatized version of the old idea
that it is ostension that provides the basic semantical links between language
and reality. Wittgenstein held it for a while—rather a long while, if I am right.
However, he eventually came to reject it, for reasons that at least *prima facie*
apply quite as well against Kripke.

To put the same point in different terms, to say that "a" behaves like a rigid
designation in b's knowledge worlds is to say that

$$(\exists x)K_b(a = x) \tag{1}$$

But what this expresses is the fact that b knows what a is (see later.) And this
cannot be guaranteed by the meaning of "a" alone. Whether or not (4) is true
depends crucially on the identification system one is relying on.

In this sense, epistemic logic provides strong evidence against any theory
of direct reference. No wonder, therefore, that the new theorists of reference
have studiously neglected it, in spite of its importance for applications of logic.

2. The Promises

Now, what are the promises of such an epistemic logic? What questions does it help us to answer? Well, what questions are we likely to ask in epistemology? One of the first concerns surely the objects of knowledge. When one knows something, what is the knowledge about? Interesting *prima facie* distinctions are codified in the syntax of ordinary language. We speak of knowing truths, propositions, and facts. Such knowledge is expressed by the *knows that* construction that is incorporated in our epistemic logic. But how can we express what might be called "knowledge of objects"—that is, the kind of knowledge expressed in English by what is known as simple *wh*-constructions such as *knowing who, what, where, when* and so on. In the simplest cases, the answer seems obvious. If K expresses it is *known that* and the variable x ranges over persons, then the sentence

$$\text{It is known who murdered Roger Ackroyd} \tag{2}$$

can be expressed by

$$\text{It is known of some particular person x that x murdered}$$
$$\text{Roger Ackroyd} \tag{3}$$

Or, more explicitly, by

$$(\exists x)K(x \text{ murdered Roger Ackroyd}) \tag{4}$$

which has the form

$$(\exists x)KM(x, r) \tag{5}$$

For what else could be meant by *knowing who* did the dastardly deed than *knowing of some particular individual x* that x did it?

Indeed, this is a viable analysis of simple *wh*-knowledge. The simplest case of such simple knowledge is knowing the identity of an individual.

By the same token as before,

$$\text{It is known who b is} \tag{6}$$

is equivalent to

$$\text{It is known of some particular individual x that b is x} \tag{7}$$

which has the form

$$(\exists x K(b = x) \tag{8}$$

All that is presupposed by such analyses is some systematization of the logic and semantics of the logic of knowledge along the lines indicated here. What this amounts to is some version of what is known as "possible worlds" semantics for epistemic logic, including a system of reference and a separate system of cross-identification. (If one shares my distaste for the "possible worlds" terminology, one may speak of possible scenarios instead.)

Knowing what an entity of a higher type is can likewise be expressed in terms of K, but now we have to quantify over higher-order entities. For instance, *knowing which function* $g(x)$ *is* can be expressed by

$$(\exists f)K(\forall x)(g(x) = f(x)) \tag{9}$$

where f is a function variable. This might be abbreviated as

$$(\exists f)K(g = f) \tag{10}$$

which brings out the parallelism between (10) and (8).

Unfortunately, this analysis of what it means to know the identity of a function is in terms of higher-order quantification (quantification over functions). Such quantification promptly leads to an avalanche of difficult problems. Which higher-order entities exist? If we know an answer to that question, we could decide what axioms to posit in set theory. What does it mean for a higher-order entity to exist, anyway? We would obviously be much wiser if we could dispense with higher-order quantification.

The distinction between knowledge of propositions (or truths) and knowledge of entities has many intriguing applications. Here I will mention only one. It is obvious that intuitionistic mathematics is calculated to deal, not so much with mathematical truths, as with our knowledge of mathematics. But if this knowledge is assumed to be propositional, very little seems to be accomplished. Indeed, S is provable in the usual epistemic logics if and only if *KS* is provable.

The real novelty is, I have argued, that intuitionists (the original ones, not the *soi-disant* ones of our day and age) were not concerned with our knowledge of mathematical propositions, but with our knowledge of mathematical objects. Consider, for example, the axiom of choice. Does a choice set always exist? We can consider this question till we are blue in the face without finding an easy answer. In contrast, it is easy for someone to admit that we do not always know what a choice function would be. I will not pursue this matter here, and use it only to illustrate the tremendous interest of the distinction between knowledge of truths (propositions) and knowledge of objects (entities).

This distinction between the knowledge of propositions and knowledge of entities is thus of considerable philosophical and other theoretical interest. For another application, it shows that at least in the simplest cases, we can analyze knowledge of objects in terms of knowledge of propositions. This is shown by expressions like (8) (or perhaps also (5)–(7)), in that the only epistemic element they contain is the *knowing that* operator K.

More generally speaking, one thing that epistemic logic seems to promise is an analysis of different kinds of knowledge in terms of the single operator K. This project can be carried out in some cases, in addition to the analysis of simple *wh*-knowledge just outlined. For instance, *why*- and *how*-knowledge is obviously more complex conceptually, but can be brought within the scope of such analysis. (See, e.g., Hintikka and Halonen 1995.) Most importantly, an insight into the possibility (and indeed presence in our actual discourse) of the different modes of identification opens up possibilities of analyzing different types of knowledge by acquaintance—that is, of the kind of knowledge that is in natural languages expressed by a direct (grammatical) object construction. (see Hintikka 1975, chs. 3–4, and 1990; Hintikka and Symons 2003.)

Such analyses have a philosophical interest that goes way beyond whatever logico-linguistic relevance they may have. For instance, the fact that the only epistemic operator we need is the *knows that* operator suggests strongly that propositional knowledge can be thought of as the only basic kind of knowledge. This meshes well with the initial observations earlier concerning the pragmatic function of the notion of knowledge.

For another thing, it is obvious on the basis of the model theoretical meaning of propositions like (7) that they express what in the current jargon is called *de re* knowledge. The possibility of a uniform analysis in terms of a single epistemic operator shows that there is no irreducible *de re* knowledge. Such a notion is a figment of certain philosophers' imaginations—or so it seems on the basis of our observations so far. And since the postulation of such direct reference is the lynchpin of the so-called New Theory of Reference, this theory is thus seen to involve a serious confusion.

Likewise, the possibility of an analysis of the kinds of knowledge that rely on different modes of identification by reference to a single epistemic operator shows that what is involved in acquaintance-type knowledge is not a different kind of *knowledge*, but a different mode of identification. This difference in identification manifests itself in the form of a difference between the (correlated pairs of) quantifiers involved, not in the form of a difference in the kind of information (knowledge). This particular insight turns out to be relevant even for neuroscientific theorizing, as is shown in Hintikka and Symons (2003).

Unfortunately, it is not immediately obvious that such analyses can always be carried out. Thus, the promises I have described threaten to remain only promises. For instance, the analysis exemplified by (5) and (6) works naturally only in the case of simple *wh*-knowledge. For how can we analyze more complex types of knowledge in the same spirit? How can we represent knowledge statements such as the following?

$$\text{Mary knows whose advice every young mother should trust.} \quad (11)$$

$$\text{It is known how the observed variable y depends on the controlled} \\ \text{variable x in such-and-such experimental situation.} \quad (12)$$

Needless to say, we understand (11) in the sense in which *prima facie* answers to it have the form "her mother" rather than "Dr. Spock." In view of this explication, one might try to express the logical form of (11) as follows:

$$(\forall x)(M(x) \supset (\exists y K_{Mary} T(x, y))) \quad (13)$$

But (13) does not say the same as (11). In (11), Mary's knowledge is about all actual young mothers, all of whom must therefore be known to her in order for (13) to be true. This is not implied by (11).

This point is important enough to be elaborated by means of further examples and explanations. For one thing, if (13) were equivalent to (11), the latter would imply

> If Celia is a young mother, Mary knows whose advice
> Celia should trust.   (14)

But this may very well be false—namely, if Mary does not know Celia.

In general, we might say that knowing something about each individual (as in 13) is different from knowing the same thing about all individuals (as in (11)). Aristotle already knew better than to assimilate the two to each other; see *Posterior Analytics*, A1, 71a25-b9.

On a purely linguistic level, Elisabet Engdahl already argued (1986) that the logical form of sentences such as (11)–(12) cannot be represented on the first-order level.

Semantically speaking, the reason for all this can be said to be that when we "quantify into" a construction governed by an epistemic operator, the values of variables must be the same in all of the relevant knowledge words—in other words, such values must be known to the agent in question. A solution might seem to be to make explicit the dependence of the trusty advisor on the young mother in question, perhaps as follows:

$$(\exists f)K_{\text{Mary}}(\forall x)(M(x) \supset T(x, f(x)))\qquad\qquad(15)$$

This is obviously a much better reading. For Mary's knowledge amounts to picking out an advisor for each young mother, and of course such picking out is mathematically speaking precisely what a function does. However, it now sounds strange to say that the object of Mary's knowledge is a certain function, not certain advisors. In other words, it is puzzling that no first-order translation of (11) into the language of epistemic logic seems to be possible.

Obviously an analysis that dispenses with quantification over higher-order entities would be preferable. For one thing, such an analysis would be free of all the difficult problems that are associated with questions of existence of higher-order entities. All told, it is not clear how our distinction between different types of knowledge can be made general.

Similar difficulties emerge with the other philosophical and other conceptual insights promised by the original "first-generation" epistemic logic. Many of these promises concerned the application of epistemic logic to the theory of questions and answers. This theory can be made virtually a part of epistemic logic by construing a direct question as a request to bring about a certain epistemic state. (There will be restrictions on how this state of affairs is to be brought about.)

A specification of this epistemic state is called the *desideratum* of the direct question in question. It ought to be representable by means of a satisfactory epistemic logic. Much of the logical theory of questions and answers can be formulated in terms of the desiderata of questions.

For instance, (6) is the desideratum of the direct question

$$\text{Who murdered Roger Ackroyd?} \tag{16}$$

Likewise, the first-person version of (11) namely,

$$\text{I know whom every young mother should trust} \tag{17}$$

expresses the desideratum of the direct question

$$\text{Whom should every young mother trust most?} \tag{18}$$

For simple *wh*-questions, epistemic logic enables us to define some of the most important concepts in the theory of questions and their answers. In particular, we can define the presupposition of a simple *wh*-question. In the case of (16) it is obviously

$$K(\exists x)M(x, r) \tag{19}$$

But it is not obvious how this notion could be defined more generally. Furthermore, the all-important question–answer relationship can be formulated for simple *wh*-questions. Suppose the addressee of the question (16) responds by offering a singular term—say, "b"—as the hoped for answer. Assuming that the reply is true and accepted by the questioner, he, she (or, it, if the inquirer is a computer) can now say

$$\text{I know that b murdered Roger Ackroyd} \tag{20}$$

In brief:

$$K_I M(b, r) \tag{21}$$

When does this satisfy the questioner? When is it a true or *conclusive* answer, as I will call it? Not always, for the questioner might fail to know who b is. In view of the meaning of the desideratum of a question, the answer is if and only if it implies the desideratum of the question; in this case if and only if it implies

$$(\exists x)K_I(b = x) \tag{22}$$

When does this implication hold, then? The semantics of epistemic logic described earlier yields the answer: If and only if it is the case that

$$(\exists x)K_I(b = x) \tag{23}$$

In other words, (23) must be available as an extra premise. Our semantical common sense agrees with this diagnosis.

In brief, the "reply" (21) $K_I M(b, r)$ entails the desideratum

$$(\exists x) K_I M(x, r) \tag{24}$$

only in conjunction with the extra conclusiveness condition (23).

In the case of simple *wh*-questions, we can thus characterize explicitly the relation of questions to their (conclusive) answers.

This result opens a highly interesting epistemological perspective. The question (16) is a factual question. Answering it requires providing the questioner with the factual information codified in (24). It also requires providing the questioner with the conclusiveness condition (23). Now, what (23) expresses is not purely factual knowledge. It involves also conceptual (in this case, lexical) knowledge—namely, knowledge of who it is that is being referred to.

This is especially clear when "b" is a proper name. (It can be one, as pointed out before.) There the knowledge expressed by the conclusiveness condition is purely conceptual—namely, knowledge of the meaning of the proper name "b."

Such conceptual knowledge is *a priori* as far as the usual factual discourse is concerned. Hence we have located a role for *a priori* knowledge smack in the middle of empirical questioning and *a fortiori* empirical inquiry. *A priori* knowledge is needed to secure the conclusiveness conditions, in effect to convert arbitrary responses to genuine answers. I find it hard to think of a more interesting perspective into the epistemology of empirical inquiry.

But, alas, an attempt to generalize these observations to all kinds of questions, and ergo all kinds of inquiry, faces the same problems as were discussed in connection with different kinds of knowledge.

These observations illustrate and reinforce what was said earlier by way of criticizing philosophers' *de dicto* versus *de re* distinction. In what was just discovered, there is implicit an interesting logico-semantical insight. In a reply such as (21) to a simple *wh*-question, one is clearly speaking of b *de dicto*, as this term is currently used. Otherwise, no collateral conclusiveness condition (23) would be needed. Indeed, according to the usual terminology, in the desideratum such as (24) of a simple *wh*-question, the kind of knowledge required is *de re* knowledge. But when the conclusiveness condition (23) is adjoined to (21), the knowledge involved in (23) is transmuted to a *de re* knowledge. This naturally does not affect the kind of knowledge or the kind of reference involved in (21). What this shows is that there is no such thing as irreducibly *de re* or *de dicto* knowledge, or even *de re* or *de dicto* reference in the case of simple *wh*-questions. However, it is not obvious how this striking result can be extended to all epistemic contexts.

Other epistemological applications of epistemic logic seem to fall into the same category of interesting but unfulfilled promises. One general novelty is to try to model knowledge-seeking in general by construing it as a questioning process. Of course, such an approach is in a sense no novelty for it goes back to the very first explicit model of reasoning in Western philosophy—that is, to the Socratic method of questioning, or *elenchus*. In the briefest possible terms, this method amounts to modeling all inquiry as a questioning process. In fact, Aristotle had already suggested that all the first principles of science could be obtained by such a questioning process.

The same Aristotle in effect refined this model by noting that the answers to certain questions are predictable independently of the particular answerer. They are the answers that, from one perspective, are logically implied by earlier answers. Such logical inference steps can be separated from the (true) interrogative steps. They are governed by the rules of inference of deductive logic.

When we are recording the successive steps of interrogative inquiry on paper (or on a computer disk), logical inference steps and interrogative steps look rather similar. The former are steps from a premise (or number of premises) to a conclusion; the latter are steps from the presupposition(s) of a question to its answer.

There are even closer analogies between some of the most important types of logical and interrogative steps. For one thing, in an application of the rule of existential instantiation we move from a sentence of the form

$$K(\exists x)F[x] \tag{25}$$

or perhaps

$$K(\exists x)F[x] \tag{26}$$

to an instance of the form

$$F[a] \tag{27}$$

or perhaps

$$KF[a] \tag{28}$$

where a is a new individual constant, in some treatments a member of a special class of individual constants called dummy names. Their m.o. is very much the same as the John Does and the Jane Roes of legal parlance.

In a comparable interrogative step, the inquirer moves from the presupposition of a simple *wh*-question, which is of the form (25) or (26), to an answer of the form

$$F[a] \tag{29}$$

or perhaps

$$KF[a] \tag{30}$$

If this is to be a genuine answer, there must also be available the conclusiveness condition

$$(\exists x)K(a = x) \tag{31}$$

The main function of (31) is merely to make a available as a substitution value
of various future steps of logical inference.

Now, these two kinds of steps not only look alike, there is a deeper connection between them. This connection can be seen best by raising two important
general questions that turn out to be interrelated. One of them concerns the
role of logic in inquiry in general. At first sight, it might seem that the last word
on the question was put forward by Aristotle when he separated the necessitated answers—that is, logical inference steps—from the unnecessitated ones–
that is, from interrogative steps. In Aristotle's terminology, the former can be
judged *ad argumentum* without considering the answerer, whereas the latter
can be fully evaluated only *ad hominem*. It might seem that Aristotle was seriously biased in weighting the two kinds of answers, in that he devoted most of
his attention to syllogistically construed logical inference steps. Even though
this impression may not be entirely correct historically, the fact remains that in
actual real-life inquiry, the most important job is done by interrogative steps.
Only in them does new factual information enter into the inquirer's line of
thought.

Accordingly, deductive logic seems to play a rather modest role in inquiry in
general. And this result seems to belie the widespread popular image of logic
as the "secret" of all good reasoning. This view is epitomized by the stories
of the clever "deductions" of real or fictional sleuths such as the proverbial
Sherlock Holmes. We might in fact call this suspect perspective the "Sherlock
Holmes view of reasoning." The Sherlock Holmes view on the role of logic in
inquiry can be said to be mistaken only as long as we do not consider strategies
of inquiry and inference. Such strategies manifest themselves in the form of
answers to the problem as to what to do next in the course of actual inquiry. The
normal situation is that the inquirer has reached a number of propositions that
he, she, or it can use as premises of logical inferences or also as presuppositions
of questions. Indeed, we have two separate strategic questions here depending
on whether the inquirer is restricted to purely deductive means or whether the
inquirer is trying to find the best questions to ask. In other words, the one
problem is to locate the best deductive premise, and the other to find the best
presupposition for the question to be asked next.

It can be shown that in neither case can we find an effective (computable)
rule that would provide the correct answer in all cases. So is there anything
concrete and constructive that can be said about the strategies of inquiry in
general? Even though neither of the two questions just mentioned is mechanically answerable in general, there is a most remarkable thing than can be said
of their answers. Subject to certain conditions to be explained, *the answer is the
same for both questions.* Or, rather, this is what is suggested by the parallelism
just mentioned. Compare here (27)–(28) and (29)–(30). The two outcomes
of the next step differ only in having a different individual constant in the
same position. This usually makes little difference to the rest of the inquiry.
Hence, if the best way to shorten the rest of a deductive inquiry is to reach

(27) through a logical inference step, the best way of shortening it by means of an interrogative step is to use the same sentence as the presupposition of the question that would yield (29).

This interesting strategic parallelism between deduction and interrogation requires explanations and qualifications. Some of the qualifications needed here are inessential. For one thing, it might make a difference to the rest of the inquiry if the individual a obtained in the answer to the inquirer's question is not new but identical with one of the individuals already considered. But if the inquirer must ask a question here, he, she, or it does not usually know sight unseen whether that is the case. Hence the inquirer has in his or her strategic thinking taken into account the possibility that the answer individual is a new one.

Most importantly, the parallelism is complete only if the inquirer never has to reject ("bracket") one of the answers he, she, or it receives. Hence, what has been said applies only to types of inquiry in which we are dealing with what in the traditional jargon would be called "contexts of (pure) discovery." However, this important qualification does not reduce the interest of our results.

The parallelism between question–answer steps and deductive steps can be extended to propositional questions and the deductive rule for disjunctions. Consider, for example, the propositional question, Is it the case that S_1 or is it the case that S_2? Its presupposition is obviously

$$(S_1 \vee S_2) \tag{32}$$

(possibly prefixed by K). Its desideratum is

$$(KS_1 \vee KS_2) \tag{33}$$

A deductive rule for disjunctions splits the argument into two branches initiated by S_1 and S_2, respectively.

An answer introduces here either S_1 or S_2 into the inquirer's line of reasoning. In other words, the rest of the inquiry is the same as in the case of a deductive step, except that in the case of an answer, the inquirer can dispense with one of the two branches. But since the inquirer did not in general know ahead of time which branch he or she could disregard, the inquirer would have to consider in a strategic context both possibilities. Thus we find here the same kind of parallelism as in the case of existential instantiation.

But what about questions that do not have non-vacuous presuppositions? Now, what are such questions like? They are of course yes-or-no questions. (The term yes-or-no has to be taken in the logical rather than grammatical sense here.) But in the same way as in the case of propositional questions, a yes-or-no question such as "Is it the case that S?" corresponds to a tautology introduction rule in deductive logic—that is, to the introduction of $(S_1 \vee \neg S_2)$. This starts two branches (lines of thought) in the way illustrated by the tree method. Only one of them corresponds to the rest of the inquiry initiated by an answer to the yes-or-no question, but in the inquirer's strategic planning (prior to the answer), he or she has to consider both possible answers, thus creating an analogue to the deductive situation.

However, the parallelism that has just been discussed apparently cannot be generalized. It is not even clear in general what answers to more complex questions will look like logically, nor is it clear what their presuppositions might be. And even if answers to these questions were available, there apparently are no rules of logical inference that could parallel the relevant complex question–answer steps. This might seem to jeopardize the entire strategic analogy deduction and interrogative inquiry.

Other limitations are likewise conspicuous. Perhaps the most important shortcoming of first-generation epistemic logic confronts us when we begin to emulate Socrates and Aristotle and model all inquiry as a questioning process. Such a model is straightforward to implement as long as the inquirer is given a fixed conclusion that it be established through an interrogative process starting from given initial premises. This may be enough to answer *why*-questions through a questioning process. However, there does not seem to be any way of analyzing similarly the all-important method of answering questions—that is, initial "big" or principal questions, by means of a number of "small" or operative questions. This would be a serious limitation to any application of the logic of questions and answers to epistemology.

In view of such applicational shortcomings of first-generation epistemic logic, it might in fact look as if the philosophical community could be excused when it has so far turned a deaf ear to the interesting and important philosophical vistas suggested by the observations so far described.

3. Promises Fulfilled by Means of the Notion of Independence

I have so far been telling a story that is partly historical, partly systematic. That story has led us to a tantalizing impasse. On the one hand, by considering simple examples, we can discover highly interesting philosophical suggestions apparently implicit in our epistemic logic. On the other hand, these suggestions apparently cannot be generalized from the simple cases, in which they are more or less obvious, to more complex cases. Sometimes such an extension can apparently be accomplished only by appealing to higher-order entities that lead us to problems that are at least as recalcitrant as the ones we were trying to overcome. What are we to do?

The most popular response in this day and age seems to be to throw up our hands and claim that conceptual realities in epistemology are just too complex and too context-dependent to be captured by the clumsy tools of epistemic logic. Apparently it would be politically correct in this situation to evoke such phrases as "family resemblance" or "fuzzy logic."

Alternatively, some philosophers might decide to evoke more examples and to develop much more detailed taxonomy and other theory for these realities, in the style of empirical linguists.

The main message of this chapter is that both reactions would be dead wrong. Not only can all the difficulties I have described be solved, they can be solved in one fell swoop. This swoop is provided by the same approach that has prompted a revolution in the foundations of ordinary non-epistemic first-order logic. It is usually referred to as game-theoretical semantics, but what is important in it is not the use of game-theoretical ideas per se. Rather, the crucial insight is that the dependence of real-life variables on each other is expressed in a logical notation by the formal dependence of the quantifiers on each other to which they are bound. This insight motivates a change even in the notation of first-order logic. In the usual notation, the dependencies between quantifiers are indicated by the nesting of their scopes. But such a nesting relation is of a rather special kind. Among other things, it is transitive and asymmetrical. Hence not all patterns of dependence and independence can be expressed by its means. And hence the received logical notation does not do its job adequately, and has to be made more flexible. Since the problem is to enable us to structure our formulas more freely, it could in principle be solved without introducing any new notation and merely relaxing the scope rules—that is, the formation rules for the pairs of parentheses that indicate the dependence relations between quantifiers. In practice, it is more perspicuous to introduce instead a special independence indicator (Q_2y/Q_1x) that expresses the independence of the quantifier (Q_2y) of the quantifier (Q_1x). Game theory comes in in that such independence can be modeled in game-theoretical semantics by the informational independence of the move mandated by (Q_2y) of the move mandated by (Q_1x), in the general game-theoretical sense of informational independence. The systematic use of this notation results in the first place in what is known as independence-friendly (IF) first-order logic.

The use of the slash (independence) notation is not restricted to the usual extensional first-order logic, however. One remarkable thing here is that this notion of independence applies to all semantically active ingredients of a sentence whose semantics can be formulated in terms of a semantical game rule. The epistemic operator K_a is a case in point in that it mandates a choice by the falsifier of one of a's knowledge worlds with respect to which a semantical game is to be continued. Accordingly, the slash notation makes sense also in epistemic logic.

How, then, does it help us? Consider, in order to answer this question, sentence (7):

$$(\exists x)\,K\,M(x, r)$$

It expresses its intended meaning "it is known who murdered Roger Ackroyd" because the "witness individual" value of x must be chosen before the choice of a possible world (scenario) mandated by K. Hence this individual must be the same in all of them.

But for this purpose the value of x must not necessarily be chosen in a semantical game before the choice of the scenario (possible world) connected with K. It suffices to make the choice independently of the scenario choice. Hence (7) says the same as

$$K(\exists x/K)M(x, r) \tag{34}$$

Likewise in (17), the choice of the witness individual (the trusted person) depends on the mother in question but not on the choice of the possible world prompted by K_I. Hence the right logical form of (17) is

$$K(\forall x)(\exists y/K)T(x, y) \tag{35}$$

As can be seen, this is a sentence of IF first-order epistemic logic, and hence independent of all the problems connected with higher-order quantification.

It is easily seen that (35) and its analogues do not reduce to a slash-free notation. Hence the criticisms reported earlier are valid, albeit only as long as the IF notation is not used. But as soon as this notation is available, we can solve one of the problems posed in Section 2—namely, the problem of expressing the desiderata of complex *wh*-questions on that first-order level.

The same notation can be extended to propositional connectives. For instance, we can write

$$K(S_1(\vee/K)S_2) \tag{36}$$

This is readily seen to be equivalent to

$$(KS_1 \vee K)S_2) \tag{37}$$

In more complex examples, however, the slash notation is not dispensable. An example is offered by

$$K(\forall)(F_1(x)(\vee/K)F_2(x)) \tag{38}$$

In general, we can take any sentence of the form

$$KS \tag{39}$$

where S is a first-order sentence in a negation normal form. If in (39) we replace one or more existential quantifiers ($\exists x$) by ($\exists x/K$) and/or one or more disjunctions ($F_1 \vee F_2$) by ($F_1(\vee/K)F_2$), we obtain an epistemic sentence that can serve as the desideratum of a (usually multiple) question.

The possibility that there are several slashes in the desideratum means the possibility of dealing with multiple questions. Their behavior in natural language turns out to be a most instructive chapter of epistemic logic, as documented in Hintikka 1976. In this chapter, I will not deal with sentences with multiple K's—that is, with iterated questions.

Thus the received terminology already embodies a mistake. What happens in quantified epistemic logic is not "quantifying into" an opaque context, but quantifing *independently* of an epistemic operator and the moves it mandates.

The resulting logic of K-sentences can be considered a second-generation epistemic logic (or a fragment of such a logic). In that logic, the most important concepts relating to questions and answers can be defined for all different kinds of questions. For one thing, if the desideratum of a question is (39), its presupposition is obtained by dropping all the slashes /K. A reply to such a question brings about the truth of a sentence in which each slashed existential quantifier sub-formula

$$(\exists x/K)F[x] \tag{40}$$

is replaced by

$$F[g(y_1, y_2, \ldots)] \tag{41}$$

where (Qy_1), $(Qy_2), \ldots$ are all the quantifiers on which the quantifier $(\exists x/K)$ in (40) depends in (39). Likewise, each disjunction $(F_1(\vee/K)F_2)$ occurring as a sub-formula of (39) is replaced by

$$((g(y_1, y_2, \ldots) = 0 \,\&\, F_1) \vee (g(y_1, y_2, \ldots) \neq 0 \,\&\, F_2)) \tag{42}$$

where (Qy_1), $(Qy_2), \ldots$ are all the quantifiers on which the disjunction in question depends in (39).

This reply amounts to an answer if and only if the conclusiveness conditions of the form

$$K(\exists f/K)(g = f) \tag{43}$$

are satisfied. Instead of (43), we could write

$$K(\forall y_1)(\forall y_2)\ldots(\exists z/K)(g(y_1, y_2, \ldots) = z) \tag{44}$$

Whenever there are no quantifiers (Qy_1), $(Qy_2), \ldots$ the function term $g(y_1, y_2, \ldots)$ is replaced by an individual constant.

This shows also how knowing the identity of a function can be expressed on the first-order level, thus removing one of the limitations of the first-generation epistemic logic.

This generalizes the notions of presupposition, desideratum, conclusiveness condition, and the question–answer relation to all questions, with the partial exception of *why-* and *how-*questions, which have to be dealt with separately. With this qualification, it can be said that we have reached the first fully explicit and general logic of questions and answers. This generality is of considerable interest for the purposes of both philosophers and linguists. For philosophers, one of the many interesting things about this second-generation epistemic logic is that it is a *first-order* logic. All quantification is over individuals, thus avoiding all the difficult problems concerning the existence of higher-order entities.

Linguists might be interested in the fact that in the framework of semantic representation provided by epistemic logic, the slash (/) is the embodiment of the question ingredient. Applied to disjunctions (as in $(\vee/-)$), it creates propositional questions, and applied to the existential quantifiers (as in $(\exists x/-)$), it creates *wh*-questions. This also throws light indirectly on the semantics of the question ingredient in natural languages.

The independence notation has further uses. For one thing, it enables us to express what is commonly referred to as common knowledge. In the case of knowledge common to two agents, a and b, it means that they not only share the same information, but that each of them knows that the other one knows it, and that each knows that the other one knows that the other one knows it, and so on. This is achieved by making the order of the initial K's irrelevant and also using as the *wh*-ingredient $(-/K_a K_b)$. For instance, the following sentence expresses the idea that it is common knowledge between a and b whether it is the case that S:

$$K_a(K_b/K_a)(S(\vee/K_a K_b) \neg S)$$

This shows that in order to express common knowledge in general, we have to make sure that the relevant knowledge operators are on a par in the slashes, and not only when they are prefixed to a sentence. And, if so, we can see that common knowledge could not have been formulated in general terms in the first-generation epistemic logic.

The result of this liberalization of epistemic logic is a simple but powerful logic of knowledge, including a logic of questions and answers. This second-generation epistemic logic fulfills the promises that the first generation suggested but did not deliver. By its means, we can carry out the promised analyses of all different kinds of knowledge and all different kinds of questions, using the *knows that* operator K as the only epistemic ingredient.

Thus, for instance, knowledge *de dicto* and knowledge *de re* are but different variants of the same basic notion of knowledge. Moreover, the important difference between two different modes of identification can be seen not to imply any differences in the kind of information (knowledge) involved in them. This fact turns out to have interesting consequences even outside logic and philosophy in neuroscience, where it helps to understand the two visual cognition systems sometimes known as the *where*-system and the *what*-system. (See Hintikka and Symons 2003.)

The notion of independence also enables us to deepen the analysis of the *de dicto* versus *de re* contrast sketched earlier. It is possible to assume that in a semantical game, the non-logical constants are not initially interpreted by the participants. Instead, the references that are assigned to them are chosen by the verifier as a move in the game. In fact, Hintikka and Kulas have shown that this assumption serves to throw light on certain regularities in the semantics of ordinary language. It is perhaps not obvious that such mileage can be obtained from the assumption, for there is clearly only one choice that can win—namely, to assign to the constants their linguistically determined references. The extra mileage is nevertheless real, for once there is a game rule for the interpretation (i.e., assignment of references), applications of this rule may or may not be independent of other moves in the game. (This is the opening utilized by Hintikka and Kulas. In particular, the choice of the reference of b in a sentence such as (21) may or may not be independent of the choice of the scenario prompted by K_I. Earlier, it was assumed to be dependent on the choice of the scenario. It can be made independent notationally by replacing (21) with

$$K_I M((b/K)r) \qquad (45)$$

This is obviously what is meant by taking b to be *de re*. Almost equally obviously, (45) is logically equivalent to the conjunction of (21) and (23).

General terms can be treated in the same way. This possibility is perhaps somewhat more conspicuous in the case of belief than of knowledge, but this is merely a matter of degree. For instance, consider the statement

$$K_a(P/K)(b) \qquad (46)$$

It says that a knows that b is one of the individuals who or what in fact are P. It does not require that a *know* that they and only they have the property P.

These extensions of the independence notation show several interesting things. It reinforces my earlier result concerning the definability of the *de dicto* versus *de re* contrast. It also shows that this contrast is not restricted to singular terms. Furthermore, we can now see that the familiar contrast between the referential and predicative uses of singular terms such as definite descriptors is not an irreducible one but is rather a matter of different construction in terms of the same basic notions.

An especially interesting generalization of earlier insights that is now brought out into the open is the partly conceptual character of the conclusiveness conditions of all *wh*-questions, simple and complex. For instance, a reply to an experimental question whose desideratum is of the form (12) is a function-in-extension—that is to say, a mere correlation of argument values and functions-values like a curve on graph paper. Such a reply does not qualify as an answer because the questioner might not know which function is represented by the correlation or by the graph. Knowing its identity is conceptual— in this case, mathematical—knowledge. This throws into a strikingly sharp profile the role of mathematics in experimental (and hence presumably empirical) science and even the indispensability of mathematics in science in general. Likewise, the partial strategic parallelism between deduction and questioning can now be generalized. As the first step, we can epistemologize the questioning processes in the following way:

(i) Every initial premise S is replaced by $K_I S$.
(ii) Every answer A is replaced by $K_I(A \& C(A))$, where $C(A)$ is the conjunction of all the conclusiveness conditions for A.

This does not yet generalize the parallelism between question–answer steps, and logical (deductive) steps, which suggested a strategic near-identity of interrogation and deduction. We have generalized the rule for question–answer steps in inquiry, but we do not have any rule of deductive inference that would match it. Such a parallel rule can be obtained by generalizing the rules of purely deductive reasoning. The original analogy was between existential instanti-ation and simply *wh*-questions. The existential quantifier whose variable is instantiated must occur sentence-initially in the received rule applications of existential instantiation. Why can we not instantiate also inside a larger formula? (Surely an existential quantifier expresses there, too, the availabil-ity of truth-making individuals.) The answer is that the "witness individual" in question will then depend on certain other individuals. Hence the instantiating term must be a function of those individuals. Formally speaking, we can extend the rule of existential generalization so as to allow to replace a sub-formula of the form

$$(\exists x)F[x] \tag{47}$$

of a larger formula by a formula of the form (41), except that now g must be a new function symbol or a "dummy function symbol," if they are used as a separate category of symbols. Some people might want to call them names of "arbitrary functions," in analogy with "arbitrary individuals."

This clearly serves to extend the parallelism between deduction and ques-tioning discussed earlier. In a context of pure discovery, the optimal strate-gies of questioning parallel the optimal strategies of deductive inference, in the sense explained. Even though deductive steps and interrogative steps in inquiry are different from each other, they are, in the case of pure discovery, governed by the same rules. As I sometimes have put it, Sherlock Holmes was right: All good thinking is logical thinking. More cautiously speaking, we have located one important role of deductive logic in inquiry—namely, the role of providing strategic advice for reasoning in general.

Along the same lines, we can also at once remove the most important limita-tion to the applicability of the logic of questions and answers and hence of the applicability of epistemic logic. We can now reconstruct the process of answer-ing principal questions by means of operative questions. How can we do it? Simply by using the desideratum of the principal question as the target propo-sition to be established by the interrogative process. Naturally this involves making the epistemic element explicit throughout, as indicated earlier. For instance, the initial premises are not now first-order sentences $T_1, T_2, \ldots$, but their epistemic forms $KT_1, KT_2, \ldots$ Answers to questions will likewise all begin with K, as in examples like the resulting logic is, as we may put it, the first gen-eral reconstruction of the *elenchus* of the Platonic Socrates, who was already trying to cope with large-scale principal questions ("What is knowledge?" "What is piety?") by means of putting small questions to his interlocutor. This opens up the possibility of constructing a genuine epistemology of knowledge-seeking over and above the epistemology of knowledge-justification, which what current epistemology almost entirely is.

Thus the second-generation epistemic logic serves to carry out all the major philosophical promises that were made but not fulfilled by the first-generation version. The crucial concept in this generational jump is the notion of informational independence, which thus emerges as the key idea in the logic of knowledge. It is clearly impossible to develop a general logic of knowledge without the help of the notion of independence. This role of the notion of independence has some methodological interest of its own. It turns epistemic logic into an ally in the revolution in ordinary non-epistemic logic that has been instigated by the same notion of independence. This notion is in turn possible to formulate only if we are using some form of game-theoretical semantics. Whatever successes the second-generation epistemic logic can score therefore provide evidence of the usefulness of game-theoretical concepts in logic. At the same time, the second-generation epistemic logic provides evidence of the importance of the notion of independence in general, including its prevalence in the semantics of an actual "ordinary" working language.

Last, but not least, we have in epistemic logic a vivid reminder of the aptness of the Wittgensteinean wonder at how much metaphysics can be condensed in a drop of logic (Wittgenstein called it "grammar"). In the spirit of Wittgenstein's dictum, perhaps I can conclude with a list of some of the drops of insights that the original epistemic-logic promised but that were delivered only by the second-generation one.

1. Distinction between propositional knowledge and knowledge of objects (entities).
2. Uniform analysis of all different kinds of knowledge in terms of a single *knows that* operator.
    (a) The basic kind of knowledge is propositional.
    (b) There is no irreducible *de re* knowledge.
3. An analysis of the basic notions concerning questions and answers, including the notion of presupposition and the question–answer relation.
4. Answers (conclusive answers) to empirical questions often require *a priori* conceptual knowledge (e.g., mathematical knowledge).
5. A method of answering (principal) questions by means of (operative) questions.
6. A partial strategic parallelism between questioning and deduction. ("Sherlock Holmes vindicated.")

References

Aristotle, 1994, *Posterior Analytics, second edition,* translated with a commentary by Jonathan Barnes, Clarendon Press, Oxford.

Böer, Stephen E., and William G. Lycan, 1986, *Knowing Who,* MIT Press, Cambridge.

Boh, Ivan, 1993, *Epistemic Logic in the Later Middle Ages,* Routledge, London.

Bühler, Axel, 1983, *Die Logik kognitiver Sätze,* Duncker and Humboldt, Berlin.

Engdahl, Elisabet, 1986, *Constituent Questions: The Syntax and Semantics of Questions with Special Reference to Swedish,* Reidel, Dordrecht.

Fagin, R., J. Y. Halpern, Y. Moses, and M. Y. Vardi, 1995, *Reasoning about Knowledge*, MIT Press, Cambridge.

Gabbay, Dov, and John Woods, editors, 2003, *Handbook of the History and Philosophy of Logic*, North Holland (Elsevier), Amsterdam.

Gochet, Paul and P. Gribomont., 2002, "Epistemic Logic," in Gabbay and Woods, editors (2003).

Hintikka, Jaakko, 1990, "Cartesian Cogito, Epistemic Logic, and Neuroscience," *Synthese*, vol. 83, no. 1, pp. 133–157.

Hintikka, Jaakko, 1976, *The Semantics of Questions and the Questions of Semantics: Case Studies in the Interrelations of Logic, Semantics, and Syntax: Acta Philosophica Fennica*, vol. 28, no. 4, Societas Philosophica Fennica, Helsinki.

Hintikka, Jaakko, 1975, *The Intentions of Intentionality*, D. Reidel, Dordrecht.

Hintikka, Jaakko, 1962, *Knowledge and Belief: An Introduction to the Logic of Two Notions*, Cornell University Press, Ithaca, New York.

Hintikka, Jaakko, and Ilpo Halonen., 1995, "Semantics and Pragmatics for Why Questions," *Journal of Philosophy*, vol. 92, pp. 636–657.

Hintikka, Jaakko, and Jack Kulas, 1985, *Anaphora and Definite Descriptions*. D.Reidel, Dordrecht.

Hintikka, Jaakko, and Gabriel Sandu, 1995, "The Fallacies of the "New Theory of Reference," *Synthese*, vol. 104, pp. 245–283.

Hintikka, Jaakko, and John Symons, 2003, "Systems of Visual Identification in Neuroscience: Lessons from Epistemic Logic," *Philosophy of Science,* vol. 70, pp. 89–104. And as Chapter 6 in this volume.

Knuuttila, Simo, 1993, *Modalities in Medieval Philosophy*, Routledge, London.

Kripke, Saul A., 1972, "Naming and Necessity," in D. Davidson and G. Harman, editors, *Semantics of Natural Language*, D. Reidel, Dordrecht, pp. 253–355.

Laux, Armin, and Heinrich Wansing, editors, 1995, *Knowledge and Belief in Philosophy and Artificial Intelligence*, Akademie-Verlag, Berlin.

Lenzen, Wolfgang, 1978, *Recent Work in Epistemic Logic*, Acta Philosophica Fennica, vol. 30, no. 1, Societas Philosophica Fennica, Helsinki.

Lenzen, Wolfgang, 1979, Epistemologische Betrachtungen zu (S4, S5), Erkenntnis, vol. 14, pp. 33–56.

Lenzen, Wolfgang, 1980, *Glauben, Wissen, und Wahrscheinlickkeit: Systeme der epistemische Logik*, Springer-Verlag, Berlin.

Lepage, François and Serge Lapierre, 2000, *Logique partielle et savoir: Essai de philosophie formelle*, Bellarmin Vrin, Montreal/Paris.

Meyer, J.-J.Ch., and W. van der Hoek, 1995, *Epistemic Logic for AI and Computer Science*, Cambridge University Press, Cambridge.

Stelzner, Werner, 1984, *Epistemische Logik*, Akademie-Verlag, Berlin.

van der Hoek, Wiebe, 1993, "Systems for Knowledge and Belief," *Journal of Logic and Computation*, vol. 3, pp. 173–195.

von Wright, G. H., 1951, *An Essay in Modal Logic*, North Holland, Amsterdam.

Williamson, Timothy, 2000, *Knowledge and Its Limits*, Oxford University Press, Oxford.

4

Presuppositions and Other Limitations of Inquiry

1. Presuppositions as a Crucial Limitation of Inquiry

Socrates was right. All rational knowledge-seeking can be conceptualized as a questioning process, with question–answer steps interspersed with logical inference steps. "Rational" here means "capable of epistemological evaluation." This is what I have argued in Hintikka 1998. Here I will not review the arguments for this view of "inquiry as inquiry," as I have called it, but instead examine some of its implications. In any case, I am not the first philosopher by a long shot to defend the omnipresence of questioning in our knowledge-seeking. Aristotle modeled both his methodology and his logic on the different aspects of the Socratic questioning process, or *elenchus*. One of the better known—albeit not one of the best appreciated—later representatives of similar views is R. G. Collingwood, who went even further and asserted that "[e]very statement that anybody ever makes is made in answer to a question." (Collingwood 1940, p. 23.)

Or is Collingwood perhaps merely echoing Aristotle according to whom all the propositions used as dialectical premises originate from questions? (See *Topics* I, x.) In any case, Collingwood had something of an ulterior motive in conceiving of all propositions as answers to questions. This ulterior motive is a legitimate one. He wanted in this way to subject to philosophical examination the limitations that characterize a certain line of inquiry or the thought of some individual thinker or even the intellectual stance of an entire era. These limitations are, according to Collingwood, due to the presuppositions of questions. As he puts it, "Every question involves a presupposition." (Collingwood 1940, p. 25.) A question can be meaningfully asked only if its presupposition is available. Hence the need for a presupposition limits our questions, and consequently, since all propositions are answers to questions, limits the propositions we can propose.

Whatever one may say of the details of Collingwood's ideas, his main conception is correct if I am right in construing all rational inquiry as an

interrogative procedure. For then the limits of inquiry are obviously determined to a large extent by the available presuppositions of questions and
answers. (The qualifications this statement needs are discussed later, especially in Section 7.) It follows that all doctrines concerning the limitations of
scientific or other kinds of knowledge-seeking will have to be discussed by
reference to the presuppositions of questions and questioning.

But where do we get the presuppositions of our questions that enable us to
ask them? This question can be raised either apropos Collingwood or absolutely. In some cases, the presupposition of a question can be an answer to an
antecedent question. That antecedent question must have its own presupposition. But according to Collingwood, such a regress of presuppositions will
come to an end. Thus at the far end of a Collingwoodean hierarchy of presuppositions there are what he calls "ultimate presuppositions." They are not
answers to any prior questions. They determine the character of the thought
of the thinker who presupposes them. They are therefore crucial, according
to Collingwood, to any study of how a thinker's thought is restricted by his or
her own assumptions. Hence, one can add that they are among other things
crucial to any understanding of the entire issue of epistemological relativism.
In a different direction, the role of presuppositions is relevant to the problem
of demarcating science from metaphysics. For it is not unnatural to suggest
that what supposedly makes metaphysical questions meaningless is that their
presuppositions have not been established.

Thus, configurations of Collingwoodean ultimate presuppositions are not
entirely unlike Kuhnian paradigms. Both are supposed to guide inquiry and
mark its limits in ways other than acting as premises of inferences. However,
Collingwood is one up on Kuhn in this department, the reason being that
presuppositions of questions can—and should—be made a part of a systematic theory of questions and answers. Indeed, Collingwood in so many words
called his study a "logic of questions and answers." In contrast, paradigms
are such wild and woolly animals as not to allow much rational discussion. It
ought not have come as a surprise that Kuhn himself abandoned his notion of
paradigm, albeit only in favor of an almost equally mysterious idea of "disci-
plinary matrix." Collingwood's approach thus exhibits a much greater promise
than Kuhn's. For instance, a careful study of the logic of questions and answers
in the spirit of Collingwood has a much better chance of eliciting the actual
conceptual presuppositions of different inquiries and inquirers, including the
presuppositions of our own discourse, than any kind of "paradigm research."
It would be highly salutary to recast such an enterprise as "presupposition
research."

Needless to say, Collingwood's "logic" is still not an explicitly formulated
logic in a sense that would have satisfied a Tarski. This is not merely a matter
of cosmetic exactness or architectonic organization. It will turn out that some
of Collingwood's explicit statements are not exceptionlessly true. For instance,
pace Collingwood, there are questions without non-trivial presuppositions, as

will be pointed out in Section 7. For another instance, one and the same state-ment can be an answer to more than one question. Collingwood is not free from confusion, either. I cannot help suspecting that when he speaks of pre-suppositions of questions he is sometimes, in effect, thinking of what might be called "presuppositions of answers" but which I have (perhaps unfortunately) called the "conclusiveness conditions of answers." (See Section 12.) All these shortcomings affect the evaluation of Collingwood's idea of the ultimate pre-suppositions of questions as determining the limits of our thinking.

In the logic of questions and answers, we do in fact have an instructive example of how bright and shiny logical tools can be of help to understand and master important epistemological and other philosophical problems. But in order to make full use of the logic of questions and answers for epistemological purposes, we must also consider how sequences of questions and answers contribute to—and almost virtually constitute—a line of inquiry. This is spelled out by setting up what I have called an "interrogative model of inquiry." In principle, this model at first looks exceedingly simple. It is like a deductive argument, except that at any time, new premises may be introduced in the form of answers to questions—assuming that the questions in question are answerable.

As a bookkeeping device, we can use a semantical *tableau* in the sense of E. W. Beth (1955). It turns out to be advisable to rule out any traffic between the left-hand and right-hand sides of any *tableau* (or *subtableau*). A question can be raised only if its presupposition is on the left side, and if an answer is forthcoming, it will likewise be added to the left side. The details of logical bookkeeping are nevertheless technicalities that do not matter to the main ideas involved in interrogative inquiry.

Such an inquiry can be thought of as a game against nature in the sense of the mathematical theory of games. A play of such a game starts from a number of *initial premises* on the left side and the conclusion to be established on the right side. If the inquirer manages to close the *tableau*, he wins and his opponent ("nature") loses. The precise determination of payoffs is in most cases not crucial. Also, and most importantly, the set of available answers will have to be specified.

Speaking more generally, a word on answers and answering might be appro-priate here. The first modern philosopher to have compared scientific inquiry to questioning seems to have been Francis Bacon. He gave the likeness a nasty turn, however, comparing as he did an experimentalist with an inquisitor who forces a prisoner to reveal the truth. For the analysis undertaken here, we do not need to assume the role of a torturer, but we have to postulate a minimal consistency on the part of the answerer. We will simply assume that in each inquiry, a certain set of potential answers is given. (We can call this the "answer set") When a question is asked, the respondent will provide an answer to it as soon as there is one in the answer set. This may be considered as a generaliza-tion of the requirement of the repeatability of scientific experiments. It might be of interest to ask whether certain closure conditions should be imposed on the answer set. We will not discuss that question here, however.

As Collingwood's case shows, many questions concerning the presuppositions of questions, and more generally the presuppositions of inquiry, are relevant to the larger philosophical and methodological questions about the intrinsic limitations of inquiry, including the problem of relativism, and even more generally to the problem of historical understanding and its limitations. This is because Collingwood is essentially correct in considering any rational inquiry as a questioning process.

2. Utilities in Inquiry

At the same time, the interrogative model shows that the presuppositions of questions and answers are not, on the face of things at least, the only parameters restricting inquiry. This fact also suggests that the theories of Collingwood and Kuhn cannot be the whole story about the limitations of inquiry.

What are the other limitations? Let us return to the idea that in any one inquiry, the set of available answers must be fixed. This stipulation of a fixed store of available answers can nevertheless be relaxed. If we are thinking in game-theoretical terms, we can allow the inquirer to "purchase" the right to ask certain questions, in the sense that asking them will reduce the potential payoff resulting from the outcome eventually reached. This is not unnatural. For instance, improved (but more expensive) experiments can extend the range of answers a scientist can receive from nature.

From game theory we know that the strategy choices of different players are importantly dependent on their utilities. Hence it follows that an inquirer's strategies, and *a fortiori* the course of an inquiry, are affected by the inquirer's utilities. These can be partly determined by extra-scientific factors. Hence, in the interrogative model, we can take fully into account the role of non-epistemic aims of inquiry. However, contrary to what many people, including prominently Thomas Kuhn, believe, this does not imply that the choice of strategies of inquiry is not fully determined by logical and epistemological principles. The possibility of a fully rational methodology of inquiry is entirely compatible with the influence of values on the utilities associated with the different outcomes of inquiry, and indeed more generally with the utilities characterizing an entire course that inquiry may take. Notions such as "paradigm" thus harbor, as they are typically used, an important fallacy.

3. Availability of Answers

The availability or non-availability of answers affects the inquirer's strategy choice also independently of any variation in utilities. If a fixed store of available answers is thought of as characterizing an interrogative "game," this store constitutes a major limitation on inquiry. If this supply of answers is extended, new opportunities are opened to investigation.

This store of answers is nevertheless not fixed by our language or by our conceptual scheme. Its extent is a matter of fact or, rather, a complex of matters of fact. Since nature's answers are often outcomes of experiments, this complex may include prominently the state of scientists" experimental technology. And this is a most familiar feature of the actual history of science. The progress of science has repeatedly been made possible by advances in our techniques of observation, measurement, and experiment. Kepler would never have been able to formulate his laws if Tycho Brahe had not improved the accuracy of astronomical measurements. It has been said that when a Ptolemaic astronomer and a Copernican astronomer looked at the heavens, they saw different things. Such statements are usually employed to illustrate the theory-ladenness of observations. So used, they are highly misleading. Admittedly, in a different sense, it is the case that even when Tycho Brahe and one of his predecessors made "the same" astronomical observations, they were doing different things. But this means only that they ended up making different entries (entries of different precision) in their observation logs because of differences in the degree of accuracy of their observations.

Saying this might seem painfully obvious. However, once again it does have repercussions on what philosophers are saying and doing—or trying to say and to do. The set of available answers determines partly the set of presuppositions that an inquirer has access to. Hence the questions that one can legitimately ask will depend on factors such as the state of experimental technology. Ergo, it is futile to set limits to an inquirer's inquiries in logical or other purely conceptual terms. Hence the problem of demarcation that loomed so large for Popper, and to a lesser extent for the logical positivists, is not a purely philosophical one. Any full answer to it will depend on the current state of scientific research.

4. Knowledge Statements

In order to make progress here, we have to investigate further the nature of interrogative inquiry. We have to uncover the logical form of questions, answers, and their presuppositions. For one important thing, what can be said of the presuppositions of questions? First, I have to explain what the true logic of questions and answers is, which in practice means showing how questions and answers are treated in the right kind of epistemic logic. (For a fuller account, see Hintikka 2003; Hintikka, Halonen, and Mutanen 1998.) In using this logic, the ingredients of one's language include the resources of some fixed first-order language plus a sentence-initial epistemic operator K. Since the particular knower we are talking about is largely irrelevant, for the purposes of this chapter this operator K can here usually be thought of as expressing an impersonal "it is known that." Its meaning can be captured by thinking of it as a universal quantifier ranging over the scenarios (courses of events) left possible by what is known. In game-theoretical semantics, K mandates a choice by the falsifier of one of those epistemically possible scenarios.

For simplicity, in what follows, our formulas are always assumed to be in a negation normal form—that is, in a form where the logical constants are

$$\sim, \ \&, \ \vee, \ (\exists x) \ \forall x, \ =$$

and where all negation-signs ($\sim$) occur prefixed to an atomic sentence or an identity.

The novel ingredient in my epistemic logic is the independence indicator / (the slash). Its meaning can be seen from an example or two. The sentence

$$K(\exists x) \ S[x] \tag{1}$$

says that in every possible scenario compatible with what is known, there exists among its members an individual, call it x, such that S[x]. What this amounts to is saying that it is known that there exists an x such that S[x].

But what does it mean to assert the following?

$$K(\exists x/K) \ S[x] \tag{2}$$

Here, the independence of ($\exists x$) of K indicated by the slash (/) means that the individual x satisfying S[x] must be chosen independently of the choice of any particular scenario compatible with what is known. Hence the choice of x might as well be made before the choice of a scenario signaled by K. In other words, there is some one and the same individual x that in all those scenarios satisfies S[x]. In other words, (2) means that it is known of some particular individual x that S[x]. And this is unmistakably what it means to know who or what satisfies S[x]. In brief, if the variable x ranges over persons, (2) says that it is known who (call him or her x) is such that S[x].

Ordinary language examples of (1) and (2) might be:

It is known that someone murdered Roger Akroyd   (3)

It is known who murdered Roger Akroyd   (4)

Or, if the question is raised personally,

I know who murdered Roger Akroyd   (5)

Here, the difference between ($\exists x$) and ($\exists x/K$) is essentially that between someone and who (in other examples some other *wh*-word, such as *what, where, when, ...*). The same difference can be said to separate knowledge of propositions from knowledge of objects (of any logical type)—in other words, knowledge of entities that perhaps could also be called knowledge of id-entities.

Similar remarks apply to subordinate propositional questions. Consider the following propositions:

$$K(S_1 \lor S_2) \tag{6}$$

$$K(S_1(\lor /K)S_2) \tag{7}$$

The former says that it is known that S_1 or S_2. The latter says that it is known whether S_1 or S_2. Thus the relation of $\lor$ to $(\lor/K)$ is like the relation of *that* to *whether*.

These concepts and distinctions can be generalized. Excluding nested interrogative constructions (as well as constructions with *why* or *how*), any knowledge statement can be said to be of the form

$$KS \tag{8}$$

where S is like a first-order sentence (in negation normal form) except that some existential quantifiers $(\exists x)$ have been replaced by $(\exists x/K)$ and some disjunction signs $\lor$ by $(\lor/K)$. These slashed expressions constitute the question ingredient in our formal (but interpreted) language. The propositional question indicator $(\lor/K)$ expresses knowledge of propositions whereas $(\exists x/K)$ expresses knowledge of objects (entities; in this case, individuals).

5. Questions and Their Desiderata

This explains the nature of knowledge statements. But what do they have to do with questions? The answer is very simple. Semantically speaking, a question is, at bottom, a request for information (knowledge). To specify this information is to specify the epistemic state that the questioner wants to be brought about. Any first-person knowledge statement can serve this purpose. A knowledge statement corresponding to a direct question is called its *desideratum*. For instance, the desideratum of the question

Who murdered Roger Ackroyd? (9)

is

I know who murdered Roger Ackroyd (5)

or, if the question is an impersonal one, (3). And the logical form of (3) or (9) is, of course, (2).

Different questions correspond to non-equivalent desiderata and equivalent questions to equivalent desiderata. One way in which the notion of desideratum helps our analysis of interrogative inquiry is that it enables us to deal with ways of answering questions by means of questions. In the original explanation of inquiry by questioning, some fixed conclusion was postulated as being given at the outset of the inquiry. This might seem to restrict the applicability of interrogative inquiry tremendously, for only in the case of *why*- and *how*-questions do we know at the outset of an inquiry what its conclusions will be. This apparently restrictive assumption can be disarmed by assigning the desideratum of a question to the role of the "conclusion." The entire inquiry will then amount to our attempt to answer this "big," or *principal question*, with the help of answers to several "small," or *operative questions*.

A question can thus play two different roles in inquiry. Answering it may be the aim of the entire game—namely, in the case of a principal question. But answering an operative question is merely one step in the process of hopefully answering the principal question. Again, the distinction between principal and operative questions is not recent news. For instance, as Richard Robinson (1971) has shown, Aristotle's injunction against the fallacy of *petitio principii* was originally a warning against asking ("petitioning") the principal question when asking a number of the operative ones is in order.

In general, the desideratum of a question determines much of its logical behavior and most of its logical properties. An important example is offered by the very notion of presuppositions we are interested in here. The presupposition of (9) is

> I know that someone murdered Roger Ackroyd.   (10)

More generally, the presupposition of a question whose desideratum is of the form (2) is (1).

6. Presuppositions of Questions

The general characterization of the presupposition of a question is now easy. As you can see, the presupposition (1) of the question whose desideratum is (2) is obtained from (2) by leaving out the slashed /K. This holds in general. If the desideratum of a question (8), its presupposition is obtained from (8) by omitting all expressions of the form /K. This is a good example of how the independence (slash) notation enables us to carry out a simple and uniform treatment of most of the different kinds of questions.

This analysis of the presuppositions of questions deserves a few comments. First, it is perhaps in order to note that many linguists use a notion of presupposition that pertains only to the existential presuppositions of different kinds of sentence or utterances. In a way, presuppositions of questions also vouchsafe existence, as one can see from such presuppositions as (1). But the existence in question is not so much the existence of individuals or of objects of some other sort, but the existence of answers to a question. If Roger Ackroyd were not murdered, there simply is not a satisfactory answer to the question as to who murdered him.

Of course, people actually do ask questions whose presuppositions have not been established. If so, the "if" presupposition is not in fact satisfied, and no answer to the question will be available. Hence, asking the question whose presupposition has not been established can have a purpose altogether different from obtaining a true answer. By answering such a question, the respondent will consent to the truth of the presupposition. And such a presupposition. especially when it is self-referential, can have surprising consequences. For instance, anyone who promises to answer the following yes-or-no question is in trouble:

Will you answer this question falsely or give me $1,000?

For the only way of keeping the promise is to give the questioner $1,000. Raymond Smullyan has cleverly exploited the logic of such self-referential questions in what he calls "coercive logic." This "logic" is a vivid illustration of the role of presuppositions in questioning. (See Smullyan 1997.) In a different direction, real-life cross-examiners in a court of law know all too well how to extract admissions from witnesses by inducing them to answers whose presuppositions they would not have agreed to if asked directly. Thus the logic of presuppositions is fully as important in the pragmatics of questions as they are in their semantics.

One important thing that the interrogative model of inquiry shows is that the presuppositions of such questions that play a role in an inquiry cannot be combined into one super-presupposition, whether we call it an ultimate presupposition, a paradigm, or an interdisciplinary matrix. They do not depend on each other in a way that would enable us to integrate them in the kind of way in which the premises used in a branch of science can typically be integrated into an axiom system—if we are to believe Hilbert. One reason is that presuppositions of questions do not depend only on presuppositions of earlier questions, but also on answers to earlier questions and ultimately also on the initial premises. I will return to this matter in Section 11.

What has been found out helps to put into perspective Collingwood's idea of ultimate presuppositions. Naturally, many questions need a presupposition, but this presupposition does not typically come from an earlier presupposition. This means that presuppositions do not form a simple hierarchy, as Collingwood seems to assume. Of course there can also be (and sometimes must be) a number of initial premises of the entire inquiry. But since the presuppositions of the actual operative questions cannot always be traced back to these initial premises, it is not clear that they can play the role of Collingwood's ultimate presuppositions. Admittedly, they can provide presuppositions to the inquirer's initial questions, but they also serve as premises for the deductive steps of the inquiry.

Be this as it may, it is instructive to compare Collingwood's ultimate presuppositions with the initial premises of an interrogative inquiry, no matter how Collingwood's idea of presuppositions is to be interpreted in detail. Are the initial premises perhaps what Collingwood thinks of as ultimate presuppositions? If so, we are dealing with presuppositions of an entire inquiry, not of isolated questions. Furthermore, we are then dealing with two different kinds of presuppositions here. If Collingwoodean presuppositions are conceptualized as initial premises of inquiry, they do not in a real-life situation constitute an insurmountable obstacle to inquiry. For what, as was pointed out earlier in Section 3, can be established by the interrogative depends on two different parameters, not merely on the initial premises but also—and more importantly—on the totality of available answers. A restriction on initial premises can be compensated by widening the class of available answers. Indeed, this is virtually a fact of life for a historian of science. The rise of empiricism—that is, abstention from *a priori* assumptions—has gone hand in hand with the development of an improved technology of observation and experimentation.

Conversely, arguments for the need of *a priori* assumptions in science and in learning theory are sensitive to the range of questions that are answerable. For instance, Chomsky (1959) has argued that presuppositionless learning models cannot account for the speed at which a child learns his or her first language, and that we must therefore postulate innate grammatical ideas. This argument depends heavily on the assumption that the input into the learning process (that is, in effect, the language community's answers to the learner's tacit questions) consists of particular data. Chomsky's argument does not go through if these "answers" can be conceptualized as including general laws or regularities. This illustrates the way in which an extension of the range of available answers enables an inquirer or learner to dispense with initial premises.

But if the limitations imposed on inquiry by the initial premises can be overcome by such means, these premises cannot be ultimate presuppositions in Collingwood's sense in that they do not restrict inquiry in the way he obviously thought.

Another consequence of these observations is that initial premises of inquiry are also a far cry from presuppositions of inquiry of the kind Thomas Kuhn wanted us to consider. In order to overcome limitations of inquiry resulting from a given set of initial premises, we do not have to be converted to a new overall "paradigm" or a new way of thinking and arguing. In some cases, what is needed for such liberalization is better techniques of observation and experimentation. In philosophy of science, what is needed might be a realization that scientific inquiry can be conceptualized as an inquiry where the answers a scientist receives are often laws of at least partial generality.

Perhaps the best way of making sense of Collingwood's idea of ultimate presupposition is to evoke the distinction between principal and operative questions, and understand him as speaking of the presuppositions of the different principal questions that an inquirer raises. But if so, the presuppositions of the questions that are asked during actual inquiry are not necessarily related in any substantial way to the presuppositions of the principal question of the inquiry in question. Furthermore, the different principal questions that one and the same inquirer, or same tradition of, inquirers, is pursuing need not be related to each other logically or epistemologically. In particular, they need not be subsumable under a single ultimate presupposition. Perhaps we can thus suspect Collingwood of, in effect, assimilating principal questions and operative questions to each other. And perhaps Thomas Kuhn can find here an application for his concepts so as to supplement a Collingwoodean conception of ultimate presuppositions.

7. Presupposition-Free Questions?

The most interesting things about the presuppositions for the purposes of this chapter are nevertheless the differences between different kinds of questions. Here is a list of the desiderata of some types of questions and their corresponding presuppositions:

Question	Desideratum	Presupposition	(11)
Propositional	$K(S_1(\vee /K)S_2)$	$K(S_1 \vee S_2)$	
Simple *wh*	$K(\exists x/K) S[x]$	$K(\exists x) S[x]$	
Complex *wh*	$K(\forall x) (\exists y/K) S[x, y]$	$K(\forall x) (\exists y) S[x, y]$	
Mixed	$K(\forall x) (S_1 [x](\vee /K)S_2[x]$	$K(\forall x) (S_1[x] \vee S_2[x])$	

The first kind of question in this list is a propositional or *whether*-question. As a special case, we obtain a yes-or-no question whose desideratum is of the form $K[S] \vee K) \sim S)$ and presupposition $K(S \vee \sim S)$. But $(S \vee \sim S)$ is tautologically true, and yes-or-no questions hence have an empty presupposition. This gives the lie to, among other things, Collingwood's claim that every question has a presupposition.

But having to fault Collingwood is not the only disconcerting thing here. Consider any question whatsoever, with a presupposition as complex as one can imagine. Suppose one raises it and receives an answer, say S. Now one could have asked, instead of the original question, the yes-or-no question, "Is it the case that S or not?" Since S was available as an answer to the original question, it must also be available as an answer to this yes-or-no question.

For instance, in an experimental question to nature, a scientist might ask: How does the observed variable y depend on the controlled variable x? Such a question has a complex presupposition expressible only by a general proposition. An answer to this question will then be a function f such that $y = f(x)$ expresses the intended dependence. But we could have asked instead the presuppositionless question, "Does y depend on x according to the law $y = f(x)$?" If the former answer is correct, then nature must reply to the latter one, "Yes."

But this seems to mean that in an inquiry, any question whatever can be replaced by a yes-or-no question. And since yes-or-no questions do not have any non-vacuous presuppositions, it looks as if any inquiry can be conducted without resorting to any presuppositions at all. Both Collingwood's project and mine seem to be misconceived.

Or is there a fallacy in the line of thought just carried out? No, there is not, but we have to put its result in a wider perspective. What does it mean to say, as we did earlier, that we *could* have asked the presuppositionless yes-or-no question instead of the presupposition-laden original one? It means that there is nothing that prevents us from asking the yes-or-no question, that it is not forbidden by any law, be it logical, natural, human, or divine. But such a *de jure* possibility does not mean that the question was *de facto* epistemically possible in the sense that we could have known to ask this particular question without already knowing its answer. In my example, we would have not known to ask the yes-or-no question about the particular function f if we had not antecedently obtained it as an answer to the experimental question.

This puts the entire matter of presuppositions of questions in a new light. The source of this light can be taken to be the crucial distinction that can be made in practically any rational goal-directed process, including interrogative inquiry. It is instructive to conceptualize such processes as games. Then, as in a typical game, we must distinguish from each other, on the one hand, the rules that define admissible moves, winning and losing, and so on, and by so doing define the game, and, on the other hand, the rules (or principles or whatever one calls them) that tell one how to play the game well. The former will be called *definitory* rules of the game and the latter, *strategic* rules. Both kinds of rules can in principle be formulated explicitly. In this sense, strategic rules are not merely heuristic, even though often optimal strategic rules may not be computable or may not be applicable directly for some other reason, and hence in practice have to be used via approximations and rules of thumb. For instance, the optimal strategies in the "game" of deductive theorem-proving are not computable, although they are codified by perfectly well-defined mathematical functions, and hence are not always directly applicable. For a different example, since there is a finite upper bound to the length of a chess game, the optimal chess strategies are recursive, even though no one knows precisely what they are and what the outcome would be of a play in which the antagonists use them.

By means of the game-theoretical framework, we can express the insight we have just reached. Limiting one's questions to yes-or-no questions that do not require presuppositions does not restrict the range of results one can establish (prove by an interrogative argument), but it does restrict one's strategies, in the sense that if one tries to dispense with these presuppositions, one is restricted to clumsy and, in more complicated cases, unmanageable strategies. In the worst case, one cannot even formulate such strategies—for instance, when one does not know all the individuals in one's universe of discourse.

Thus, the advantage of relying on strong presuppositions in inquiry is a strategic one. This is best seen in what an inquirer's strategies might be in different types of inquiry. If I am not allowed to use non-trivial presuppositions in asking the question

> Who murdered Roger Ackroyd?   (12)

I am reduced to asking of one person after another,

> Did a_1 murder Roger Ackroyd?
> Did a_2 murder Roger Ackroyd?
> ......   (13)

And if one does not think that this is tedious enough, think of what the corresponding procedure would be in the case of an experimental question concerning the dependence of a real-valued variable y on another variable x. Without non-trivial presuppositions we would be reduced to asking the question whose desideratum is

$$K(\forall x)(f(x) = g(x)) \tag{14}$$

for each function f one by one, where y $= g(x)$ specifies the actual (observable) dependence of y on x. Yet this enormous task can be replaced by asking of a simple experimental question if we have at our disposal the appropriate presupposition.

This strategic power of experimental questions can be considered as the epistemological explanation of the success of early modern science. The methodological "secret" of scientists such as Galileo and Newton is not their empiricism, but their use of experiments, especially controlled experiments. Such experiments can be thought of, it was seen earlier, as *wh*-questions with a functional (general) answer.

In sum, insofar as presuppositions of questions (or, rather the unavailability of presuppositions of questions) restricts our strategies of inquiry, not what it is possible in principle to establish interrogatively.

8. Socratic Questions

As far as the role of yes-no questions is concerned, the history of philosophy offers us an instructive subject for a case study. The name of this subject is Socrates. In construing all rational knowledge-seeking as questioning, we are merely following the precedent of the Platonic Socrates. Socrates claims that he does not know anything. (Indeed, this pretended ignorance is the original meaning of Socratic irony, or *eironeia*.) All the conclusions he puts forward and makes his interlocutor aware of—often painfully aware of—he deduces from the interlocutor's answers. Indeed, what we find in a Socratic dialogue are many of the ingredients of the interrogative model outlined here. There is a principal question, usually a definitory one such as "What is knowledge? "What is piety?" and so on. There are operative questions, put by Socrates to his interlocutor. Logical inferences are drawn at the end of a dialogue, sometimes introduced by statements by Socrates such as, "Let us now add our admissions together." Furthermore, logical conclusions are sometimes also drawn in the form of an answer to a question. Several examples of such inferences-as-answers-to-questions are found in the slaveboy episode of the *Meno*.

One of the most conspicuous features of Socratic questioning is that he uses for the most part only yes-or-no questions. This feature is shared by Aristotle's dialectical method as it is expounded in the *Topics*. It has prompted a lot of commentary. For instance, Gilbert Ryle writes (Ryle 1971, vol.1, p. 90) apropos Platonic questioning games:

The questioner can only ask questions; and the answerer can, with certain qualifications, answer only "yes" or "no." "So the questioner's questions have to be properly constructed for "yes" or "no" answers. This automatically rules out a lot of types of questions, such as factual questions, arithmetical questions, and technical questions. Roughly it leaves us only with conceptual questions, whatever they may be.   (15)

But what has been found out in this chapter shows that Ryle is wrong, and indeed diametrically wrong. An answer to any question can also be obtained as an answer to a yes-or-no question. Hence Socrates's questions are not restricted to conceptual questions. On the contrary, suitable *wh*-questions are obviously much more closely related to conceptual matters, such as the definitions of different concepts. Indeed, the principal questions of Socratic inquiry are *prima facie* requests of definition and as such *wh*-questions rather than yes-or-no questions.

One reason why Socrates is asking yes-or-no questions is that they do not need presuppositions. They are the only questions that an *eiron* who professes ignorance can consistently ask. But they do not restrict their answers to some particular subject matter. They can therefore be raised at any time, without needing any preparatory argument to establish their presuppositions. Yet there is little that distinguishes formally or materially answers to yes-or-no questions from answers to other kinds of questions.

In any case, it is not true that Socrates asks only yes-or-no questions. We have to be careful here, however, in view of the distinction between principal and operational questions, for it is conspicuous that Socrates's principal questions are typically *wh*-questions in that they are definitional "what" questions. Hence what I am saying is merely that the operative questions Socrates asks are mostly (but not all) yes-or-no questions.

It is in fact not true that the Platonic Socrates asks only yes-or-no questions, even if we restrict our attention to operative questions. For instance, at *Gorgias* 474B and at *Charmides* 159C, Socrates asks a propositional question that is not a yes-or-no question. He also asks repeatedly *wh*-questions. Cases in point are found at *Apology* 20B, *Euthyphro* 5D, *Hippias Major* 304E, *Laches* 192B, and *Phaedo* 105C-D. I would go as far as to assert that much of the knowledge and wisdom that Socrates typically is looking for is obtainable more naturally through a *wh*-question—if its presupposition were available—than through a yes-or-no question. But precisely for the purpose of avoiding those presuppositions, Socrates replaces other kinds of questions by yes-or-no ones, in the way we discussed earlier. For this reason, *wh*- questions are the exceptions that prove the rule in Socratic questioning. In some of the Socratic questions, one can, as it were, capture this transition *in actu*: "For what is being miserable but desiring evil things and possessing them?" (*Meno* 78A.) Here, Socrates first raises a *wh*-question—namely, "What is it to be miserable?" However, he immediately transforms it into a yes-or-no question concerning the answer he expects to receive—namely, "Is being miserable to desire evil things and to possess them?"

Similar steps from a *wh*-question to a yes-or-no question concerning the intended answer to it are taken by Socrates elsewhere. For instance, in *Phaedo* 76C, Socrates asks, "When did our souls acquire the knowledge of them [recollected things]? Surely not after we were born as human beings." He receives the answer, "Certainly not." But "not" is not an answer to a *wh*-question but to a yes-or-no question.

Other problems concerning Socrates and his method are likewise illuminated by what has been found. To say that Socrates does not need any presuppositions in his inquiry amounts to saying that he does not need any factual knowledge in his enterprise. He does not need to know anything. Here we have an explanation of Socrates's ironic professions of ignorance. Such professions serve to highlight one of the merits of Socrates's method—namely, its freedom from presuppositions.

Otherwise Socrates's pretended ignorance is hard to understand, as witnessed by scholars" contrived comments on it. For instance, Richard Robinson accuses Socrates of moving illicitly back and forth between information-seeking questioning and examiner's questioning. Vlastos tries to defend Socrates by attributing to him a special strict sense of knowledge. There is no direct basis for such views in the text, and in any case, all such accounts are dispensable in favor of the one according to which Socrates is highlighting one of the most important features of his operative questions—namely, their independence of background knowledge. Socrates' irony llustrates an important feature of epistemic logic.

Of course, Socrates had to possess knowledge of a different kind—namely, strategic knowledge. He did not use in his interrogative argument any answers that his interlocutor does not give. He does not have to claim that he knows anything. But he has to know which questions to ask. This is precisely the gist of a good interrogative strategy. But does it not amount to knowing what the answer will be? In the passages just quoted, Socrates first raises a *wh*-question and then moves on to ask the yes-or-no question concerning the very answer he expects. How can he do this without knowing the answer? Isn't Socrates therefore disingenuous when he pleads ignorance? The answer is that all good questioning strategies involve some amount of anticipation of what the interlocutor's answer will be. For instance, in a court of law, a cross-examiner must anticipate what the witness will say or else he or she is likely to be in dire trouble. Yes, Socrates must have knowledge in order to practice *elenchus* successfully, but *his knowledge is strategic, not factual knowledge*—which is precisely my point. In an epistemological perspective, Socrates' irony is but a way of highlighting the distinction between definitory and strategic rules or perhaps between factual and strategic knowledge.

9. Strategic Knowledge as Logical Knowledge

Now, what is this strategic knowledge like? Strategic knowledge will in interrogative inquiry ultimately come down to a method answering questions of
the following form: Given the list of the propositions one has reached in a line
of inquiry, which question should one ask next? In view of the need of presuppositions, this amounts to asking: Which proposition should one use as the
presupposition of the next question? This strategic problem has a counterpart
in deductive logic. This counterpart problem is: Which proposition should one
use as the premise of the next logical inference? In neither case does there exist
a mechanical (recursive) method of choosing the right proposition—that is, the
optimal strategy is not mechanical in either case. But in one type of inquiry
there obtains a remarkable connection between the two strategic choices. This
case is a context of pure discovery. In technical terms, this means a type of
inquiry in which all answers are known to be true, or at least can be treated as
being true. If so, all we need to do is to find out what the truth is; we do not have
to worry about justifying what we find. And this is indeed how Socrates treats
his interlocutor's answers, if only for the sake of argument. This is admittedly
a special kind of case, but an especially interesting one, one reason for this
interest being that according to a widespread view, contexts of inquiry cannot
be dealt with by rational logical or epistemological means.

In this case of pure discovery, there is a remarkable relation between the
two strategic choices. *The optimal choice is the same in both kinds of inquiries.*
In other words, even though interrogative (question–answer) steps and logical
inference steps in inquiry must be sharply separated from each other, they
are governed by the same strategic principles, insofar as the inquiry has the
character of pure truth-seeking, freed from all worries about the veracity of the
answers the inquirer is receiving. This insight was adumbrated for the first time
in Hintikka (1989) and spelled out more fully in Hintikka (1999 and 2003).

We also receive here an incisive answer to the question of the nature of
Socratic strategic knowledge: It is, in effect, logical knowledge in the sense of
knowledge of strategies of logical (deductive) reasoning. More generally, optimal strategies of interrogative reasoning approximate the optimal strategies
of deductive reasoning insofar as we can trust the answers we are receiving.

This throws an interesting light not only on the character of Socrates's
wisdom but on the nature of strategic knowledge in general. In particular, it
shows that our strategic knowledge does not have intransgressible limits. In
principle, it can be enhanced by learning more about logic, in the sense of
knowledge of strategies of logical reasoning.

10. Yes-No Questions and the Sub-Formula Requirement

What has been said does not close all the issues. Among the ones that have
to be reopened, there are the prospects of tracing presuppositions back to

the initial premises, the partial parallelism between interrogative inquiry and deduction, and the presuppositionlessness of yes-or-no questions. Let me start from the last issue. It is obvious that a tautological presupposition $(S \vee \sim S)$ cannot fail to be true. But can it fail to be known? It can be argued—I would say, can be shown—that interrogative inquiry should be construed as an epistemic enterprise. What this implies for an explicit treatment of interrogative inquiry is not hard to work out. For instance, each initial premise should be prefixed by an implicit or explicit epistemic operator K, and likewise for the ultimate conclusion of the inquiry. This need of epistemification is instantiated by the necessity of using the desiderata of questions as ultimate conclusions of inquiry mentioned in Section 5. Indeed, this epistemification is in keeping with the treatment of questions, their presuppositions and their answers by means of epistemic logic outlined in Sections 4–6.

But, if so, presuppositions of operative questions will require that a certain statement be known, not merely that it is true or assumed to be true. And, if so, the presuppositions of yes-or-no questions will be of the form $K(S \vee \sim S)$, not of the form $(S \vee \sim S)$. Now, there is a viable notion of knowledge according to which one has to be aware of what one knows. If so, even the presuppositions of yes-or-no questions must be assumed as initial premises or derived from them like all other presuppositions. This would appear to vindicate Collingwood, for it would mean that all presuppositions can often be traced back to the initial premises, albeit usually with the help of answers to earlier questions.

However, a closer look at the structure of interrogative inquiry belies this pretty Collingwoodean picture. The talk of tracing propositions figuring in interrogative inquiry back to the initial premises makes obvious sense only if (definitory) rules of the "game" are such as to satisfy the sub-formula property. What this property means here is that (the non-epistemic part of) each sentence occurring in one's tableau of inquiry is a sub-formula of an earlier one, or else a substitution-instance of such a sub-formula. The usual tableau rules of ordinary first-order deductive logic satisfy the sub-formula principle. And since they constitute a complete system of deduction in ordinary first-order logic, no rules violating the sub-formula principle are needed there. Many formulations of first-order logic admittedly employ further rules of inference, rules that do not satisfy the sub-formula principle. But the result known as Gentzen's first *Hauptsatz* and others like it show the dispensability of those additional rules, exemplified by unrestricted *modus ponens*, the so-called cut rule of proof theorists, and so on.

It is here that a subtle difference between deductive inquiry and interrogative inquiry emerges. The basic form of the assumptions that violate the sub-formula property is the introduction of tautological disjunctions $(S \vee \sim S)$ or in its epistemic variant, $K(S \vee \sim S)$ into the left side. But even though such additional rules do not add to the power of deductive inquiry (in the sense of adding to the range of propositions that are provable by deductive means), they do increase the scope of interrogative inquiry. There are ultimate conclusions that can be proved only by means of such additional quasi-tautological assumptions. The reason is obvious on the basis of what has been said. The newly introduced propositions K(S ∨ ∼S) are precisely the presuppositions of yes-or-no questions. If they are not subject to any restrictions, the inquirer may ask any yes-or-no question. And any proposition available as an answer to any question can be obtained as an answer to such yes-or-no question. (See Section 7.)

These matters, and indeed the entire theory of questions and answers, could be streamlined and perhaps also clarified by using as the underlying logic independence-friendly first-order logic rather than the received first-order logic. (For independence-friendly logic, see, for example, Hintikka 1996.) in this logic, we have to distinguish from each other two different negations. The natural semantical rules define a strong (dual) negation ∼ which does not obey the law of excluded middle. Of course we need also the contradictory negation ¬.

Then a yes-or-no question "Is it the case that S" is answerable only if S is true or false. This is expressed by (S ∨ ∼S). Hence the presupposition of the yes-or-no question (in the sense of this chapter) is K(S ∨ ∼S). Unlike K(S ∨ ¬S), this is not logically true. Hence, in independence-friendly logic, yes-or-no questions, too, have their non-trivial presuppositions, just like other kinds of questions. These presuppositions must be established by previous inquiry before the question may be asked. Thus yes-or-no questions are not always permitted any longer. However, this does not break the strategic analogy with deduction, in that disjunctions (S ∨ ∼S) are not logically true. Rules like the modus ponens and the cut rule hold for ¬ but not for ∼.

This change of logic does not change the theoretical situation, however. What it does is to enrich the expressive potentialities of our logical language. For instance, the range of answerable questions (see Section 3) in an interrogative game now need no longer be specified from the outside as a part of the definition of the game. Available answers can be characterized as those presuppositions for which the law of excluded middle holds.

In any case, the advantages of rules such as the tautology-introduction rule and the cut rule in deductive logic are essentially strategic. In ordinary first-order logic, they typically make it possible to shorten and to simplify proofs, even though in such a logic, they do not allow proving any logical truths that are not provable without them. They are dispensable, but only at the cost of longer proofs.

At the same time, such additional rules as do not obey the sub-formula principle complicate the strategic situation enormously. In deductive tableaux, each formula introduced by the original rules was a sub-formula of one of the earlier ones, and its introduction could therefore be thought of as a step in analyzing the situation described in the initial premises or in the ultimate conclusion. In contrast, the earlier history of a tableau construction does not

restrict the choice of the proposition S in the tautology (S ∨ ~S) being introduced. This opens the floodgates for a deluge of new strategies. Moreover,
since these new strategies are less strictly determined by the given initial data
of the problem, tautology introduction and unrestricted yes-or-no questions
allow much more scope for creative imagination and invention than the steps
satisfying the sub-formula property.

11. Presuppositions of Presuppositions

One thing we can now also see is that the presuppositions of yes-or-no questions K(S ∨ ~S) cannot normally be traced back to the initial premises that
express the epistemic starting points of inquiry. For facts as to what questions are answerable are normally determined by the context of the inquiry
independently of our thinking. And since they are sometimes indispensable
in inquiry, not all presuppositions have a precedent in the initial premises of
inquiry. There is no set of absolute presuppositions that would restrict inquiry.
Collingwood's notion of *absolute* presupposition is not viable.

To return to the main theme of this chapter, we have reached an unequivocal
answer to the question as to whether rational epistemological inquiry is subject
to intransgressable restrictions such as are supposed to be dictated by Collingwood's ultimate presuppositions or by Kuhn's paradigms. The approach used
here has so far followed Collingwood in construing limitations of inquiry as
presuppositions of questions. What has been found by means of an examination of the presuppositions of questions is that these presuppositions do
play an important role in inquiry, but that they restrict strategies and do not
impose limits to what can be established by means of the inquiry. Moreover,
the effect of the restrictions can be compensated for, not only by liberalizing
the restrictions in the sense of assuming stronger initial premises but also by
increasing the range of answerable questions. This can be established perfectly
naturalistically—for instance, through improved experimental and observational techniques. Hence what has been found here tells against all theories of
unavoidable restrictions to inquiry, relativistic or not.

We have also seen in this section that there is no way of tracing all the
presuppositions relied on in an inquiry to its initial premises. The notion of
ultimate presuppositions is unworkable.

12. Presuppositions of Answers

But must all presuppositions of inquiry in the sense intended by the likes of
Collingwood be construed as presuppositions of questions in the logical sense
used earlier? This is a pertinent question. On the one hand, Collingwood
not only speaks in so many words of the presuppositions of questions but
often has obviously in mind the same sorts of presuppositions as have been

considered here. He even uses some of the traditional examples of violations of such presuppositions—for example, examples of the type, "When did you stop beating your wife?"

On the other hand, however, it seems to me that Collingwood is assimilating to each other presuppositions of questions in the sense used here and what might be called "presuppositions of answers." In order to avoid confusion, I have nevertheless called them "uniqueness conditions." They have been discussed elsewhere (see especially Hintikka 2007) and hence I can be relatively brief here. An example can convey the main point.

As perceptive philosophers from Francis Bacon to Immanuel Kant to R. G. Collingwood have pointed out, one can—and ought to—construe controlled experiments in science as questions put to nature. Such a question has the form, "How does the variable y for a certain quantity depend on another one, say x, for a different variable?" (It is probably the very fact that the experimenter can in fact control one of the variables that prompted Bacon's metaphor of an investigator forcing nature to reveal her secrets.) The experiment succeeds in providing an answer to this question if the function expressing the dependence is known. Technically this means that the desideratum of the question becomes true. This desideratum can be expressed logically in any of the following forms:

$$(\exists f)K(\forall x)\, S[x, f(x)] \tag{16}$$

$$K(\exists f/K)(\forall x)\, S[x, f(x)] \tag{17}$$

$$K(\forall x)\, (\exists y/K)\, S[x, y] \tag{18}$$

Here, K is the knowledge operator ("It is known that") and / the independence operator. What an experiment ideally achieves can be thought of as a function-in-extension—that is to say, an infinite list of correlated arguments values and function values. If this function-in-extension is g, then the purely observational components of an experimental answer is

$$K(\forall x)\, S[x, g(x)] \tag{19}$$

One can think of (19) as being illustrated by an infinitely sharp curve on a graph paper.

But (19) does not logically imply (16)–(18). This fact has a concrete interpretation. Even if we abstract from all limitations of observational accuracy and of the accuracy with which on can manipulate the controlled variable, still "Nature's response" (17) will not satisfy the experimentalist unless he or she knows or finds out what the function g is, mathematically speaking. In terms of the hypothetical illustration, even if there is an arbitrarily accurate curve on the experimentalist's graph paper, he or she may still fail to know what the function is that the curve represents. Only if the scientist knows or is shown what that function is has he or she reached a conclusive answer to the experimental question.

This additional information is expressed by what I have called the "conclusiveness condition." In an example, this condition can be expressed in any of the following four forms:

$$(\exists f)K(\forall x)(g(x) = f(x)) \tag{20}$$

$$K(\exists f/K) \, (\forall x) \, (g(x) = f(x)) \tag{21}$$

$$K(\exists f/K) \, (g = f) \tag{22}$$

$$K(\forall x) \, (\exists y/K) \, (g(x) = y) \tag{23}$$

Even though (19) alone does not entail (16)–(18), it does so in conjunction with (20)–(23). This shows that (20)–(23) constitute a kind of presupposition of answers to an experimental question. Such "presuppositions" (conclusiveness conditions) limit the possibility of answering questions somewhat in the same way as the presuppositions of questions we encountered earlier. Hence they are relevant to the over-arching theme of this chapter, which concerns the limitations of inquiry. In what way does the need of conclusiveness conditions like (20)–(23) limit our quest of information?

What kind of knowledge is it that the presuppositions of answers such as (20)–(23) express? This knowledge concerns the identity of certain mathematical objects—namely, functions. It is hence conceptual and *a priori* in character. Indeed, we have found one of the main gates through which mathematical knowledge enters into the very structure of empirical science. Such knowledge is needed to answer scientific questions, typified by experimental questions. This knowledge does not come to a scientist automatically. It has to be gained. But such knowledge is not uncovered in a laboratory or found codified in a textbook of experimental physics. It is obtained in departments of mathematics or from textbooks and treatises of mathematics and mathematical physics. Hence we have found here a very real constraint on an empirical inquirer's ability to answer experimental questions, and indeed a constraint on inquiry in general. Moreover, what is especially interesting here is that this constraint is conceptual rather than factual in nature. In the case of an experimental scientist, the restriction is imposed on him or her by the limit of their mathematical knowledge. Any particular scientist labors under restrictions on his or her knowledge of the relevant mathematical knowledge. But these personal restrictions are not inevitable or incorrigible. They can be overcome by increasing one's knowledge of the relevant functions or by consulting suitable sources of mathematical information. Hence, once again we are not dealing with absolute limits of inquiry, only epistemic ones.

These limits are nevertheless a very real factor in the history of science and mathematics. Repeatedly, the need of knowing what a function is that has been encountered by physicists and other empirical scientists has not only prompted mathematicians to come to know it better, it has prompted them to ask which function it is in the first place.

Likewise, the role of conclusiveness conditions ("presuppositions of answers") is highly important in experimental science. Everybody seems to agree that one of the most important kinds of progress in science is the introduction of new concepts. It is also thought fairly generally that such an introduction typically happens when a new theory is introduced. What is seen here is that mathematical concepts that facilitate the investigation of new and often more complicated structures often take place for the purpose of answering new experimental questions.

All these remarks can be extended from experimental questions to all complex scientific *wh*-questions.

An interesting feature of our results resolved so far is that the mathematical or other conceptual knowledge that is required to reach conclusive answers to empirical questions is not *knowledge that*—that is, knowledge of facts, propositions, or truths—but identificatory *knowledge of* certain kinds of mathematical *objects*—in the first place, functions. This observation can be taken as further evidence of the independence of the identificatory system of the referential system in our actual semantics.

Knowledge of the identity of objects (of different logical types) can be thought of as definitory knowledge, at least in the sense that it answers questions to the form "What is ....?" It is scarcely accidental that such questions play an important role in the questioning method of the Platonic Socrates. The importance of these questions is not due merely to the fact that their answers are definitions, but first and foremost to their role in all questioning as unavoidable "presuppositions" (conclusiveness conditions) of answers to all questions. More generally speaking, this role of the knowledge of identities helps us to understand the important role of definitions in the thought of Plato and Aristotle. The more important questions and questioning are for a thinker, the more important is identificatory knowledge likely to be for him or her.

The need to know the mathematical identity of the function-in-extension g, as in (19), has a counterpart in the case of simple *wh*-questions such as (8). There the conclusiveness condition that a response—say "b"—has to satisfy can be expressed in any of the following two forms:

$$K(\exists x/K) (b = x) \tag{24}$$
$$(\exists x) K(b = x) \tag{25}$$

where the variable ranges over persons. If so, (24)–(25) obviously amount to saying that

$$\text{I know who b is.} \tag{26}$$

The need of these requirements is obvious. If I do not know who b is, the response "b" to the question (8) will not fully satisfy me.

When "b" is a proper name, (24)–(25) will express semantical knowledge. They do not give anyone any factual information about the bearer of the name "b." It only tells one who is referred to by it. This kind of knowledge is a counterpart to the mathematical knowledge expressed by (20)–(23). This analogy throws some light on the nature of both kinds of knowledge, and raises intriguing questions that I deal with in the next chapter.

It can be seen that this kind of identificatory knowledge is needed both when the identity of a particular object is at issue and when the object in question is a universal—for instance, a function. Indeed, one of the most interesting results we have reached is the close parallelism between simple *wh*-questions and complex experimental *wh*-questions. Such results throw interesting light on the old interpretational problem concerning the *what*-questions of the Platonic Socrates, recently rehearsed in Benson 1992(b), as to whether he was identifying particulars or universals.

Once again we have found genuine presuppositions of empirical inquiry. Once again, they are factors operative in actual scientific inquiry. The restrictions in question result from the limitations of our knowledge of mathematical functions. But such restrictions are not unavoidable. They can be escaped by means of whatever mathematical research it takes to come to know previously unexamined functions typically resulting from a controlled experiment.

If there are any absolute limitations to empirical inquiry that result from the presuppositions of answers, they can be traced back to the limitations of our mathematical knowledge, in particular our knowledge of functions. Are there such restrictions? An answer depends on what we take it to mean to know which mathematical function it is that expresses a given mode of dependence— in brief, what it means to know a certain mathematical function.

But even without having any detailed answer to this question (sic), it is clear that the scope of one's knowledge of the identity of various mathematical functions can be enlarged and that the knowledge required for the purpose—as well as the knowledge acquired in the process—is mathematical in character, not empirical. Hence the limitations to our knowledge acquisition imposed by the conclusiveness conditions of answers are not eternal and immutable, but can be removed step by step by acquiring more mathematical and other conceptual knowledge.

In sum, limitations to inquiry resulting from the initial premises can be overcome by making more questions answerable. Limitations resulting from presuppositions of questions present only strategic difficulties, not barriers to what can be accomplished by inquiry, and limitations resulting from the "presuppositions of answers" (i.e., conclusiveness conditions) can be overcome by gaining more mathematical and other conceptual knowledge. And one does not seem to face any intrinsic limitations in such a quest of mathematical knowledge, either. Even restrictions on available answers can in principle be removed by improved techniques of inquiry.

Acknowledging these limitations does not aid and abet in the least skeptical or relativistic views, including the views of the "new philosophers of science" à la Kuhn. I am even prepared to say more here, and to ask: "In view of the results reported here, is it any longer intellectually respectable to hold relativistic views or otherwise believe in unavoidable restriction on our knowledge seeking and knowledge acquisition"? The answer is, of course: "Only if you can provide a better analysis of the presuppositions of questions and answers than the one given here."

References

Plato is cited in the Loeb Library translations (Harvard University Press).

Benson, Hugh H., editor, 1992(a), *Essays on the Philosophy of Socrates*, Oxford University Press, New York.

Benson, Hugh H., 1992(b), "Misunderstanding the 'What-is-F-ness" question," in *Benson*, 1992(a), pp. 123–136.

Beth, E. W., 1955, "Semantic Entailment and Formal Derivability," *Mededlingen van de Koninklijke Nederlandse Akademie van Wetenschappen*, Afd.Leterkund. N. R. vol. 18, no. 13, Amsterdam, pp. 309–342.

Chomsky, Noam, 1959, "Review of Skinner: Verbal Behavior," *Language*, vol. 35, pp. 26–58.

Collingwood, R. G., 1940, *An Essay on Metaphysics*, Clarendon Press, Oxford.

Collingwood, R. G., 1993, *The Idea of History*, revised edition, Clarendon Press, Oxford.

Hintikka, Jaakko, 2003, "A. Second-Generation Epistemic Logic and its Theoretical Significance," in Vincent Hendricks et al., editors, *Knowledge Contributors*, Kluwer Academic, Dordrecht, pp. 33–55.

Hintikka, Jaakko, 1999, *Inquiry as Inquiry*, Kluwer Academic, Dordrecht.

Hintikka, Jaakko, 1998, "What Is Abduction? The Fundamental Problem of Contemporary Epistemology," *Proceedings of the Charles S. Peirce Society*, vol. 34, pp. 503–533. A revised version entitled "Abduction—Inference, Conjecture, or an Answer to a Question" appears as Chapter 3 in this volume.

Hintikka, Jaakko, 1996, *The Principles of Mathematics Revisited*, Cambridge University Press, New York.

Hintikka, Jaakko, 1989, "The Role of Logic in Argumentation," *The Monist*, vol. 72, pp. 3–24.

Hintikka, Jaakko, Ilpo Halonen, and Arto Mutanen, 1998, "Interrogative Logic as a General Theory of Inquiry," in *Hintikka*, 1999, pp. 47–90.

Kuhn, Thomas, 1970, *The Structure of Scientific Revolutions*, second edition, University of Chicago Press, Chicago.

Robinson, Richard, 1971, "Begging the Question 1971," *Analysis*, vol. 31, no. 4, pp. 113–117.

Robinson, Richard, 1953, *Plato's Earlier Dialectic*, Clarendon Press, Oxford.

Ryle, Gilbert, 1971, *Collected Papers I-II*, Hutchinson, London.

Sentas, Gerasimos Xenophon, 1979, *Socrates*, Routledge and Kegan Paul, London.

Smullyan, Raymond, 1997, *The Riddle of Scheherazade*, Harcourt Brace, New York.

Vlastos, Gregory, 1971, "The Paradox of Socrates", in Vlastos, editor, *The Philosophy of Socrates: A Collection of Critical Essays*, University of Nortre Dame Press, Notre Dame, Indiana, pp. 1–21.

5

The Place of the *a priori* in Epistemology

1. The Unreasonable Effectiveness of the *a priori* in Epistemology

Aristotle said that philosophy begins with the experience of wonder. But different phenomena are experienced as wondrous by different thinkers and to a different degree. The wonder that is the theme of this chapter seems to have struck some non-philosophers more keenly than most professional philosophers. Indeed, the most vivid formulation of the problem is probably in the title of Eugene Wigner's 1960 paper, "The Unreasonable Effectiveness of Mathematics in the Natural Sciences." Historically speaking, Wigner's amazement is nevertheless little more than another form of the same reaction to the success of mathematics in science as early modern scientists' sense that the "book of the universe is written in mathematical symbols." For a philosopher, this question is in any case a special case of the general problem of the role of our *a priori* knowledge, mostly codified in the truths of logic and mathematics, in the structure of our empirical knowledge.

This overall philosophical problem assumes different forms in different contexts. Wigner's puzzle has been taken up in the same form by relatively few philosophers, most extensively by Mark Steiner in his 1998 book, *The Applicability of Mathematics as a Philosophical Problem*. This problem can be given technical turns—for instance, by asking whether scientific laws can be expected to be computable (recursive), and even more specifically by asking which known laws are in fact computable. (See, e.g., Pour-El and Richards 1989.)

More commonly, philosophers have adopted a narrower and more skeptical stance. They have raised the question as to whether *a priori* theories, in the first place mathematical theories, are really indispensable in science. The extensive discussion of this question has been prompted largely by what is usually referred to as Quine's argument for the indispensability of mathematics in science. (See e.g., Quine 1981(b); Colyvan 2001.) In the light of hindsight—or perhaps in the light of a more general perspective—this has turned out to be

107

an inauspicious beginning in more than one respect. Quine's indispensability claim has deep roots in the idiosyncrasies of his overall philosophy. Quine had to resort to the kind of argument he used because of the poverty of his epistemological theory. In a nutshell, this theory can be explained in terms of Quine's famous "world wide web" metaphor. The structure of our total system of knowledge is like a huge net that is held in place at its boundaries by observations (sense-registrations). Its different nodes are connected with each other by relations of logical implication. But what is the place of mathematics in Quine's picture? There does not seem to be much left for mathematics to do in such a scheme. On the face of things, the Quinean picture is not so far from Ernst Mach's idea of science as an economic description of our experiences. And Mach, too, leaves next to nothing for serious logic and mathematics to do. For him, all deductive reasoning, explicitly including mathematical reasoning, is tautological. Similarly, Quine's analogy does not seem to leave any place for mathematical knowledge.

What lies behind this predicament is Quine's rejection of the analytic–synthetic distinction. According to him, the network itself is our creation. We can in principle change the inferential links between its nodes. Mathematics is simply the best possible way we have of organizing those links—and thereby organizing the entire texture of our empirical knowledge—in the best possible way. The indispensability of some mathematics or other is thus simply part and parcel of this overall epistemology and philosophy of science. We need logic and mathematics in order to connect the nodes of the net with each other. In other, more commonplace words we need mathematics in science for the purpose of deductive systematization. This is not a conclusion of Quine's theory; it is its presupposition. It is in this sense that philosophers have been able to speak of a "failure to explicate what is meant by 'indispensable' in Quine's argument" (Colyvan 2001, p. 76.) It can only be evaluated as a part of Quine's overall epistemology.

It follows that Quine cannot offer any explanation as to why this or that particular mathematical theory is useful or perhaps indispensable in science. Quine offer no solutions to Wigner's problem.

2. The Nature of Deductive Systematization

Even though Wigner's and Quine's puzzles offer a handy introduction to the problem of this chapter, the way of solving the problem is not to pursue their lines of thought further. The reason is that the solution of the problem of the role of the *a priori* in epistemology has to be looked for elsewhere. In order to clarify the problem situation, a brief discussion of Quine's approach is nevertheless in order. This discussion will focus mostly on ideas that have not figured prominently in the earlier literature on the indispensability problem.

First, Quine's web analogy does not bear critical scrutiny. It is part and parcel of the analogy that the consequence relations holding the net together are syntactical and recursive or at least recursively enumerable (axiomatizable). Otherwise, human reasoners do not have any general method of deciding which node is connected with which other one. The resulting overall view is so unrealistic that it is to my mind surprising that it is still being taken seriously. For one thing, it is totally alien to all serious logical semantics. After the work of Gödel and Tarski, it simply is impossible to maintain that the meaning of propositions is constituted via their inferential relations to other propositions. Meaning is a matter of semantics, and the overwhelming impact of the work that began with Tarski and Gödel is to make it clear that the semantical relationships cannot be reduced to syntactical ones. Furthermore, any associative relationship must be grounded in syntactical relations as providing the clues that prompt those inferences or associations, and *a fortiori* fails to serve as a ground of meaning. Instead, its "lateral" relations to other propositions, the semantical properties of a proposition, are determined by its truth conditions or its other "vertical" relations to reality. Small wonder, therefore, that Quine's ideas in language theory have for a long time been totally alienated from all real work in logical or linguistic semantics.

We can thus see that Quine's entire "world wide web" picture is predicated on his syntactical and inferential viewpoint. This viewpoint is inadequate, however, and once its inadequacy is realized, the motivation for Quinean holism evaporates. The truth-conditions of a given sentence do not refer to its deductive relations to other sentences. One can do model theory without ever mentioning rules of inference, but in the last analysis, one cannot understand, let alone justify, one's inference rules except model-theoretically. The same holds, of course, for scientific theories employing more powerful mathematics than elementary arithmetic. In brief, the Quinean argument for the indispensability of mathematics in science is predicated on an antiquated pre-Gödelian dogma. It may be that the function of logical words in guiding logical inferences is of great practical interest to philosophers and scientists who are applying logic. But philosophically, this function is secondary in relation to the role of logical words in determining the meaning, including the truth-conditions, of the sentences in which they occur. To think that this determination takes place via inferential relationships is to fail to appreciate the insights reached in logical theory in the last eighty or so years.

This point becomes evident when we scratch the surface of any particular problem about the relationship of inference rules and meaning. For instance, intuitionists do not mean something non-classical by their statements because they are using different inference rules. They have to use different inference rules because their statements are not only calculated to assert the truth of a certain mathematical statement S. They assert that the truth-making functions (witness functions, Skolem functions) of S are known. (See Hintikka 1996(a) and 2002(b).)

In any case, the last nail in the coffin of the idea that inferential relationships can serve to systematize a theory is contributed by independence-friendly (IF) first-order logic. This logic has a much better claim to be our true unrestricted basic logic than the so-called ordinary first-order logic (predicate calculus), which is only a fragment of IF logic and which should really be referred to as dependence-handicapped logic. IF logic is not axiomatizable, and therefore there cannot be any set of inferential relationships that fully characterize our basic logic. In brief, the web of logic itself cannot be held together by inferential relations. If so, it is *a fortiori* futile to expect that a set of inferential relationships could hold together a scientific theory and its different concomitants.

Another way of seeing that Quine's idea of a web of knowledge held together by relations of logical implication is not only misleading but *grund-falsch* is to note that these relations of logical implication are tautological. If F logically implies G, the information that G can yield is merely a part of the information content of F. How such empty relations can create the kind of connecting links required by Quine's metaphor is a mystery, and is bound to remain one.

This may sound too general and too abstract to be convincing, and perhaps it is. But it can be particularized in a way that has a direct impact. Quine's web analogy is but an expanded form of the old idea that theoretical concepts, even though their objects are not observable, can receive their meaning from the logical connections between the propositions that contain them and observation statements. Indeed, Quine compares in so many words the postulation of mathematical object to the postulation of theoretical entities in physics. (Quine 1981a, pp. 149–150.) But if so, then in view of the crucial role of the "vertical" connections between propositions and reality, it might be expected that we could separate what a proposition says about observables from the rest of it, and replace the proposition by the outcome of that reduction. The result would have the same observable consequences as the original proposition, leaving the theoretical concepts of the original proposition unemployed without any work to do. Indeed, this is what it was hoped that the so-called Ramsey reduction would accomplish. A Ramsey reduct is obtained from the sentence—say, $S = S[T_1, T_2, \ldots]$—where $T_1, T_2, \ldots$ are all the theoretical terms of S—by replacing $T_1, T_2, \ldots$ by replacing them by variables—say, $X_1, X_2, \ldots,$—and then binding those variables to sentence-initial existential quantifiers. We can call this reduct

$$(\exists X_1)(\exists X_2) \ldots S[X_1, X_2, \ldots] \tag{1}$$

In brief, (1) is the Ramsey reduct of $S[T_1, T_2, \ldots]$. The reducer's hope was that (1) would have the same observable consequences as $S[T_1, T_2, \ldots]$ and thereby show that theoretical concepts are unnecessary in science. In terms of Quine's metaphor, even the propositions in the middle of the web, away from the observational rim, could be said to receive their empirical meaning directly from observable consequences—namely, from the consequences of (1), without having to consider the logical relations of $S[T_1, T_2, \ldots]$ to any other propositions. This would have pulled the rug out from under Quine's idea that the empirical meaning of a proposition is constituted by means of its relations to other propositions. And this would have in turn vitiated Quine's argument for the indispensability of mathematics in science.

At first, this attempted refutation of Quine could not be carried out, however. For if $S[T_1, T_2, \ldots]$ is a proposition of a first-order language using the usual logic, (1) does not always have an equivalent in the same language. In other words, the Ramsey reductions cannot be carried out in the same language. Hence, we apparently cannot get rid of the existential quantifiers $(\exists X_1)$, $(\exists X_2) \ldots$ But these range over the kinds of theoretical entities we were trying to get rid of.

However, this counterattack in defense of Quine fails. (See Hintikka 1998.) For it turns out that the failure (1) to have an equivalent on the first-order level is merely a result of the unnecessary restrictions that Frege and Russell imposed on first-order logic and that have only recently been lifted. If we make it possible to have arbitrary patterns of dependence and independence between quantifiers represented on the first-order level, we obtain a stronger logic, which is known as the IF first-order logic and which is still a *first-order* logic. By its means, (1) can be expressed on the first-order level, hence eliminating all quantification over theoretical entities in the sense of references of theoretical terms. For reasons indicated earlier, this deprives Quine's line of thought its *raison d'être*. The indispensability of mathematics may be a fact, but it cannot be defended à la Quine. According to Quine's own lights, a theory is committed to the existence of the entities over which its quantified variables range. Accordingly, for Quine, (1) involves a commitment to the existence of theoretical entities, but its translation to the corresponding IF first-order language does not, for there we quantify only over individuals.

3. Are Mathematical Objects Dispensable?

The origins of the indispensability problem in Quine's philosophy show up here in another way, too. Since Quine has no sharp distinction between analytic and synthetic truths, he cannot distinguish mathematical and empirical knowledge from each other, either. Hence he cannot very well speak, much less argue for, the indispensability of mathematical knowledge in science, even though this is arguably the crucial question here. Quine can distinguish mathematical propositions from experimental and observational propositions only in terms of the objects they pertain to. In this way, the problem has come to be construed as the problem of the indispensability of mathematical objects in science. In particular, the critics of indispensability have typically formulated their arguments as showing how mathematical objects can be dispensed with in science.

These efforts are not much more convincing than a Quinean defense of indispensability. One problem here is the relevance of the ontological problem of the dispensability of mathematical objects to mathematical practice, and in particular to the usefulness (reasonable or not) of mathematical knowledge in science. This is obviously a highly complex matter. Does the use of mathematical reasoning in science commit a mathematician to the existence of mathematical objects? No simple answer is in the offing. According to a quip by Tom Lehrer, doing arithmetic in base eight is just like doing it in base ten—if you are missing two fingers. Perhaps we can take his quip to illustrate the fact that, if the missing two fingers were to make a difference to the preferential base, their existence or non-existence does not affect the actual arithmetic. Would the similar absence of two entities called numbers from the number sequence make a difference to the uses of arithmetic in science? Obviously we have a most complex problem here. It is made more difficult by the common failure to distinguish our knowledge of mathematical truths from our knowledge of the identity of mathematical objects. (For this distinction, see Hintikka 1996 (b).) I will return to these problems later in this chapter. (See Sections 11–12)

Thus I find some of the typical recent arguments for the dispensability of mathematics in science shallow. By and large, what they are calculated to establish is that we need not assume in scientific theories any individual objects called numbers. A characteristic example is offered by what might be called "reverse representation theorems." (See Hartry Field 1980, 1989 and Colyvan 2001, chapter 4.) A typical ordinary representation theorem might show that a certain purely relational structure—for instance, the system of Euclidean geometry axiomatized by Hilbert—is equivalent to a structure characterized by metric notions such as distance. The values of such metric functions are, of course, numbers. A reverse representation theorem might show that such numerical-valued functions as distance can be eliminated in favor of purely relational concepts.

Such results can be interesting and illuminating. However, to proffer them as arguments for the dispensability of mathematics in science presupposes a narrow conception what mathematics is. Admittedly, mathematics used to be considered as the "science of numbers," but that conception was superseded more than a hundred years ago by the rise of what has been called "conceptual mathematics." (See, e.g., Laugwitz 1996.) If there is a notion that epitomizes this more abstract, and at the same time more comprehensive, idea of mathematics, it is not the concept of number but the concept of *function*, naturally understood in the wide sense, that is not restricted to numerical functions. The dispensability of mathematics in science will then mean the possibility of managing without functional concepts. Such a possibility is totally unrealistic. If a historical perspective is needed to illustrate this irreducibility, an early one was provided by Ernst Cassirer in 1910. The history of the concept of function is in fact one of the most crucial aspects of the development of modern mathematics. (See Youschkevich 1977; Hintikka 2000.)

In logical theory, much of the metatheory of first-order logic can be developed in the format of a theory of the Skolem functions. This is natural, because the existence of Skolem functions can be considered as an implementation of our pre-theoretical ideas about the truth of quantificational sentences. (The Skolem functions of a sentence S produce as their values the "witness individuals" that must exist for S to be true.) The perspective provided by Skolem functions is also especially illuminating, when more patterns of dependence and independence between quantifiers are considered than are allowed in the needlessly restricted "ordinary" Frege-Russell treatment of the logic of quantifiers. Thus, functions turn out to be the most important part of the ontology of logic and mathematics. And, hence, the entire discussion of the indispensability or dispensability of mathematics in science should be addressed to the question of the role of functions in the language of logic and mathematics, rather than to the question of the existence of objects (individuals) called numbers. One of the first results that follows when this is done is that a reduction of some part of mathematics to logic does not *ipso facto* show the indispensability of such abstract entities as functions in that part of mathematics.

It is thus instructive to study the role of the idea of function in our usual logical notation involving quantifiers. This notation is also the basis of much of the usual language of mathematics, as was first spelled out in the process of the "arithmetization of mathematics" in the nineteenth century. In hindsight, this process might almost as well have been called the logization of mathematics, where the logic of that logization is essentially the logic of quantifiers. Hence the key question here is the role of quantifiers in determining the ontology needed in science.

Now, what both the defenders and the critics of the indispensability have failed to see is the main reason why complex sentences cannot be tested directly for truth. This reason is not always or even typically the presence of theoretical concepts in them or their being connected with testable sentences only inferentially, but their quantificational structure. One cannot verify or falsify a sentence of the form

$$(\forall x)(\exists y)S[x, y] \tag{2}$$

directly, in one fell swoop, not because it contains unobservable non-logical concepts or because it is connected with observables only inferentially, but because the semantical game it involves has at least one dependent move made by the verifier. From this it follows that the strategies the verifier uses in dealing with (2) can only be represented by functions. These functions cannot be grasped at first one glance. The "theoretical concepts" that a sentence such as (2) involves are its Skolem functions. These functions are imported by quantifiers, not by non-logical theoretical concepts occurring in a proposition or by its logical consequences.

Because of this crucial role of functions in logic and mathematics, the entire project of eliminating numbers or other particular mathematical objects from science is of a strictly limited interest. Such elimination uses our customary logical apparatus, including quantifiers. Since the use of quantifiers was seen to rely on Skolem functions, the apparent elimination merely replaces one type of mathematical objects by another class of abstract entities—namely, functions. One can dispense with Skolem functions only if one can dispense with quantifiers, which in effect means dispensing with logic.

Thus, any elimination of mathematical objects in favor of theories involving quantifiers (or equivalent) fails to get at the bottom of the problem of the role of mathematics—and of other *a priori* knowledge—in epistemology. Such an elimination leaves us with the most important logico-mathematical entities playing a role in which they appear absolutely uneliminable. What will be done next is to try to diagnose the role of mathematics in knowledge acquisition in general.

4. Mathematical Knowledge in Knowledge Acquisition

Among the most important weaknesses of the indispensability dispute is the way questions are posed in it. As was seen, the lion's share of attention in it is focused on ontology, first on the role (if any) of mathematical objects in science. Because of this direction of interest, the role of mathematical *knowledge* in science is easily obscured. And even when the discussion has conceived (or can be interpreted as having conceived) the role of mathematical knowledge in scientific knowledge, the questions raised have concerned the role of mathematical theories in scientific theorizing. In spite of the lip service paid to scientific and mathematical practice, very little serious thought has been devoted to the role of mathematics in the processes of knowledge acquisition in science or elsewhere. This role is what is studied next in this chapter. It will be shown that mathematical knowledge plays an essential role in the typical procedures that introduce new information into scientific reasoning—to wit, in experiments and observations. The results of this inquiry will also show what the nature of this indispensable mathematical knowledge is.

One reason why this study has not been attempted before is that there has not existed an explicit logical and epistemological theory of knowledge acquisition. It even used to be generally maintained that there cannot exist a rational theory of such high-grade acquisition of new knowledge that can be called discovery. The slogan was that only a theory of justification is possible in rational epistemology, but not a theory of discovery.

But how, however, a logic of discovery is known to be possible, the reason being that it is actual. This actual theory of discovery is an application of the theory of information acquisition by questioning, also known as the "inter-rogative model of inquiry." (See, e.g., the papers collected in Hintikka 1999.) This approach is a straightforward application of the logic of questions and answers, otherwise known as "erotetic" logic. This logic at once reveals, when correctly developed, the role of mathematical knowledge in empirical inquiry, especially clearly in experimental inquiry.

The consequences of this analysis can be appreciated even without considering the details of erotetic logic used to uncover them. It will be shown that the results reached here put the paradigm case of ampliative empirical reasoning, experimental induction, and thereby the entire concept of induction, into an importantly new light.

5. On the Logic of Questions and Answers

In order to carry out this project, it may be noted that there is a simple but profound argument that shows that mathematical (logical, conceptual) knowledge is indispensable in empirical science. As was indicated, this argument is based on the logic of questions and answers. Even though the most general formulation of this logic is not yet generally known, I can only, for reasons of space, explain the main points by means of examples. (Brief expositions of the underlying logical theory can be found in Hintikka 2003 and in Hintikka, Halonen and Mutanen 1998.)

The crucial matter concerns the requirements for satisfactory (conclusive) answers to questions, especially *wh*-questions. Ever since Aristotle, logicians have recognized, more or less clearly, that in order to ask a factual question and to be entitled to expect an answer, the presupposition of the question must have been established. Nevertheless, not until the advent of contemporary epistemic logic was it realized that in a different sense, satisfactory answers, too, need presuppositions of sorts. These presuppositions of answers have to be distinguished from the presuppositions of questions. In order to highlight the difference, I have called the quasi-presuppositions of answers "*conclusiveness conditions.*"

In order to see how these quasi-presuppositions of answers enter the problem situation, suppose that I ask:

Who will win the gubernatorial race?

In the eyes of an epistemic logician, the intended result of asking this question is one that enables the questioner to say, truly,

I know who will win the gubernatorial race. (3)

Such a specification of the intended epistemic result of an adequate answer to a question is called the desideratum of the question. It determines the logical behavior of the question in question as well as the behavior of its answers. In order to see how, suppose that you answer: "The democratic candidate." Then, assuming that I know that you are honest and knowledgeable, I can now say, truly,

I know that the democratic candidate will win the (4)
gubernatorial race.

But (4) is not yet what I wanted to accomplish by my question. The outcome of the response—that is, (4)—is not automatically the desired one. It is not the desideratum (3), nor does it imply (3). The reason is that I may fail to know who the democratic candidate is. In order for the answer to be conclusive, it must be the case that

> I know who the democratic candidate is.   (5)

This requirement is called the "conclusiveness condition" of the answer. It is the "presupposition" of an answer mentioned earlier. If your task is to provide a conclusive answer to my question, you must bring about the truth of (5) and not only of (4), unless you can assume it.

In the notation of epistemic logic (including the independence indicator/), (3)–(5) can be said to instantiate the following forms:

$$K_I(\exists x/K_I)W[x] \tag{6}$$
$$K_I W[d] \tag{7}$$
$$K_I(\exists x/K_I)(d = x) \tag{8}$$

(See Hintikka 1992.) These forms have equivalents in the old-fashioned epistemic logic that tries to dispense with the independence indicator (slash). These equivalents are:

$$(\exists x)K_I W[x] \tag{9}$$
$$K_I W[d] \tag{7}$$
$$(\exists x)K_I(d = x) \tag{10}$$

A clue to the meaning of the independence indicator is in order here. The equivalence of (6) and (18) with (9) and (10) in fact illustrates this meaning. The basic idea is simple. In a semantical game with (9), the value of x has to be chosen before the possible scenario ("possible world") that is imported into a semantical game by K_I is chosen, as indicated by the left-to-right order. But the same effect is in this case reached by requiring that, even if the value of x is chosen after the choice associated with K_I, it be selected in ignorance of the scenario, and in that sense independently of it. This independence is what the slash expresses. In this case, (6) can be expressed in a traditional first-order epistemic logic as (9). But elimination of the slash is not possible in more complicated cases. Once again the reason is an intuitive one: that not all types of independence can be expressed simply by changing the order of K and ($\exists$ x)—that is, merely by changing the relative linear order of different logical notions. For not all types of dependence are transitive, let alone linear.

To return to the example, questions whose desideratum is of the form (6) or (9) are known as simple *wh*-questions. The equivalence of (6) and (8) with (9) and (10), respectively, shows that the independence notation is not needed when dealing with simple *wh*-questions. However, it turns out that this notation is indispensable for the purpose of bringing out an analogy between simple and complex *wh*-questions and of otherwise generalizing the treatment of simple *wh*-questions.

The intuitive relationships between (3)–(5) explained here are reflections of the logical relationships between (6)–(8). The result (6) of the response does not alone logically imply the desideratum (6), but it does so in conjunction with the conclusiveness condition (8). All these relationships are corollaries to a right kind of formulation of epistemic logic.

6. The Conceptual Element in Conclusive Answers

All this does not yet touch on the crucial philosophical issues. What can be said of the epistemology that is revealed by our fragment of epistemic logic? The response "d" ("the democratic candidate") might look perfectly unproblematic. It specifies correctly an individual satisfying the condition that the inquirer ("me") was interested in. Why does it not automatically satisfy the questioner? What has been found shows why. The knowledge expressed by (3) or (5) is not exclusively factual. It involves a conceptual component. This component is brought out by the need to have the conclusiveness condition satisfied. It is not enough for me (the questioner) to have a way of referring to the right entity. I must also know who or what is being so referred to. This knowledge is no longer completely factual in the same sense as (4) or (7). It can be thought of as being partly semantical (conceptual). Hence all the knowledge sought for in asking a simple *wh*-question is not factual. In order to receive an answer to the question, the inquirer must possess or receive also certain conceptual knowledge.

This is seen even more clearly in the case in which the noun phrase replacing "d" is a proper name. If I ask, "Who won the race?" and you answer, "John Doe," I am not any wiser unless I know ahead of time who John Doe is or unless you bring me to know who he is. And this knowledge is now purely semantical. It does not amount to knowing any facts, but to knowing who is being referred to by a proper name. Such knowledge is of course linguistic (semantical, conceptual) and hence *a priori* in relation to the facts that are involved in the question and its answers.

Some philosophers will be puzzled by the fact that, while what is said to be known in a proposition such as

$$\text{Tom knows who Dick is} \tag{11}$$

(expressed in symbols)

$$K_{\text{Tom}}(\exists x / K_{\text{Tom}})(\text{Dick} = x) \tag{12}$$

is a conceptual truth, it is not a necessary truth. But there should be nothing surprising here. Insofar as we can speak by means of our language about that very same language, including different people's knowledge of the language, we inevitably have truths—namely, truths about what the expressions of our language mean, that are conceptual and yet not necessary. Such linguistic truths are *a priori* in relation to the factual truths that the language in question can convey, but that does not make them necessary in the usual epistemological sense—that is, in the sense of being unavoidable. For what we mean by our symbols is, of course, a contingent matter. Only poorly educated philosophers who are assimilating to each other the obviously different notions of conceptual truth, necessary truth, and analytically established truth will be puzzled by the non-necessary character of some conceptual truths.

The conclusiveness conditions of answers to simple *wh*-questions are thus partly conceptual in nature, as was seen. Hence the analysis of the question-answer relation in the case of simple *wh*-questions has brought out a remarkable fact of an epistemologist's life. It has shown that there is inevitably a conceptual and, in a sense, *a priori* component to all such knowledge that can serve to provide conclusive answers to simple *wh*-questions. Here, even the most elementary parts of epistemic logic can be seen to bring out an important epistemological insight.

The distinction between responses such as (7) and the corresponding uniqueness conditions (8) amounts to a kind of separation of a factual ("synthetic") component and a partly conceptual ("analytic") component of a conclusive answer (5) from each other. Is the denial of the possibility of a separation between the two therefore due merely to a superficial analysis of the logic of questions? I will leave the question to my readers to answer.

The only comment I will make here is to remind the reader of the views of philosophers such as Collingwood, according to whom every serious proposition is an answer to an explicit or implicit question. If they are right, the distinction reached in the logic of questions between the two components of a conclusive answer to a question has a much wider applicability—it applies to all propositions actually and seriously propounded.

This interplay of conceptual and factual knowledge in simple empirical *wh*-questions should not come as a surprise to any perceptive intensional logician. As soon as the semantics of one's concepts involves more than one possible scenario (philosophers' grandiloquent terminology—more than one possible world), one's semantics has two different dimensions. On the one hand, it has to specify reference—that is, specify which denizen of each scenario is picked out by a given term or phrase. On the other hand, it has to be specified which individuals in two different scenarios are identical and non-identical with each other. These two tasks can be called "reference" and "identification." Their criteria are largely independent of each other both in theory and in practice. For instance, if (3), then the reference of "the winner of the gubernatorial race" is determined for each scenario compatible with everything I know. In each possible scenario, it picks out the person who in that particular scenario is nominated by the democratic party. But this does not yet specify the identity of the person in question because I may fail to know who the happy nominee is. For this purpose, the winner of the nomination race will have to be the same in all my epistemically possible worlds. In terms of possible-worlds semantics, the response to a question must somehow fix a world line of cross-identification whose nodes in different "worlds" are the individuals that the term in question refers to in the different scenarios. Their being manifestations of one and the same individual is what is required by saying that they must be connected with each other by a world line. For instance, what (5) or (8) requires in that the term "d" ("the democratic candidate") picks out the same individual in all the scenarios compatible with what I know.

Mastering the identification system constitutes an essential part of the *a priori* knowledge that is needed for the purpose of using a language. This system is what is involved in the conclusiveness conditions or answers. It is largely independent of the reference system. In fact, a modicum of analysis shows that the way in which the world lines of identification are drawn is in our actual conceptual practice largely independent of the way in which the references of our terms in different scenarios ("possible worlds") are determined.

Thus the distinction between the factual and the conceptual component in *wh-* questions and in their answers results from the very nature of epistemic logic as involving several "possible worlds" or, more accurately speaking, as always involving the class of all scenarios compatible with what someone knows (on some particular occasion).

Here we can also see that Quine's failure to countenance the distinction is not a simple oversight but a consequence of a deeper assumption—namely, Quine's refusal to traffic in unrealized (but nevertheless realistic) scenarios. This refusal is what I have elsewhere called (Hintikka 1997) his one-world assumption.

7. Experimental Questions

This analysis of simple *wh*-questions can be extended to all questions, with the partial exception of why- and how-questions. (For them, see Hintikka 1999, and especially Hintikka and Halonen 1992.) The generalization is again best indicated by means of suitable examples. Consider, as such an example, an experimental question that an empirical scientist puts to nature in the form of a controlled experiment. It can be taken to be, in the simplest case, of the form:

> How does the observed variable y depend on the controlled   (13)
> variable x?

The desideratum of (13) can be taken to be of the form

$$K_I(\forall x)(\exists y/K_I)S[x, y] \tag{14}$$

which is equivalent to

$$K_I(\exists f/K_I)(\forall x)S[x, f(x)] \tag{15}$$

or

$$(\exists f)K_I(\forall x)S[x, f(x)] \tag{16}$$

The analogy with simple *wh*-questions is obvious. However, the desideratum cannot now be expressed on the first-order level without the slash (independence) notation, which is therefore indispensable for the purpose of generalizing the treatment just given of simple *wh*-questions to all other *wh*-questions.

What kind of reply can nature provide to an experimental question such as (13)? In practice, an experiment usually provides a few points on the x-y plane that represent the results of observations or measurements. They are, furthermore, only approximations within the limits of experimental errors. The scientist then tries to find a curve that best fits these approximate observations. There is an extensive epistemological and methodological literature on the problems of such curve-fitting. These problems are often thought of as the paradigmatic epistemological problems of what used to be called "inductive sciences."

It is nevertheless important to realize that they do not exhaust the important philosophical questions that arise here. Let us suppose that we idealize boldly and look away from all the restrictions on observational accuracy and on the number of observations that can be made. Then we can think of the absolute limit (ideal case) of nature's response to an experimental answer to be a function-in-extension—that is, to say, a set of pairs of all possible argument values and the corresponding function values. Such an infinite class of pairs (satisfying certain obvious conditions) of argument values and correlated function values is, of course, what a function is, set-theoretically speaking. A function in this sense can be thought of as being represented by a curve in the x-y plane. No curve-fitting is any longer needed, for the totality of the measurement points is the curve. The result of such an idealized reply is that the scientist can now say of the relevant function-in-extension g

$$K(\forall x)S[x, g(x)] \tag{17}$$

where the set of the pairs $<x,g(x)>$ is the function in question ("function-in-extension").

But even if the scientist manages to find this function-in-extension—that is, manages to make (17) true for some particular class of such pairs, can he or she claim to know how the second variable depends on the first? In other words, has the experiment conclusively answered the initial question (11)? Obviously not. The result (17) will leave a serious scientist puzzled *unless he or she knows which function* g(x) *is, mathematically speaking.* The situation with experimental (AE) questions is precisely analogous to—nay, precisely the same as—the case of simple *wh*-questions just examined. In both cases, a response that only specifies a correct entity of the appropriate logical type is not enough. The questioner must also know, or must be brought to know, who or what this entity is. This quandary might be called, with an apology to Heine, the Lorelei problem. ("Ich weiss nicht was soll es bedeuten....") If I am looking at the graph of a function without knowing which function it represents, I am reduced to saying, "I don't know what it is supposed to mean."

This requisite collateral knowledge can be expressed by a sentence of the form

$$K(\forall x)(\exists y/K)(g(x) = y) \tag{18}$$

which is equivalent to

$$K(\exists f/K)(\forall x)(g(x) = f(x)) \tag{19}$$

or

$$(\exists f)K(\forall x)(g(x) = f(x)) \tag{20}$$

which may be written elliptically as

$$(\exists f)K(g = f) \tag{21}$$

Here, (17) is analogous with (7), and (18) = (19) with (8) = (10). In other words, experimental questions behave in the same way as simple *wh*-questions except for the logical type of the entities (individuals versus functions) involved in the two cases.

8. Identification of Second-Order Entities and Essentialism

We have thus found a strict parallelism between the identification of individuals and the identification of higher-order entities, such as functions. Admittedly, I have explained the parallelism only for functions, but an extension to other kinds of second-order entities is obvious. This parallelism, thought deceptively simple, has major philosophical consequences. It shows once and for all the hopelessness of all essentialist accounts of identification. These accounts rely on the predicates and relations that individuals have for the purpose of determining their identity in different scenarios. Such an approach works only if the identity of those predicates and relations is unproblematic. What has been seen here shows that the identification of functions and—by parity of cases— of predicates and relations—is not always automatic, but involves in principle the same kinds of questions as the recognition of individuals. An essentialist approach hence merely replaces one identification problem with another. Even if this move marks progress towards solving the problem—as I believe it does not—it will not alone amount to a solution.

In principle, some philosopher might try to make use of the identity of individuals picked up by a predicate as a means of identifying the predicate, instead of basing the identification of individuals on their essential properties. There is, in fact, a sense in which Aristotle can be said to have tried to do so. Contrary to the usual superficial interpretations, a predication such as

A is B

is for Aristotle essential only if the *is* in it has identificatory force and hence picks out a definite substance or class of substances. The basis of this procedure of Aristotle's is that he does not make the Frege-Russell assumption that words for being are ambiguous between expressing identity, predication, and existence. An Aristotelian *is* or rather, *estin* can have all these senses as its components, but it can also lack some of them. (See Hintikka, 2006.)

9. The Nature of the Conclusiveness Conditions

It is important to realize what the need of the conclusiveness condition (18) means and what it does not mean. One thing it does not mean is that we are considering functions otherwise than merely extensionally, let alone that we are somehow smuggling intensional entities into mathematics. The values of the function variable f in (19)–(21) are functions-in-extension, not any kind of intensional entities, quite as fully as the values of the variable x in (8) or (10) are ordinary flesh-and-blood human beings, not ghosts called "possible individuals." The additional force conditions such as (8), (10), or (18)–(21) is merely that the identity of these ordinary extensional entities must be known to the questioner.

There is admittedly a temptation to think that the idealized experimenter who has constructed a perfect graph of the dependence of y on x on his or her graph paper must know the function that codifies the dependence, so that (18)–(21) are for him or her true, after all. For surely such an idealized experimenter can be said to know the full set of pairs of argument values and corresponding function values that *is* the function, extensionally or set-theoretically speaking, or so it seems.

This temptation is a nice illustration of the complexity of the conceptual situation, and also an illustration of the distinction between two different senses of identification that I have made and applied elsewhere. (See, e.g., Hintikka 1989 and 1996(b).) They have been called public and perspectival identification. A factually omniscient deity sees the entire function-in-extension in one fell swoop and consequently can identify it perspectivally. But even such an omniscience about matters of observable fact would not automatically enable the deity to identify publicly the entity whose world line it is. For the deity in question need not be mathematically omniscient. Even a fictional compleat experimenter is still in the same position as we humans are in that he or she sees the function but does not see (visually know) which function it is, just as one can see (in the sense of laying one's eyes on) the murderer of Roger Ackroyd without seeing who he or she is. Hence the correctly diagnosed temptation under scrutiny does not in reality show that any non-extensional entities are involved in the identification of functions.

The distinction between the two modes of identification and its applicability here can be illustrated in different ways. One set of clues is yielded by the reflexions of the distinction in natural language. Yes, perhaps the experimenter may be said to come to *know the function*, but that does not amount to *knowing what function* it is. This seemingly minor grammatical contrast signals in reality a distinction of major importance between two modes of identification. (See, e.g., Hintikka 1989 and 1996(b).) Suffice it to point out merely that there is a distinction between seeing a person and seeing who he or she is and likewise between knowing a person (being acquainted with him or her) and knowing who he or she is. The same distinction can be made—and must be between knowing a function and knowing what function it is.

The point I am making here perhaps becomes clearer if one thinks of graphs of functions as one notation among many in which one can deal with functions. If this is legitimate, then an experimenter's case is strictly parallel to that of an inquirer who asks a simple *wh*-question and receives a reply. Like such an inquirer, an experimentalist can refer correctly to nature's answer to his or her question; that is what the graph does. But that does not automatically (read: logically) enable the experimenter to know what is referred to (represented) by the reply.

The distinction between the two modes of identification can be used to put the dual nature of a controlled experiment into a perspective. It may not be far-fetched to suggest that the primary "inductive" purpose of the physical performance of a controlled experiment is to identify the dependence function perspectivally. Then one could describe the step from an observed function-in-extension to the mathematical law governing it as an inference from a perspectival identification to public identification.

The sense in which a function-in-extension does not alone constitute an adequate answer to an experimental question can be seen in different ways. For a simple historical instance, it was not difficult for scientists and mathematicians to produce good graphs of the curve formed by a perfectly flexible uniform hanging chain. But it took a significant ingenuity on the part of early modern mathematicians to figure out what the function is that was represented by such graphs. (See Mach 1960, pp. 85–87.) This example illustrates a more general point. Only if a scientist knows what the function is that an experiment has yielded can he or she predict what the function-in-extension is that another experiment concerning the same variables is likely to produce. For knowing what a function is is logically speaking nothing but being able to recognize it (its manifestation) in a variety of different circumstances. For instance, unless one knows the function that specifies the shape of one's hanging chain, one does not know what to expect of other hanging chains with a different length and with different endpoints. In more general terms, the mathematical function identified in a controlled experiment will contain parameters characterizing the particular set up used in the experiment. (In the case of the hanging chain, these would be the length of the chair and the distance between the hanging posts.) The values of these parameters are not ordinary observable quantities, but can serve to define one particular application of the relevant laws and theories. The logical status of such applications is discussed in Hintikka 2002(a).

Generality with respect to such parameters is thus, in effect, generality with respect to the possible scenarios presupposed by the concept of knowledge. Thus the Lorelei problem is thus very much a fact of life—or at least of fact of epistemology—for practicing scientists.

In general, a scientist can generalize from a single experiment only if he or she knows the law governing the functional dependence that an experimentalist has found. The identificatory knowledge encoded in the conclusiveness condition is not only indispensable for a genuine answer to our experimental question, it is also indispensable for the purpose of using the outcome of an experiment as a stepping-stone to an inductive generalization. Paraphrasing Euler (see Youschkevich 1977, p. 68), one might say that the graph of an unidentified function not determined (at least not yet determined) by any known equation is, as it were, traced by a free stroke of the hand. (Of course, in the case of an actual experiment, the hand is nature's.) I do not know what the same hand will draw next time unless I know the rule it is following. Even more generally, how can one as much as to discuss a function-in-extension? One can assign a name to it, but one can define it only in a purely nominal sense. Such a naming does not in principle help me at all to know how the same variables depend on each other in another experimental situation. Hence the conclusiveness condition makes a real difference in the case of experimental questions, too. For if I can identify the function represented by a graph in one experimental situation, I know its graph in other possible situations. Indeed, this is what identificatory knowledge means in correctly interpreted possible-worlds semantics, for the intended "possible worlds" are precisely the different occasions of use of the concepts in question. (See Hintikka 2002(a).)

And this difference is precisely what the failure of (18)–(21) amounts to. For to know what an entity—in this case, the function g—is, in other words, to know what "g" means, is to know what it refers to in different circumstances of use. And what one's knowledge of the mere function-in-extension fails to provide (as was seen) is precisely knowledge of what that dependence function (even only the function-in-extension) is in other situations in which the dependence is manifested. As was seen earlier, such different circumstances of use might be manifested by different values of the parameters that identify different particular experimental contexts.

The difficulty of the Lorelei problem is easily underestimated. A historical example of this is the difficulty that Kepler had in finding the right mathematical law that captures Tycho Brahe's observations concerning the orbit of Mars. Yet no lesser a figure than Peirce had to confess that he had initially and mistakenly thought of Kepler's work as little more than "to draw a curve through the places of Mars." (Peirce 1931–35, 3.362.)

A partial analogue of the difference between knowing the function-in-extension and knowing its mathematical law is receiving a coded message and decoding it. This analogue is apt precisely in that it illustrates the complexities of the Lorelei problem. Indeed, some early modern scientists compared the task of a scientist to deciphering the "Book of Nature." This simile perhaps has—or can be interpreted as having a more specific meaning than we first realize.

10. The Conceptual Component of Experimental Answers is Mathematical

The same analogy serves to extend the distinction between conceptual and factual components of an answer from simple *wh*-questions to experimental questions. In the case of simple *wh*-questions, the indispensable collateral knowledge concerned the identity of individuals, and can be thought of as semantical. But now the entities whose identity is at issue are functions, not individuals, as is seen from (18)–(21). Accordingly, the requisite identificatory knowledge is in this case mathematical, not semantical in a narrowly linguistic sense. In any case, whatever one takes the relation of these two kinds of knowledge to be, the identificatory knowledge needed here is not physical knowledge. That is, finding out what mathematical function is represented by a given experimentally established curve is not a problem to be solved by an experimental physicist. It is a task for mathematicians, or mathematical physicists, not for experimental scientists, even though knowledge of the relevant physical laws may be needed to solve it. Solving the problem of the identity of a curve produced by a controlled experiment can indirectly increase our factual knowledge, even though in a different sense it does not. By itself, identifying a function (coming to know it) contributes only our mathematical knowledge, in other words, to conceptual (*a priori*) knowledge. Such an identification typically means finding a place for the function to be identified within the framework of some theory of similar functions. Developing a theory that enables a mathematician to do so is no mean feat in most cases. Yet such is this mathematical knowledge that has been found to be indispensable in experimental science. Indeed, this need of being able to tell physicists what the functions are that their experiments have produced has been an important incentive in the actual development of mathematics. (See Hintikka 2000.)

In brief, the requisite knowledge of the identity of experimentally discovered functions is not factual, but mathematical in nature. Lorelei problems are solved in departments of mathematics, not in physics laboratories. Yet such mathematical knowledge is needed for the purpose of conclusively answering empirical, especially experimental, questions. What an experimental physicist is trying establish is not just a smooth curve on a graph paper indicating his or her data, but establishing what function it is that governs the dependence of different variables on each other. For one small example, when a co-discoverer of Wien's radiation law reported his findings, he did not just communicate a function-in-extension to other physicists, he gave them a mathematical law: "Furthermore, I am pleased to inform you that I have found the function I of Kirchoff's law. From my observations, I have determined the emissitivity function $I = (c_1/\lambda^\alpha) \, e(\exp(c_2/\lambda \, T))$." (Paschens to Kayser, June 4, 1896; quoted in Hermann 1971, p. 6.)

The mathematical character of the knowledge of conclusiveness conditions of experimental questions is also of interest from the vantage point what used to be called *historisch-kritisch*. Michael Friedman has aptly argued that the most important ingredient of the philosophy of logical positivists was their conception of the *a priori* element as being mathematical and logical. What has been found vindicates this conception in the instructive test case of experimental knowledge in a literal sense. The *a priori* knowledge needed in experimental science is the knowledge codified by conclusiveness conditions, and this knowledge has been seen to consist, in this case, of knowledge of mathematical functions.

11. The Indispensability of Mathematics

Thus, even though identifying the function which an experiment yields is a mathematical problem, it is an integral part of conclusively answering a physical (experimental) question. Hence, mathematics is indispensable in science. Without its help, we literally could not answer conclusively perfectly empirical scientific questions. And hence Quine was right: Mathematics is indispensable in science, just as he claimed. We have not only found a place for *a priori* knowledge in the world of facts, we have shown the indispensability of such knowledge.

It is nevertheless of interest to see precisely what that place of the mathematical and other *a priori* knowledge is in science. The role of logic and mathematics in science is often thought of as consisting in relating different propositions to each other. We encountered this view in the beginning of this chapter as a foundation of Quine's belief in the indispensability of mathematics in science. Now we have found another role of mathematics in experimental science—namely, conclusiveness conditions for the answers to experimental questions. In less technical terms, mathematics is needed in order to express adequately the answers to empirical questions. This role of mathematics in science is different from its deductive role. The knowledge that mathematics provides is about the identity of mathematical objects, including functions, not about deductive connections.

It is not obvious, however, what such an indispensability of mathematical knowledge in experimental science implies about realism vis-à-vis mathematical objects. Indeed, our rejection of the Quinean picture of mathematics as holding together of the fabric of science might seem to destroy all such implications. Quine's idea seems to be that whatever is indispensable in science must enjoy the same objectivity as science. This assumption can perhaps be accepted. But in order to obtain an argument for ontological realism, one has to assume also that whatever is indispensable for scientific purposes must enjoy the same kind of reality as the (other) objects of science. This assumption has been seen to be false. The kind of knowledge codified in the conclusiveness conditions is indispensable, and it may be as objective as scientific knowledge in general. But it is not factual knowledge, but conceptual knowledge, and it is not about the natural objects that science is normally thought of as dealing with. The indispensability of mathematics in science is a fact, but it does not imply that mathematical and scientific knowledge are ontologically on a par, and hence it does not imply ontological realism, either, with respect to mathematical objects—or so it seems.

Furthermore, my reason for indispensability differs sharply from Quine's. The argument presented here does not depend on a denial of a distinction between conceptual (analytical) and factual (synthetic) truths. It discourages any such denial. The conclusiveness conditions (18)–(21) are mathematical and *a fortiori* conceptual in an even clearer sense than the conclusiveness conditions (10) of simple *wh*-questions. In contrast, an unidentified function-in-extension is merely a summary of the raw data yielded by the experiment. Hence there is an unmistakable consequential difference between the two.

But even though the argument so far presented for the indispensability of mathematics in science does not yield reasons for ordinary ontological realism, it shows something else. First, it shows that mathematical knowledge must have the same objectivity as experimental knowledge. Indeed, this follows *a fortiori*, for it was seen that a certain type of mathematical knowledge is a component of experimental knowledge—that is, knowledge needed to answer experimental questions conclusively. Hence, if experimental knowledge is objective, then so is mathematical knowledge.

Moreover, a review of the argument outlined earlier reveals an interesting feature of the conceptual situation. What kind of mathematical knowledge is it that was found indispensable in experimental science? A glance at such examples as (18)–(21) provides an answer. The knowledge in question pertains to the identity of mathematical objects, typically functions, rather than to the mathematical truths. In the classification of Hintikka (1996(b)), it is knowledge of mathematical objects. But there clearly cannot be objective knowledge of the identity of mathematical objects unless such objects enjoy objective existence. In epistemology, we can invert Quine's dictum and say: No identity without entity. More fully expressed, there can be no knowledge of identities without existing entities that that knowledge is about. In order to know which functions a controlled experiment (experimental question) has produced, there must be such a function, just as much there must exist the next governor of my state in order for anyone to claim truly to know who he or she will be. If the constitution of my state has been changed, and the next head of that state will be a prime minister rather than a governor, it cannot be true to say that I know the identity of the next governor—there just ain't no such person. Hence the line of thought outlined in this chapter provides a proof of the ontological realism of mathematics after all.

However, the argument presented here does not show what kind of objective existence mathematical objects enjoy (or suffer). This question calls for a separate investigation. Suffice it here to point out only that for such an investigation we need sharper distinctions between kinds of objective existence than are found in the standard literature. Objective existence does not mean existence independently of human thought and human action. We can have perfectly objective knowledge of such man-made objects as bridges, highways, buildings, and books. Non-physical existence does not have to mean existence in some supersensible "Platonic" region of the actual world, either. Conceptual objects may enjoy a reality that is not relative to a particular scenario (state of affairs, course of events, a.k.a. "possible world"). For instance, such objects may pertain to relations between different scenarios, such as identities between denizens of different "worlds."

One has to be careful here in other respects, too. One of them is the precise sense in which "there is no identity without entity." The entities relevant here are functions. As (18)–(20) illustrate, the identity of such functions can be expressed without quantifying over entities other than individuals, provided that we have an independence indicator (slash) at our disposal. We do not have to quantify over higher-order entities in the literal sense.

Moreover, I have shown in Hintikka 1998 that certain conceptual objects—namely, functions—are being tacitly presupposed already by our logic of quantifiers. This logic is not fully explainable by the feeble metaphor of quantified variables "ranging over" a certain class of values. Quantifiers are proxies for certain choice functions, known in the trade as Skolem functions, wherefore these functions are presupposed by all use of (nested) quantifiers. Hence a clever philosopher may try to eliminate numbers in favor of geometrical (space-time) objects (See Field 1980), but the very theory of such geometrical objects inevitably presupposes other kinds of mathematical objects—namely, functions.

12. Knowing What a Mathematical Object Is

A comment is in order here to avoid unnecessary misunderstandings. It might be objected to that the idea of knowing a function (knowing which mathematical function is represented by a function-in-extension) is a vague notion. (Strictly speaking, as indicated earlier, we should be speaking of *knowing what* a function is, rather than *knowing it*, for the latter expression is normally used of perspectival identification, which is not the issue here.) What precisely are the criteria of such knowledge? Admittedly, these criteria depend on the purposes of the mathematicians in question and the state of the art in the entire mathematical community. But this relativity does not imply vagueness. Once the standards are fixed, however tacitly, the conceptual situation is what has been diagnosed in this chapter. It is simply a fallacy to conclude from the fact that a concept is not sharp that it is not applicable, important, or even expressible in a logical situation

In this respect, the situation with respect to simple *wh*-questions and experimental questions is similar. For instance, people's actual choice of the operational criteria of *knowing who* someone is vary widely. (For their messy choices, see, e.g., Boër and Lycan 1986.) But even though the choice between different criteria may be underdetermined, it does not imply that each of the possible standards is not objective. The notion of *knowing who* does play a useful role in our language and in our thinking. Once the criteria of knowing the identity of entities of different logical type have been fixed, the logical relations are as I have described them. Likewise, it can make a concrete difference to mathematicians' and physicists' working life whether they know which function mathematically speaking a certain function-in-extension "really" is, even if the criteria of such "real" knowledge are different on different occasions.

This analogy between the identification of persons and the identification of mathematical functions may not be immediately convincing, however. There is more to be said here, in any case.

One unmistakable fact is that the identification of functions obtained empirically is a job that is constantly being performed by scientists and mathematicians. And whatever the precise criteria are or may be of succeeding in such an enterprise, it makes a concrete difference when one does succeed. Kepler spent years trying to find the function represented by Tycho Brahe's observations concerning the orbit of Mars, and when he reached the right one, there was no hesitation in his mind. Even experimental scientists frequently report their results in the form of a function represented by a mathematical formula, as we saw earlier. Obviously there are, in scientific practice, some objective criteria for when an empirically established dependence relation is found to be instantiating some specific mathematical function. I am not overlooking the problems occasioned by the limits of observational accuracy, presence of errors, and so on, only arguing that they present a problem different from the identification of functions.

This does not mean that mathematicians, logicians, and philosophers would not have a hard time if they were asked to specify the precise conditions in which one can be said to know a mathematical function. In this day and age, the computability of the values of the function (at least over a range of argument values) might look like a viable candidate, but I do not think that it is the right one. A mathematician can come to know more things about her favorite non-recursive function than she knows about her best friend, one might argue, though of course different kinds of things. Who am I to say that she does not know the function quite as fully as she knows her friend? Here we have a bunch of fascinating questions that ought to be grist for the mill of the fashionable students of "mathematical practice" but whose significance they blithely ignore. I will return to these questions shortly.

In one respect, it is potentially misleading to emphasize the character of the mathematical knowledge needed in science as pertaining to the identification of mathematical objects. This may very well make the knowledge in question seem trivial. In reality, the role of such identification is crucial in science. The reason is that it is the recognition of a given scientific (e.g., physical) relationship as a specific mathematical one that opens the possibility of applying mathematics to it—for instance, to draw logical inferences from it. Nor are these opportunities restricted to the deductive role of mathematics. I cannot apply mathematical concepts to empirical objects, even descriptively, unless I have recognized that they instantiate the relevant concepts. The identification of the mathematical concepts when they are exemplified in external phenomena is the *conditio sine qua non* of the applicability of mathematics to reality.

13. On the Nature of Identification

There may also seem to be intriguing dissimilarities between the identification of persons and the identification of mathematical objects. The conclusiveness condition identifying an individual d is of the form

$$K(\exists x/K)(d = x) \tag{10}$$

whereas the analogous condition on a function g is

$$K(\exists f/K)(\forall x)(g(x) = f(x)) \tag{19}$$

The information that (10) and (19) convey may seem to be radically different. In the case of the identification of an individual (10), we appear to be dealing with merely linguistic, indeed lexical, information, information about a simple relation of reference between a name "b" and the intended individual—in simpler terms, information about what the proper name "b" means. In contrast, the identification of a function (19) is apparently a complex matter, a matter of knowing certain things about the function b, perhaps something like knowing its power series expansion. Yet the two kinds of information should be logically on a par.

So what does the alleged parity between (10) and (19) mean? Does it mean that, appearances notwithstanding, the two kinds of conclusiveness conditions are at bottom identical? If so, it would follow that the knowledge needed to identify a function is at bottom merely semantical, like the knowledge expressed by (10). If not, what is the extra knowledge like? And where does the analogy between the two cases lie?

Now the common denominator of the two kinds of knowledge is that they both are about the identity of certain entities. This analogy throws an interesting light on both parties of the comparison. On the one hand, it highlights the fact that knowing the identity of an individual is not a simple matter, like knowing a referential relation between "b" and b. It is rather like locating the individual in question on some abstract or sometimes even concrete map or framework. This character of identification as locating the definendum on an appropriate "map" or "chart" (Peirce's word) or, generally speaking, in a frame of reference, was clearly already recognized and emphasized by Peirce. (See Hilpinen (1995, p. 285; Peirce MS 280, pp. 42–43.) Likewise the identification of a function can be described as locating it in some kind of space of functions. I do not even have to put the term "space" in quotes here, for many functions can literally be located in suitable abstract spaces—for instance, in a Hilbert space. This fact makes it natural to say that such an identification can in suitable circumstances be construed as the definition of the function in question—for instance, when an analytic function is thought of in a Weierstrassian spirit as being defined by its power series expansion or the zeta function by its series formulation. More generally and more abstractly speaking, the identification of a function might amount to placing it within a framework of a theory of a class of similar functions.

Logically speaking, the only essential requirement is that the same "map" be there in all the relevant scenarios. This requirement is nothing but another way of saying that the identification system is independent of the reference system.

Even the identification of an individual is not simply the recognition of a relation of reference or designation. It is more like locating the identified object in a suitable frame of reference, on an abstract "map" of some sort or other. This framework may vary from one occasion to another, but knowing what an identificatory statement means presupposes knowing what the framework is. There may even be cases in which identification of people by name amounts to putting the named person on the map, so to speak. I do not think that it is entirely an etymological accident that in the old days, the most common Finnish family names served to locate their bearers in the literal geographical sense. A family with the name "Saarinen" lived on an island (saari), a family named "Virtanen" lived next to a stream (virta), and one named "Mäkinen" on a hill (mäki), to take a few of the most common Finnish family names. Similar kinds of names are found in other languages. Perhaps one can see here a similarity with passport authorities' use of a person's place and date of birth as his or her identifying coordinates.

In other languages, spoken perhaps by people living closer to each other than the Finns of old times, names served to place their bearers on the social map of a local community. This is illustrated by such common English surnames as Smith, Miller, Taylor, Cooper, Tanner, and so on.

An instructive (though politically incorrect) example of locating people on one's social map is the sexist saw quoted by Evelyn Waugh: "Be kind to young girls. You never know who they will be." It is precisely the mode of identification that makes the adage sexist. In Waugh's world, the coordinates of young ladies are defined by their future husbands.

Another British example is found in C. P. Snow's novel *In Their Wisdom* (Charles Scribner's Sons, New York, 1974, pp. 17–18):

"You know my daughter Elizabeth, I think, don't you?"
"Of course I do."
"She's wondering whether to marry someone. . . ."
He went on: "He's a man called Underwood. I don't know who he is."
This didn't mean what it appeared to mean. Lord Hillmorton [the father] was quite certain of Julian Underwood's identity. He was saying that none of Julian's family, relatives or acquaintances had had any connection in the past with any of the Hillmorton's family, relatives or acquaintances.

"Putting someone on the map" is what happens in ordinary discourse, even when our means of identification (knowing who) are used in a non-standard way. Knowing the name is a frequent but not universal way of identifying a person, for knowing the name of a person or an object is normally most useful in solving the location task. For if you have a name, you can usually find a person's address, phone number, e-mail address, age, place of birth, and so on, and the FBI can find what there is in that person's file, and so forth. In this case, the idea of location can in fact be taken literally, not merely by reference to some abstract framework of identification. But this role of names in getting hold of the information that is needed to locate an individual is, from *sub specie logicae*, a contingent institutional fact. Indeed, knowing a person's name does not always do the identificatory job, for clearly one can fail to know the bearer of a proper name. Then one has somehow to grasp the framework that is being tacitly assumed. Witness, for example, the following examples from real life, or at least from real literature:

"I know him."
"Who is he?"
"He is called Kenneth Widmerpoole. I was at school with him as a matter of fact. He is in the city."
"I know his name of course. . . .But what is he like?"

(Anthony Powell, *At Lady Molly's*, Heinemann, 1957, p. 44)

In this example, the framework of identification is again a social one. Lady Conyers is trying to place the poor Mr. Widmerpoole in her social map of relatives, acquaintances, relatives of acquaintances, public figures, officials of different kinds, and so on.

Even though these examples are light-hearted, the "placing on a map" analogy points to the sources of the usefulness of mathematics in epistemology. For how is this analogy to be unpacked? Placing something on a map means coming to know its relationships to other entities. Such knowledge is precisely what mathematics is supposed to contribute to the structure of our scientific and other empirical knowledge. This can be thought of as vindicating a modified version of Quine's network analogy. In this corrected version, we do not create a semantical web through consequence relations. We utilize an already existing framework by locating empirical input within it.

The analogy between the identification of individuals and the identification of functions also reflects some light back on what is necessary for knowing who someone, say "b," is. What is needed is not to be able to refer to "b" in some special way—for instance, by a proper name or some other supposedly rigid designator. (See here Kripke 1972.) What is needed is to have so much information that one can rule out all those possible scenarios in which "b" refers to a different individual. Such information is needed even in the case where "b" is a proper name, and it is not gained by a Kripkean dubbing ceremony. In an analogous case, I can, so to speak, admire a beautiful curve on a graph paper, representing a function-in-extension, and solemnly pronounce: "I name you a lemniscata." Needless to say, such a ceremony has not in the least helped me to come to know what that function is, even though in the case of a mathematical object, we do not even have to worry about keeping track of its future career by means of causal links as, according to Kripke, we have to do with physical objects. In mathematical practice, curves are identified by their equations, not by their proper names. By the same token, a Kripkean dubbing act does not help me, in the least in the case of physical objects, to know who or what the dubbed individual is, in outright contradiction of the idea that a proper name so introduced is a vehicle of *de re* knowledge about that very individual.

Kripkean dubbing is at bottom nothing more than a dramatization of the old idea of ostensive definition. Now, the role of an ostensive definition can be pinpointed completely accurately. Such a "definition," like other forms of identification, locates the definiendum in a certain space. In the case of ostension, this space is one's visual space. Identification by means of such a space is a form of perspectival identification, not a public one. Visual space does not lie at the bottom of our normal identification of public entities, be they persons, physical objects, places, events, or whatnot. Kripke is simply mistaking perceptual identification for public identification.

Kripke thinks that once an entity has been ostensively identified and given a name, its continued identity is guaranteed by causal chains. This might seem to work for physical objects, but in the case of higher-order entities such as functions, there is not even a plausible candidate to play the role of causal continuity.

On the other hand, the identificatory character of the mathematical knowledge involved in the presuppositions confirms the earlier insight into their status as conceptual truths. There is perhaps not the same temptation to label our knowledge of the identity of functions linguistic or semantical, let alone lexical, as there is in the case of our knowledge of the identity of individuals. However, once the precise nature of the analogy between the two cases of identification is realized, it can be seen in what sense the identification of functions, too, is a matter of conceptual knowledge.

We are dealing here with extremely important questions. The possibility of making a distinction between conceptual and factual information in an experimental context casts a long shadow on all attempts to consider, for instance, logical truths as the most general factual truths. The two kinds of knowledge involved in answering an experimental question differ in kind, not just in degree of generality.

One more clarification is in order. I am not assuming a separate class of entities called functions-in-intension. The ways of identifying different functions-in-extension cannot be reified into a class of intensions. This is shown, among other things, by the fact that there may be more than one way of identifying a function in a full enough sense to justify one in saying that one knows what function it is. For instance, the system of spectral lines of a certain kind of atom can be considered as a function-in-extension in a sense relevant here. As far as the account given here is concerned, a scientist can prove that he or she knows what that function is either by deriving it from the Schrödinger equation or from matrix mechanics. It is a hugely oversimplified view of the actual criteria of *knowing who someone is* to think that they can be summed up in knowing some particular facts about him or her, including knowing some mythical "essence" of his or hers. Likewise, knowing what a function is does not in general reduce to knowing some one thing about that function, for instance knowing its intension.

14. Identification of Functions and the History of Mathematics

The identification of functions can also be looked upon in a historical perspective. When the needs of scientists thrust upon mathematicians functions they had not studied before, some historians of mathematics have described what happened as a gradual widening of mathematicians' idea of function. I find such a claim profoundly misleading. (See Hintikka 2000.) The general idea of a function as any conceivable correlation of argument values and function values is older than many of such alleged extensions of the concept. It certainly occurs in Euler. (See here Euler, quoted by Youschkevich 1977, e.g., pp. 62, 68.) Moreover, it is hard to imagine that Leibniz was not in effect relying on it when he spoke of all possible worlds, each of them governed by a different "law." If Leibniz did not identify these different laws with so many different functions, it is only because the term "function" was not yet a household word even in mathematical households. The so-called widening of the concept of function should be thought of as a widening of the sphere of functions mathematicians know in the sense of being familiar with. Indeed, the main engine of the extension of the class of functions considered by mathematicians was the need to master functions obtained as solutions of partial differential equations of physics. (See Youschkevich 1977, pp. 62, 66.)

The observations made here throw some light on other historical matters. A suggestion has been made by several scholars to the effect that the methodological "secret" of the early modern science was an extension of the idea of geometrical analysis to science. (See Hintikka and Remes 1974, last chapter; Beckcr 1959; and Cassirer 1944.) Indeed, Descartes acknowledges the Greek method as one of the starting points of his own thinking. (*Regulae*, Adam, and Tannery, vol. X, p. 374–378.) More fully expressed, the gist of the Greek method of analysis was systematic study of the interrelations of different geometrical objects in a configuration. "Analytic" geometry came about when Descartes undertook to represent these dependence relations algebraically. The revolution in natural sciences began when scientists began to look at physical configurations in the same way in terms of different kinds of dependence relations between their ingredients. This is what Oskar Becker called the idea of "analytic experiment." What has been seen in this chapter is that there is an intrinsic connection between the two enterprises. We cannot fully understand given physical dependence relations unless we understand the mathematical nature of the functional dependencies they instantiate.

15. Experiments and the Problems of Induction

It can also be seen here that the epistemic logic of questions and answers puts the problem of induction into a new light—or is it old light? For one thing, it shows the ambiguity of what is meant by the problem of induction. Induction is often thought of (in a situation such as a simple controlled experiment) as a step from a finite number of observations (observed points on the x-y coordinate system) to the function f that codifies the dependence of y on x, $y = f(x)$. Expressed in this way, an inductive step ("inductive inference") is by definition underdetermined, and hence no absolute *a priori* justification can be given to any particular choice of f. But what is equally often overlooked is that this underdeterminacy has two different sources. This is because the experimenter is trying to accomplish two different things. He or she is trying to find a function-in-extension, but usually also—and often in the first place—to identify this function-in-extension. This makes a concrete difference. If what the experimenter is merely looking for is the function f in extension, then the impossibility of reading off f from actual observations is due to the limitations of an experiment to a finite number of observations and to the limited accuracy of these observations. Such kinds of limitations can be reduced by better experimental techniques and by additional observations. The function-in-extension f can be approximated more and more closely through such improvements.

But if what the experimenter is looking for is—as is normal in scientific practice—a definite identification of the mathematical function in question, then he or she faces another kind of problem—namely, the step from a function-in-extension to its mathematical identity. Insofar as this step is part of an "inductive inference," then scientific induction has a mathematical (more generally speaking, conceptual) component. This mathematical component is different from the factual tasks involved in induction. One can, for instance, get closer to the function-in-extension f by improving one's experimental techniques, but the step from a function-in-extension to its mathematical incarnation is not automatically aided and abetted by such techniques. It requires enhanced mathematical rather than experimental sophistication.

Thus, two entirely different kinds of generalization are involved in induction. There is, on the one hand, the step from observed values of the function $y = f(x)$ to other observable values in the same experimental situation. On the other hand, there is the generalization required to extend the mode of dependence between two variables in one experimental set up to other situations. For the latter purpose, as was seen, an inquirer has to know the (mathematical) identity of the function observed in a given controlled experiment. This distinction between the two aspects of inductive inference can play a role in our understanding of actual scientific inference. For instance, the distinction between the two components of answers to experimental questions has a rough-and-ready counterpart in a distinction that is sometimes made, even terminologically, between two different kinds of activities of a scientist. In what are typically referred to as inductive inferences, a scientist is trying to reach the function-in-extension that is the factual component of an answer to an experimental question, or at least trying to anticipate new pairs of argument values and function values. But when a scientist is making a stab at identifying the dependence function mathematically, what he or she is doing is often not called inductive reasoning or inference but constructing a mathematical model. In this way, model construction receives a natural niche among the activities of an experimental scientist and indeed of any scientist. If one is enterprising enough, one can even try to develop along the lines indicated here a logical and epistemological theory of model building in science as distinguished from inductive inference.

Even in cases where it is not natural to speak of model building, we can, in principle, distinguish from each other two tasks involved in finding a conclusive answer to an experimental question. One task is to find the function-in-extension that codifies the looked-for mode of dependence between two variables. We might be tempted to call it the "inductive task," and I will in the following yield to this temptation. We should nevertheless keep in mind that what is usually called induction must be understood as involving both tasks. The other task is to find the mathematical identity of the function-in-extension that has been found inductively. I will call it the "identification task."

In practice, these two tasks are not usually distinguished from each other, certainly not temporally. For instance, the need for non-inferential model construction results from the fact that in actual scientific practice, an experimenter cannot wait till he or she has established an entire function-in-extension codifying the dependence of a variable on others before raising the question of its mathematical identity. But this does not eliminate the identification problem; it merely pushes it to an earlier stage of inquiry. What this means is that there is a conceptual component in inquiry over and above the usual inductive techniques, such as curve-fitting. Such techniques only serve to overcome the limitations on the number of experimental observations and on their accuracy, and cannot automatically facilitate an identification of the "curve" that directly results from the experiment. Thus, any adequate future discussion of the general problem of induction must be complemented by a discussion of the role of conclusiveness conditions—in other words, the role of the conceptual component of our empirical knowledge.

This injunction extends even to the history of the notion of induction. It is, for instance, instructive to think of Aristotle's notion of *epagoge* as not being so much induction in the twentieth-century sense as a search for the conceptual knowledge that provides the conclusiveness conditions needed to answer *wh*-questions. Aristotle thought that we can, after all, easily know which entities a concept applies to, for a rational man surely knows what he is talking about in the sense of knowing what entities he intends to talk about. But he need not thereby know what concept it is that picks out those entities from others—that is to say, he need not know the definition of this concept. Thus, as a consequence, induction is for Aristotle essentially a certain kind of search for definitions or, to put the same point metaphysically, an attempt to assemble the appropriate form in one's soul. In Hintikka 1980, I have in fact argued precisely for this kind of interpretation of the Aristotelian *epagoge*. In this form, the search for conclusiveness conditions has played an important role in the history of philosophy.

16. Comparison Between Different Cases

One of the insights we have reached is that there are two different things in the kind of reasoning that is usually called inductive. On the one hand, an inquirer is in the simple but representative case of experimental research searching for a function-in-extension. (This is the inductive problem in the narrower sense.) On the other hand, an inquirer is trying to identify the function in question. This is what I suggested calling the "identification task." These two searches are not sequential, but can go on at the same time. There can be all sorts of interplay between them and they can also proceed at different speeds. This creates an interesting perspective from which to view different kinds of scientific inquiry and even different episodes in the history of science.

One kind of interplay concerns the role of the mathematical identification of experimental dependencies in estimating the reliability of inductive inferences in the narrower sense. If I have to anticipate the value of an experimentally established function-in-extension for a previously unobserved argument value, my procedure is likely to be not only simpler but also more reliable if I have established the mathematical law that captures the observed fragment of the dependence function. This is especially clear when two fragments of a function-in-extension have been established for two separate intervals of argument values. Suppose that the corresponding mathematical functions have been identified. If they turn out to be the same function, it enhances the two partial inductions and encourages extending them to new argument values. If they are different, an experimental scientist faces the further problem of reconciling the two mathematical functions. I will return to this problem later.

Other situations call for other comments. In the schematic and highly abstracted thought-experiment described earlier, an idealized experimenter reaches a fully specified function-in extension and then tries to identify the mathematical function that it is a graph of. This thought-experiment looks more unrealistic than it need be. In some cases, only discrete values of the argument are possible. In such cases, if measurements are reasonably accurate, an experimenter can reach a fairly close approximation of the function-in-extension that codifies the results of experimentation. Then the main problem will be to find the mathematical function that captures the results of experimentation.

One can think here of the historical situation at the early stages of the development of quantum theory in this light. What happened at that time does not fit very well into the conventional picture of inductive reasoning. In so far as historians of science have diagnosed the thinking of early quantum theorists, they have typically spoken of model construction. There is more to be said here, however. Physicists had at the time a great deal of accurate information about the spectra of different atoms. Such a situation resembles one in which the relevant function-in-extension has been reached, at least in the sense that the main problem facing investigators was not to make the measurements of the spectral lines more accurate or more numerous. It was to find the law that captured a reasonable number of the already known measurements. Indeed, Bohr's theory applied in the first place only to the hydrogen atom, and accounted for its spectra, albeit not fully accurately. What was impressive about Bohr's theory was not that it predicted accurately the observed hydrogen spectrum, but that it produced an explicit mathematical formula that yielded a good approximation to this spectrum. In other words, success in solving the identification counted more than accuracy in solving the inductive problem. Bohr's theory was presented by him in the form of a physical model, but since this model was known to be impossible in classical physics, philosophically speaking it was little more than a mathematical model.

In the same way, Heisenberg and Schrödinger were later trying to find an explanation for similar observed data. Their respective mathematical laws were accepted (and were shown to be equivalent) well before there was any firm conception of what the underlying physical reality is like. (Indeed, some physicists warned their colleagues in so many words against asking too many questions about the reality behind the mathematical laws of quantum theory.) Hence it is natural to look upon their work in the first place as a search for the mathematical law that governs the relevant phenomena. All this is characteristic of the identification problem as distinguished from the inductive problem in the narrower sense.

More generally speaking, partial solutions to the two tasks—the inductive one and the identificatory one—can help each other. If a physicist has reached the mathematical function governing certain phenomena on the basis of partial evidence, he or she can use it to predict further observations that can fill in the function-in-extension. This is what happens when a novel theory is used to predict new kinds of observations or to predict the existence of previously unknown objects.

One kind of special but important situation arises when experimentalists have managed to establish a function-in-extension for more than one interval of argument values so well that even the identification is possible for each of the intervals to the limit of observational accuracy. It suffices here to consider the case in which the intervals are not overlapping. Then it may happen that the resulting mathematical functions are different for the different intervals of argument values. Then scientists are faced with a double task. Not only do they have to find the function values corresponding to all the different argument values, they have also to combine the different mathematical functions so that they become special cases of a single function (up to the limits of observational accuracy). This identification problem is typically solved initially by means of mathematical manipulation of the different functions that are applicable in the different intervals of argument values rather than by means of new observations. This illustrates, once again, the conceptual character of the identification problem.

A paradigmatic example is offered by Planck's reasoning in finding his famous radiation law. Planck had available for him two different laws of black body radiation—one of them (Wien's radiation law) holding for low frequencies and the other one (the Rayleigh–Jeans law) holding for high frequencies. No help could be expected from additional observations. Planck's initial line of thought was simply to manipulate the explicit mathematical formulas that express the two laws. Only later did he ask what possible physical significance the unified law might have. In doing so, he was led to realize that a natural quasi-argument for the integration involved the assumption of the quantization of energy. Thomas Kuhn (1978) has called attention to the remarkable fact that initially neither Planck nor any other physicist paid much attention to the idea of quantization. In the light of the structure of experimental inquiry, this is perhaps not surprising. The quantum hypothesis was completely irrelevant to the inductive task of finding a function-in-extension for the radiation law. And the other task—the mathematical identification of the radiation law—was easily thought of as being merely a matter of conceptual inquiry, with no direct connections with empirical facts. In such a perspective, the quantum hypothesis must have appeared to be only a heuristic idea that served to amalgamate the two different partial radiation laws into a single one. Admittedly, the target of the identification was an experimentally obtained function-in-extension. But the physical explanation and even the physical import of this function-in-extension might very well have seemed to Planck as hypothetical as Bohr's atom in its literal form as a miniature planetary system was later for its inventor.

The kind of reasoning involved in interpolating and extrapolating partial generalizations (in the sense of generalizations established only for different restricted classes of argument values) played an important role in earlier philosophy of science. It had a name: It was called "induction." For instance, Newton to the best of my knowledge consistently uses the terms induction (or its Latin cognate "inductio") in this way. Later, this sense of induction was forgotten, and was replaced by its Humean sense of inference from particulars to general truths or to unknown particulars. Moreover, I have argued that the older "Newtonian" sense is but a quantitative counterpart to Aristotle's *epagoge*. (See Hintikka 1993.)

Thus the perspective on experimental inquiry that has been reached throws an interesting light on different episodes in the actual history of science, and helps us to analyze them.

17. Approximating a Function-In-Extension Mathematically

The distinction between induction in the sense of a search of a function-in-extension and in the sense of a search of the mathematical function capturing this extension is not entirely new. Jevons (1877) discusses it using such terms as "empirical mathematical law" and "rational formula or function." He calls the controlled variable and the observed variable in an experiment "variable" and "variant." The first of these terms does not really refer to a function-in-extension obtained from an experiment, but to mathematical approximations to it. (The closest term for a function-in-extension in Jevons is probably the result of what he calls a "collective experiment." (See Jevons 1877, p. 447.))

Jevons' discussion of experiments brings out one aspect of the interrelation of the two different inductive tasks. In actual scientific practice, a scientist does not wait for the full function-in-extension before trying to find the corresponding mathematical function, nor treat the partial observations of the function-in-extension only non-mathematically, in contrast to the mathematical function sought for in the identificatory half of the inductive task. Instead, a scientist sets up mathematical approximations to the function-in-extension. When new observations come in, such a mathematical approximation is adjusted so as to take them into account, too. It is apparently sometimes thought—or at least hoped—that these mathematical approximations converge in the limit to the right mathematical law, Jevons' "rational formula."

Some such idea underlies the current theories of automated discovery. (See, e.g., Langley et al. 1987, Zytkow 1997, or Arikawa and Furukawa 2000.) These theories are of interest, but they do not embody a foolproof discovery method in the sense of a way of approximating asymptotically the true mathematical law. As we might say, approximating mathematically a function-in-extension does not necessarily yield in the limit the correct mathematical function. Hence the entire research project of automated discovery is subject to important conceptual limitations. *Sub specie logicae*, it flirts with a category mistake, insofar as it involves an attempt to reach new mathematical knowledge by utilizing ways of reaching new factual knowledge.

One cannot meaningfully speak of approximating a number of measurement results by a mathematical function unless this function belongs to some prescribed class of functions. Successive approximations can converge to the right function only if the true mathematical law belongs to this class or is a limit of functions belonging to it. The observed behavior of a function-in-extension can yield clues as to what a suitable class of functions may be. For instance, if the function-in-extension is obviously periodic, the relevant class might consist of trigonometric functions rather than, say, polynomials. But, in general, there is no absolutely certain method of selecting, *a priori*, a suitable class of functions.

This illustrates the difference between the two different experimental tasks. It also throws an interesting critical light on the entire project of automated discovery in science.

18. The Inseparability of Factual and Conceptual Knowledge

Another interesting feature of the conceptual situation revealed by the insights we have reached is a kind of inseparability of factual and conceptual knowledge. For instance, it was seen that both are needed to answer a perfectly ordinary *wh*-question. Any physicist who raises an experimental question in effect hopes for an answer that codifies both factual and conceptual knowledge.

We have to treat this inseparability carefully, however. Quine is often said to have pointed out the inseparability of factual and linguistic (and other conceptual) knowledge. If so, he is vindicated by the inseparability that has been identified in this chapter. But if so, he does not reach an adequate diagnosis of what is unsolved in this inseparability. To put the matter in the simplest possible terms, Quine has denied that there is any hard-and-fast distinction between the two kinds of knowledge to begin with. If this rejection is taken literally, it becomes inappropriate to speak of either inseparability or separability, for there is, according to such a view, no two things that could be separated from each other in the first place. The inseparability that has been diagnosed here is entanglement of the two kinds of knowledge in our epistemic practices, such as raising and answering questions. What is even more directly obvious, the two kinds of knowledge are distinguished in some cases by their logical form. The kind of conceptual knowledge that has been dealt with in this chapter is of the form "knowing who someone is" and its analogues for categories other than persons. In contrast, it is not clear that "knowing that" involves any conceptual knowledge. Thus, ironically, Quine's denial of any hard-and-fast difference between factual and conceptual truths has to be rejected for the very purpose of doing justice to inseparability that has been claimed to be one of Quine's insights.

This is not the end of the ironies of the situation. What was just pointed out is that factual and conceptual knowledge are, in the paradigm cases, different grammatical and logical constructions in which the notion of knowledge occurs. From this difference in construction it does not follow that a different concept of knowledge itself is unsolved in the two cases. On the contrary, drawing the very distinction between the two constructions with "knows" presupposes that this concept is the same in both. The ultimate distinction is between the reference system and the identification system mentioned earlier. In the formalism of epistemic logic, there is only one symbol "K" for knowledge, not a separate symbol for analytic and synthetic (conceptual and factual) knowledge. Hence Quine is, in a sense, verbally right in maintaining the inseparability of the two kinds of knowledge. But being right in this sense does not make Quine or anyone any wiser substantially. We can reach understanding and clarity only by analyzing the precise nature of this inseparability.

What has been done here is to clarify the distinction between factual and conceptual knowledge and then to argue that they are both nevertheless intertangled in an interesting way in scientific (and everyday) practice.

In all these different ways, the initially simple-looking logical insights expounded here have been seen to have important general consequences. The indispensability of mathematics in experimental science is an especially instructive case in point. In brief, we have seen how a great deal of philosophy of science can be distilled into a drop of logic.

References

Adam, Charles, and Tannery, Paul, 1897–1910, *Oeuvres de René Descartes*, published under the auspices of the Ministry of Public Instruction, L. Cerf, Paris.

Arikawa, S., and K. Furukawa, editors, 2000, Discovery Science (*Lecture Notes in Computer Science*), Springer-Verlag, New York.

Becker, Oskar, 1959, *Die Grösse und Grenze der mathematischen Denkweise*, Karl Alber, Freiburg.

Boër, Stephen and William G. Lycan, 1986, *Knowing Who*, MIT Press, Cambridge.

Burgess, John P., and Gideon Rosen, 1997, *A Subject with No Object*, Clarendon Press, Oxford.

Cassirer, Ernst, 1944, "Galileo's Platonism," in M. F. Ashley Montague, editor, *Studies and Essays in the History of Science and Learning Offered in Homage to George Sarton*, Henry Schuman, New York, pp. 277–297.

Cassirer, Ernst, 1910, *Substanzbegriff und Funktionsbegriff: Untersuchungen über die Grundfragen der Erkenntniskritik*, Berlin: Bruno Cassirer. Translated as *Substance and Function*, Chicago: Open Court, 1923.

Colyvan, Mark, 2001, *The Indispensability of Mathematics*, Oxford University Press, New York.

Field, Hartry, 1980, *Science without Numbers*, Princeton University Press, Princeton NJ.

Friedman, Michael, 1999, *Reconsidering Logical Positivism*, Cambridge University Press, New York.

Hermann, Armin, 1971, *The Genesis of Quantum Theory*, MIT Press, Cambridge.

Hilpinen, Risto, 1995, "Peirce on Language and Reference," in Kenneth L. Ketner, editor, *Peirce and Contemporary Thought: Philosophical Inquiries*, Fordham University Press, New York, pp. 272–303.

Hintikka, Jaakko, 2006, "Ta Meta Ta Metaphysika: The Argumentative Structure of Aristotle's Metaphysics," in Vesa Hirvonen, Toivo J. Holopainen, and Miira Tuominen, editors, *Studies in the History of Philosophy in Honour of Simo Knuuttila*, Brill, Leiden, pp. 41–53.

Hintikka, Jaakko, 2003, "A Second-Generation Epistemic Logic and Its General Significance," in Vincent Hendricks et al., editors, *Knowledge Contributors*, Kluwer Academic, Dordrecht, pp. 33–56. And as Chapter 3 in this volume.

Hintikka, Jaakko, 2002(a), "A Distinction Too Few or Too Many? A Vindication of the Analytic vs. Synthetic Distinction," in Carol C. Gould, editor, *Constructivism and Practice: Toward a Historical Epistemology*, Rowman & Littlefield, Lanham, Maryland, pp. 47–74.

Hintikka, Jaakko, 2002(b), "Intuitionistic Logic as Epistemic Logic," *Synthese*, vol. 127, pp. 7–19.

Hintikka, Jaakko, 2000, "Knowledge of Functions in the Growth of Mathematical Knowledge," in E. Grosholz and H. Breger, editors, *The Growth of Mathematical Knowledge*, Kluwer Academic, Dordrecht, pp. 1–15.

Hintikka, Jaakko, 1999, *Inquiry as Inquiry: A Logic of Scientific Discovery*, Selected Papers V, 47–90, Dordrecht: Kluwer Academic Publishers.

Hintikka, Jaakko, 1998, "Ramsey Sentences and the Meaning of Quantifiers," *Philosophy of Science*, vol. 65, pp. 289–305.

Hintikka, Jaakko, 1997, "Three Dogmas of Quine's Empiricism," *Revue Internationale de Philosophie*, vol. 51, pp. 457–477.

Hintikka, Jaakko, 1996(a), *The Principles of Mathematics Revisited*, Cambridge University Press, New York.

Hintikka, Jaakko, 1996(b), "Knowledge Acknowledged," *Philosophy and Phenomenological Research*, vol. 56, pp. 251–275.

Hintikka, Jaakko, 1993, "The Concept of Induction in Light of the Interrogative Approach to Inquiry," in John Earman, editor, *Inference, Explanation, and Other Frustrations*, University of California Press, Berkeley and Los Angeles, pp 23–43. Reprinted in Hintikka 1999, pp. 161–181.

Hintikka, Jaakko, 1992, "Independence-Friendly Logic as a Medium of Knowledge Representation and Reasoning about Knowledge," in S. Ohsuga et al., editors, *Information Modelling and Databases*, IOS Press, Amsterdam, pp. 258–265.

Hintikka, Jaakko, 1992, "Knowledge-Seeking by Questioning," in J. Dancy and E. Sosa, editors, *A Companion to Epistemology*, Blackwell, Oxford, pp. 241–244.

Hintikka, Jaakko, 1989, "Cartesian Cogito, Epistemic Logic, and Neuroscience: Some Surprising Interrelations," in Jaakko Hintikka and Merrill B. Hintikka, *The Logic of Epistemology and the Epistemology of Logic*, Kluwer Academic, Dordrecht, pp. 111–136.

Hintikka, Jaakko, 1980, "Aristotelian Induction," *Revue Internationale de Philosophie*, vol. 34, pp. 133–144.

Hintikka, Jaakko, and Ilpo Halonen , 1992, "Semantics and Pragmatics for Why-Questions," *Journal of Philosophy*, vol. 92, pp. 636–657. Reprinted in Hintikka 1999.

Hintikka, Jaakko, Ilpo Halonen, and Arto Mutanen, 1999, "Interrogative Logic as a General Theory of Reasoning," in Jaakko Hintikka, 1999.

Hintikka, Jaakko, and Unto Remes, 1974, *The Method of Analysis*, D. Reidel, Dordrecht.

Jevons, W. Stanley, 1877, *The Principles of Science*, second edition, London and Oxford. Reprinted, Dover Publications, New York, 1958.

Kripke, Saul, 1972, *Naming and Necessity*, Harvard University Press, Cambridge.

Kuhn, Thomas, 1978, *Black-Body Theory and the Quantum Discontinuity*, 1894–1912, Clarendon Press, Oxford.

Langley, Pat, Herbert A. Simon, Gary L. Bradshaw, and Jan R. Zytkow, 1987, *Scientific Discovery: Computational Explorations of the Creative Process*, MIT Press, Cambridge.

Laugwitz, Detlef, 1996, *Bernhard Riemann, 1820–1866*, Birkhäuser, Basel and Boston.

Mach, Ernst, 1960, *The Science of Mechanics: A Critical and Historical Account of Its Development*, Open Court, La Salle, Illinois. Original 1883, *Die Mechanik in ihrer Entwickelung*, F. A. Brockhaus, Leipzig.

Peirce, Charles S., 1931–35, *Collected Papers of Charles Sanders Peirce*, edited by Charles Hartshorne and Paul Weiss, Harvard University Press, Cambridge.

Pour-El, Marian B., and Jonathan I. Richards, 1989, *Computability in Analysis and Physics*, Springer-Verlag, Heidelberg and New York.

Quine, W. V., 1981(a), *Theories and Things*, Harvard University Press, Cambridge.

Quine, W. V., 1981(b), "Success and Limits of Mathematization," in *Quine* 1981 (a), pp. 148–155.

Steiner, Mark, 1998, *The Applicability of Mathematics as a Philosophical Problem*, Harvard University Press, Cambridge.

Wigner, Eugene, 1960, "The Unreasonable Effectiveness of Mathematics in Natural Science," *Communications in Pure and Applied Mathematics*, vol. 13, pp. 1–14. (Reprinted in Eugene Wigner: Symmetries and Reflections, Indiana University Press, Bloomington, 1967, pp. 222–237).

Youschkevich, A. P., 1977, "The Concept of Function up to the Middle of the 19th Century," *Archive for the History of Exact Sciences*, vol.16, pp. 37–85.

Zytkow, Jan, editor, 1997, *Machine Discovery*, Kluwer Academic, Dordrecht. Reprinted from *Foundations of Science*, vol. 1, no. 2, 1995/96.

6

Systems of Visual Identification in Neuroscience

Lessons from Epistemic Logic

Jaakko Hintikka and John Symons

The following analysis shows how developments in epistemic logic can play a non-trivial role in cognitive neuroscience. These obtain a striking correspondence between two modes of identification, as distinguished in the epistemic context, and two cognitive systems distinguished by neuroscientific investigation of the visual system (the "where" and "what" systems). It is argued that this correspondence is not coincidental, and that it can play a clarificatory role at the actual working levels of neuroscientific theory.

1. Introduction

While most work in neuroscience is conducted at the cellular and sub-cellular level,[1] brain research that catches the eye of philosophers is likely to come from a relatively recent interdisciplinary hybrid known as "cognitive neuroscience." Explanations from cognitive neuroscience are of interest to philosophers since they offer the possibility of connecting brain and behavior through the specification of the information processing properties of parts and processes of the brain. However, despite the prominence of the information-processing approach in the brain and behavioral sciences, it is difficult to know exactly what cognitive neuroscientists mean by "information." Historically, contexts in which this term has been given a precise definition include the so-called mathematical theory of communication, the theory of semantic information

---

[1] As John Bickle recently noted, a brief "perusal of this year's *Society for Neuroscience Abstracts* volume (cataloguing the 13,000+ slide and poster presentations at the year's meeting) reflects how intracellular, molecular, and biochemical mainstream neuroscience has become" (Bickle 2001, 468).

We would like to thank Bill Bechtel, John Bickle, Daniel Dennett, Jacques Dubucs, Juliet Floyd, Aaron Garrett, Shahid Rahman, and Lucia Vaina for comments on earlier drafts of this chapter. We would also like to thank two anonymous referees for very useful suggestions.

of Carnap and Bar-Hillel, and later the theories of informational complexity associated with Kolmogorov and Solomonoff. Most uses of the term "information" by cognitive scientists and neuroscientists conform to none of these three contexts.

Philosophers frequently complain of a lack of precision in scientific uses of the notion of information. For example, Fred Dretske notes: "Its use in telecommunications and computer science gives [the notion of information] a tough brittle and technical sound, and yet it remains spongy, plastic and amorphous enough to be serviceable in cognitive and semantic studies" (1981, ix). Like Dretske, Ken Sayre points out that uses of the term "information" in cognitive science are almost never connected with the mathematical definition of information as provided by Shannon and Weaver (1976).[2]

Even though the term as it is used in the brain and behavioral sciences is not well-defined, it plays a crucial role in scientific theory and practice. In addition to providing a putative theoretical connection between the goings on in the brain and intentional notions (belief, desire, representation, and the like), assumptions with respect to the nature, function, and flow of information can also be seen as shaping the scientific investigation and characterization of those same goings on in the brain itself. This chapter focuses on the concrete effect of presuppositions regarding information rather than the broader philosophical issues traditionally featured in discussions of information. Specifically, our argument suggests that errors at the conceptual level have consequences for the interpretation of empirical phenomena. While a wholesale revision of the way cognitive scientists have used the notion of information may be in order, our ambitions here are more modest. In this chapter, we focus on a particular research tradition in the brain and behavioral sciences, the so-called two-pathways approach to the visual system, and in so doing we argue that a mistaken conception of information has had a misleading effect on research.[3]

---

[2] One crucial and often ignored aspect of the mathematical theory of communication is that it deals with the statistical characteristics of a collection of messages rather than with the informational content of messages themselves. According to information theorists, no message is informative by itself, insofar as informational content is the product of the relationship between a message and the probability of other messages. The problem of the holism of informational measures leads to basic difficulties for any attempt to apply the mathematical theory of communication to cognitive science insofar as it conflicts with the basic assumptions of the kind of hierarchical and modular models of perceptual structures traditionally employed in cognitive science.

[3] It is difficult to underestimate the importance of the information-processing approach in the brain and to recent studies of the visual system. Historically, David Marr's work (See Marr 1982) helped to orient the brain sciences toward the information-processing approach by seeming to provide a bridge between computational analyses and the neuroscience of the visual system. In the early pages of his classic text, David Marr spoke for a developing consensus in cognitive science with his claim that "[v]ision is, first and foremost, an information processing task" (1982, p. 3).

While the two-pathways model of visual identification features prominently in most introductory textbooks and is often lauded as one of the great achievements of cognitive neuroscience, the approach continues to be a topic of considerable disagreement in the scientific community. Our analysis should not be read as an endorsement of any particular alternative to the textbook two-pathways model.[4] Rather than intervening in an ongoing debate in the cognitive neuroscience of vision, this chapter presents a far more general lesson about the nature of the notion of information. If our analysis is correct, then one of the basic assumptions in the brain sciences—namely, the notion that the brain traffics in different "kinds" of information—should be scrapped.

2. The "Where" and "What" Systems

While cognitive neuroscientists may have no real underlying theory of informational measure, there is one important point of agreement among them. Modern theories of perception, especially modern theories of vision, can be found to place great importance on distinctions between *kinds* of information. But what precisely does this almost universally accepted approach to information mean?

To answer this question it is important to avoid the temptation of projecting treatments of information from cognitive science or philosophy onto the activity of contemporary neuroscientists. For instance, neuroscientists, as opposed to traditional cognitive scientists, equivocate on whether information specifies the content of information-processing activity. Similarly, in neuroscience it would be difficult to find a practicing scientist who believes in the kind of informational encapsulation that we find in Jerry Fodor's work. Functional specialization in neuroscience has almost nothing in common with modularity in Fodor's sense (1983). Rather than arguing that functionally specific areas of cortex are informational modules, neuroscientists usually present the issue in far more modest, but perhaps more complicated, terms. Functionally specialized regions of the brain are said to be sensitive to information of different *kinds*. So, for example, a region of cortex might be described as being specialized for processing edge information or for information pertinent to face recognition.

While use of the term "information" in neuroscience is certainly vague, we can assume general agreement on one point. This one relatively stable point is the notion that there are different kinds of information in the brain, and that the difference in kind is relevant to scientific investigation and explanation. So, rather than beginning with a philosophical account of information processing (such as Fodor's), which has had only the most marginal influence on real neuroscience, a useful analysis of the concept of information as it actually

---

[4] Given the vast literature, our history of the topic will inevitably remain incomplete. However, this shortcoming is irrelevant to the task at hand.

functions in scientific theory and practice should begin from this basic point of consensus.[5]

To demonstrate the importance of this consensus, it is useful to examine a real dispute in neuroscience. One of the most significant and well-accepted theoretical results in contemporary neuroscience is the idea that visual processing is split into two relatively separate functional processes, the "where" pathway and the "what" pathway. Roughly speaking, the "where" system governs such things as spatial orientation and the location of objects in visual space (including prominently one's own body), as well as the relations of objects in visual space. The "what" system, by contrast, governs the identification of objects in the usual sense of identification.

The "where" and "what" systems in visual perception came to the fore through the study of the effects of brain injuries of various kinds on the behavior of people and animals. The specific distinction between "where" and "what" systems was made largely on the basis of behavioral deficits in patients suffering from damage to the ventral and dorsal extrastriate cortex. These behavioral deficits have been characterized in roughly the same terms for almost one hundred years. So, for example, in the early part of the twentieth century, the Irish neurologist Gordon Morgan Holmes (1918) described patients who could perceive and identify objects, while at the same time being unable to reach for, or properly locate, these objects in space.

Since at least the late 1960s, researchers have noticed a relationship between these two cognitive functions and damage to particular anatomical locations.[6] Following Ungerleider and Mishkin (1982) scientists now widely acknowledge (at least in very general terms) that lesions in the parietal cortex result in disturbances of the "where" system, whereas lesions in the posterior and inferior temporal cortex results in disturbances of the "what" system. This correlation between functional and anatomical distinctions is, by and large, unproblematic. So, in a sense, the "where" and "what" distinction presents a clear instance of a successful functional correlation in neuroscience. Damage to particular areas of the brain predictably result in deterioration of certain patterns of behavior. However, neuroscience has a wider theoretical ambition

---

[5] We are grateful to an anonymous referee for pointing out that for most neuroscientists, the term "module" is more often associated with Mountcastle's (1980) work than Fodor's.

[6] See Vaina 1990 for a discussion of the history and prehistory of this distinction in the anatomical context. The "where" and "what" taxonomy for cognitive systems has had a long and fascinating history. However, we will confine our discussion of the history to the recent past, focusing on articulations of the two systems stemming from Ungeleider, Mishkin, and colleagues' work in the early 1980s. We therefore cannot address earlier efforts to understand the distinction in neuroscientific terms. Most notably, in the 1960s, researchers localized the "where" and "what" systems *primarily* in the geniculostriate and tectofugal structures respectively (see Schneider 1969 and Trevarthen 1968). This approach is now widely regarded as having been superseded by more recent work. Nevertheless, the lessons that can be drawn from an analysis of more recent work can also be taken to apply to earlier efforts.

than simply to generate a catalog of correlations. In the case of the "where" and "what" pathways, as in so many other instances of well-established functional correlations, the functional correlation itself becomes a phenomenon that demands an explanation.

Given the influence of cognitive science, it was natural that neuroscientists would turn to explanations of the distinction in terms of the flow and processing of information. The two pathways are thought of as conveying two different kinds of information. In much of the recent discussion of visual perception, it has been assumed that "where" information and "what" information is conveyed along distinct neural pathways leading from the eyes to different centers in the cortex where the two functional systems seem to be implemented. The "kinds of information" approach has had an important effect on the search for a neural mechanism to support the distinction.

One of the controversial consequences of this approach to the "where" and "what" distinction is what we shall call the *P and M model* of visual identification. This choice of abbreviations is motivated by the widely accepted correlation of the "where" and "what" distinction with a division between retinal projections to the parvocellular (P) and magnocellular (M) regions of the lateral geniculate nucleus (LGN). This is a controversial account of the mechanisms underlying the "where" and "what" distinction, however. It is not universally accepted—for example, Semir Zeki and others have already criticized what we are calling the P and M model on anatomical and physiological grounds. (Zeki 1988 and 1993.) Of course, the present argument proceeds along different lines.

3. Two Systems and Behavior

Textbook presentations of the "where" and "what" pathways describe them as beginning at the third layer of cells in the retina: the ganglion cells. Axons from the ganglion cells form the optic nerve. These cells project to many different target regions of the brain.[7] However, for the purposes of the two-pathways discussion, the crucial retinal projections from the dorsal region of the LGN are divided into those that end up in the parvocellular (P) and magnocellular (M) regions of the LGN. M cells are most easily distinguished from P cells by their size; M cells are large, whereas P cells are small. Beyond this, these cells are widely interpreted as informationally specialized for location, size, and spatial information in the case of the magnocellular ganglion cells, and for color and contrast in the case of the parvocellular pathway. (Livingstone and Hubel 1987.)

---

[7] Milner and Goodale (1995) and Palmer (1999) describe the numerous connections and projections that retinal cells make to the rest of the brain. While the most widely studied projections that the retinal cells make are to the lateral geniculate nuclei, there are important connections to the superior colliculus, the pulvinar nucleus of the thalamus, and so on.

This initial division of informational labor has been understood as the beginning of a distinction that continues beyond the lateral geniculate nuclei and on into the cortical areas of the brain that subserve visual cognition. From here, the pathways are thought to divide into dorsal and ventral streams. The ventral stream, going from striate cortex into the posterior temporal cortex, is thought to be responsible for object recognition. The dorsal stream, going from pre-striate cortex into the posterior parietal cortex, is thought to be responsible for the perception of spatial relations among objects. Mishkin, Ungerleider, and Macko's (1983) account of the distinction in the rhesus monkey provides the classic portrayal of this latter half of the information-processing stream. Their account of the distinction in the monkey served as the basis for the later extension of the distinction all the way back to the M and P cells by Livingstone and Hubel.

Our simplified account of the "where" and "what" systems might give one the impression that the actual order of discovery was reversed. It is important to note that Ungerleider and Mishkin's correlation of the anatomical and functional distinction came before Livingstone and Hubel filled in the story from the retina to V1. So, in a sense, the P and M model looks like a natural extension of proposals that resulted from Ungerleider and Mishkin's studies of the "where" and "what" pathways in the rhesus monkey (1982).[8]

In order to complete our account of what we have called the P and M model of the two modes of identification in visual cognition, it is necessary to examine the most problematic extension of Ungerleider and Mishkin's analysis—namely, Livingstone and Hubel's proposal that the "where" and "what" pathways are distinguishable all the way back to the retina. The basic idea is that the two pathways that Ungerleider and Mishkin identified have their origins in the distinction between M and P retinal ganglion cells. As described earlier, the magno system, according to Livingstone and Hubel, is sensitive primarily to moving objects and carries information about spatial relations in the visual world. The parvo system is thought to be important for analyzing the visual scene in detail. (Livingstone and Hubel 1987.) It begins in the third layer of the retina and ends in the P layers of the LGN. Livingstone and Hubel base their assertion that the P system picks out details on the principle that it has characteristics making it more suitable for form and color vision. Since the P and M layers of the LGN project to V1, Livingstone and Hubel concluded

---

[8] In their famous studies, Mishkin and Ungerleider systematically damaged the brains of rhesus monkeys in search of the areas of the brain responsible for different aspects of visual identification. Their investigations followed on prior work in rhesus monkeys by Pohl and others who laid the anatomical groundwork for the proposals by Mishkin and Ungerleider. By 1972, Mishkin had already understood work such as Pohl's as proof that the inferior temporal cortex participates mainly in the acts of noticing and remembering an object's qualities, not its position in space. (For some useful historical discussion of this topic see Bechtel and Mundale 1999.) Conversely, the posterior parietal cortex seems to be concerned with the perception of spatial relations among objects, and not their intrinsic qualities (Mishkin 1972).

that the "where" and "what" distinction is best understood in terms of the distinction between the P and M pathways.

The principal argument for the extension of the two-pathways doctrine back to the earliest stages of the visual system is the notion that something like the P and M model is the only way to preserve the informational independence that the "where" and "what" distinction is thought to require. The idea is that by tracing the origin of the two pathways back to the distinction between the parvocellular and magnocellular pathways from the retina to the lateral geniculate nucleus, one can clearly distinguish the two kinds of information that are thought necessary to the possibility of distinguishing from each other the two modes of identification that the "where" and "what" contrast involves.

However, as mentioned previously, the P and M model is quite controversial. For example, Zeki has shown that P type pathways are not exclusively tuned for color and form (1993). Likewise, M type cells are sensitive to color and form in addition to motion. He concludes that the extension of the two-pathways program is untenable. In support of Zeki's objections it can be argued that the informational distinction is the result of a misguided construal of the nature of visual identification. In particular, the idea that different modes of identification rely on different kinds of information is subject to conceptual criticism in addition to empirical counterevidence.

4. Two Kinds of Information?

In his "On the Logic of Perception" ([1969]1975), Jaakko Hintikka outlined a very similar distinction to the one under consideration here. That work systematically distinguished *physical* from *perceptual* methods of cross-identification. The same distinction could be characterized as a contrast between subject-centered and object-centered modes of identification. As we shall see, Hintikka's treatment of the logic of this distinction, which he later referred to as a distinction between *public* and *perspectival* modes of identification, is directly relevant to visual identification.

In the case of vision, consider the totality of visual stimuli a certain person (or automaton) receives at a certain moment in time. Inevitably, this stimulus will not specify a unique scenario as to what the situation is in the perceiver's visual space. Instead, it leaves a number of alternatives open as to what the case is. Thus the identification that is being considered here concerns the identity of an object (in the wide sense of any kind of entity) in the different scenarios that the perceiver's visual information leaves open. These alternatives are the scenarios between which the identification is to take place. Philosophical logicians often misleadingly call these scenarios "possible worlds." Instead, we will simply call them the "perceiver's visual alternatives" at some given moment.

The crucial fact for our purposes here is that identification of objects in these visual alternatives can happen in at least two different ways. In the most general terms possible, to identify a person or an object is to place him, her, or it in some framework or "map." In perspectival visual identification, this framework is provided by the subject's visual space. Thus, while the *perspectival* or *subject-centered* mode of identification employs, as it were, a coordinate system defined by reference to a particular perceiver or knower, there is nothing subjective or private about it. Instead, it relies on objective general principles and on the possible situations between which the world lines of identification are drawn. To illustrate this, consider what a person, Jane, sees at a particular moment of time. Let's assume that she sees a man standing in front of her, but that she does not see who the man is. The man standing next to Jane occupies a particular slot in Jane's visual space and can be individuated in such a way as to allow Jane to track him through various visual alternatives. In this case, we can call him one of Jane's "perspectival visual objects," even though this locution has to be used with caution.

Of course, this man happens also to have a name, a social security number, and many other features of his public persona by means of which he can be identified. Persons and other objects so identified can be called "public objects." Public identification thus uses, in such a case as the requisite framework, something like the social organization of the people in question.[9] Public identification constitutes another way to track a person through possible scenarios—namely, by reference to who that person is. Let's imagine that this man standing in front of Jane happens to be the mayor of El Paso. Jane may have numerous beliefs and opinions about the mayor without being able to identify the man standing in front of her as the dignitary. She cannot identify, solely by means of the visual information, the perspectivally individuated object standing before her as the publicly individuated celebrity whose name regularly appears in the newspaper and for whom she voted twice. This means that in some of the scenarios that are compatible with Jane's visual information, the good mayor is elsewhere in her visual space, or even outside it. This does not exclude the possibility that she knows who the man in front of her is on the basis of other kinds of information—for instance, by having been told who he is. It is also compatible with Jane's knowing who Mr. Cabarello (the mayor) is outside the particular visual situation, for example, with being able to identify Mr. Cabarello as a public object, which in this case comes close to knowing which public official he is. She can track him through political history, she holds opinions about his policies, and is she happy that he is her mayor.

What makes it possible to speak of just two modes of identification is the role that the visual (or other) stimulus plays for the subject at a particular time. Stimuli contribute to reducing the set of alternative scenarios; the more

---

[9] In other cases, the framework of public identification almost reduces to geography, as in typical Finnish family names, which originally indicated the location of a person's homestead. Vintanen was a person living next to a stream or virta, Mäkinen one who lived on a hill or mäki and so on.

information one has, the more narrowly restricted is one's set of alternatives. For instance, when the set of alternative scenarios is so narrow that in all of them a term picks out the same person, it becomes true to say that the perceiver sees who this person is or sees this person, depending on the mode of identification. In contrast, the identificatory relations between two different scenarios are independent of the factual information an agent happens to possess.

In more general terms, one can say that in public identification, one takes a visual object and places him, her, or it on one's map of public figures in a wide sense of the expression. When this happens by means of one's momentary visual information, we can say that the perceiver *sees who* or *what* the visual object is. In contrast, in perspectival visual identification, the perceiver takes a public object and places him, her, or it among one's visual objects. The colloquial expression for this kind of feat of identification is to say that the perceiver *sees* the (public) object in question, thus illustrating the semantical import of the direct object construction with perceptual verbs.

To sum up, the distinction between *public*, or *object-centered*, and *perspectival*, or *subject-centered*, modes of identification is thus clear in the case of visual perception. There one can use one's identificatory framework as the perceiver's visual space. Persons and bodies occupying the same slot in this visual space (in the different situations compatible with what the person sees) can be considered identical, even if that person does not see who they are. This results in a perspectival, or subject-centered, identification system. Note that by identity, two different (but interrelated) things can be meant—either identity within a scenario ("possible world") or identity across the boundaries of scenarios. What is being referred to here is the latter, which might more explicitly be called cross-identity.

As already indicated, the two methods of cross-identification correspond roughly to the truth-conditions of two different kinds of linguistic expressions. A person, say b, is a perspectivally identified entity for a subject on the basis of his momentary visual information if it is true that

Jane sees b   (1)

(For a minor qualification needed here, see (15)–(17) following). Now, other propositional attitudes have analogous direct-object constructions—for example:

Jane remembers b   (2)

Jane knows b   (3)

Their semantics is parallel with that of (1), albeit a shade less obvious. In the case of (2), Jane's first-hand memories of past events provide a framework—a framework unlike a play or perhaps a long-running soap opera—in which certain persons (objects, places, etc.), as it were, play a definite role. They are the

persons Jane remembers independently of whether she remembers who they
were. It is in this sense that (2) is parallel with (1). Likewise, Jane's first-hand
knowledge, alias acquaintance, of persons, places, events, and so on creates a
framework with which she can place certain people, objects, places, and so on
but not others. In this way, (3) receives a meaning that is perhaps less clear than
that of (1)–(2), but in any case is parallel with what (1)–(2) express. For the
public mode of cross-identification, the analogous identificatory statements
are:

Jane sees who b is	(4)
Jane remembers who b is	(5)
Jane knows who b is	(6)

The criteria of identification here are the same *mutatis mutandis* as in the case
of (1).

5. Epistemic Logic and Cross-Identification

It is instructive to express statements (1)–(6) and others like them in an explicit
notation that brings out their logical form. This can be done by using the usual
first-order quantifiers. Now, in any logic, the values of quantified variables must
be well-defined individuals. Since we are speaking of them as elements of different scenarios, this presupposes that they can be identified between different
scenarios—in other words, that some particular mode of cross-identification
is assumed to be given. But this makes quantifiers, when used in the context
of cognitive concepts such as seeing, perceiving, remembering, and knowing,
relative to a method of identification. Since we are dealing with two different
modes of identification in the case of visual cognition, we must use two pairs
of quantifiers corresponding to perspectival and public identification. Hence,
if the public quantifiers are $(\exists x)$, $(\forall y)$, and the perspectival ones (Ex), (Ay),
then the formal counterparts to (4)–(6) are:

$(\exists x)$ Jane sees that $(b = x)$	(7)
$(\exists x)$ Jane remembers that $(b = x)$	(8)
$(\exists x)$ Jane knows that $(b = x)$	(9)

The last one of these will be abbreviated as

$$(\exists x)\, K_{Jane}\, (b = x) \tag{9'}$$

More generally, we obtain in this way an analysis of constructions of the form
knows plus a *wh*-clause (subordinate *wh*-question). For instance:

Jane knows who won the election	(10)

has the counterpart

$$(\exists x)\, K_{Jane}\, (x \text{ won the election}) \tag{11}$$

By contrast (1)–(3) are rough translations of the following:

$$(Ex) \text{ Jane sees that } (b - x) \tag{12}$$

$$(Ex) \text{ Jane remembers that } (b = x) \tag{13}$$

$$(Ex) \text{ Jane knows that } (b = x) \tag{14}$$

$$(Ex) \text{ } K_{Jane} \text{ } (b = x) \tag{14'}$$

However, this correspondence between (1)–(3) and (12)–(14) is not the only possible one. For example in the "translation" (12), "seeing b" is taken to require *recognizing* b—that is, seeing b as b. In the weaker sense in which "seeing b" simply means laying one's eyes on b, (1) should be expressed by

$$(Ex) \text{ } (x = b \text{ } \& \text{ } (Ey) \text{ } (\text{Jane sees that } (x = y))) \tag{15}$$

In the corresponding sense, (2)–(3) should be translated as

$$(Ex) \text{ } (x = b \text{ } \& \text{ } (Ey) \text{ } (\text{Jane remembers that } (x = y))) \tag{16}$$

$$(Ex) \text{ } (x = b \text{ } \& \text{ } (Ey) \text{ } K_{Jane} \text{ } (x = y)) \tag{17}$$

For instance, in (17), b is one of Jane's acquaintances even though she need not know b as d. Both pairs of quantifiers behave among themselves in the same way. For instance, from

$$K_{Jane} \text{ } S[b] \tag{18}$$

(where S[b] does not contain any intentional operators), we cannot infer either

$$(\exists x) \text{ } K_{Jane} \text{ } S[x] \tag{19}$$

or

$$(Ex) \text{ } K_{Jane} \text{ } S[x]. \tag{20}$$

These inferences can be vindicated however, by an additional premise, which for (19) is (9′) and for (20) is (14′). This treatment of the interplay of quantifiers and epistemic operators is easily generalized. A similar analysis can also be given of the identification of general concepts instead of individuals.

6. Formal Analysis Vindicated by Evidence

Applying this analysis of the two modes of identification to the context of actual visual cognition is relatively straightforward. To identify b in the perspectival sense means finding a slot for b among our visual objects—in other words, locating b visually. This means in effect being able to answer a "where" question. In contrast, identifying b in the sense of public cross-identification means being able to put b on the map of abstract impersonal knowledge. It means being able to answer a "who" or "what" question. This suggests strong parallels between the distinction between the two cognitive systems and the distinction between perspectival and public identification. This consilience can be extended *a fortiori* to the formal representations (7)–(20).

The appropriateness of this analysis can be seen from the fact that the functional manifestations of the two cognitive systems are precisely what we are led to expect on the basis of our analysis of the two methods of identification. This is shown vividly by subjects suffering from disturbances in the one or the other system. This identity of the semantical distinction between the two methods of identification and the two cognitive systems is so strong that such disturbances can be used to teach and to internalize the logical distinction between the two kinds of quantifiers. The most common type of disturbance is a failure to identify objects of a certain kind, for instance faces (prosopagnosia) or colors (color agnosia). When in (fortunately rare) cases a subject loses spontaneous visual object identification in general, the result is a patient like Oliver Sacks's "man who mistook his wife for a hat." (See the title essay of Sacks (1985).) This is precisely what the general-object counterparts to (1) and (12) express. Sacks's sensitive account of Dr P.'s affliction captures the difficulties faced by an otherwise normal man who is unable to determine the identity of common objects or familiar faces.

By and large he recognised nobody: neither his family, nor his colleagues, nor his pupils, nor himself.... In the absence of obvious "markers" he was utterly lost. But it was not merely the cognition, the *gnosis*, at fault; there was something radically wrong with the whole way he proceeded. For he approached these faces – even those near and dear – as if they were abstract puzzles or tests. He did not relate to them, he did not behold. (12)

Dr. P. was unable to visually recognize common objects, but he could make inferences based on certain clues that eventually led him to correctly identify the object in question. Again Sacks's account strikingly captures the affliction:

I had stopped at a florist on my way to his apartment and bought myself an extravagant red rose for my buttonhole. Now I removed this and handed it to him. He took it like a botanist of morphologygiven a specimen, not like a person given a flower.

"About six inches in length," he commented, "a convoluted red form with a linear green attachment."

"Yes," I said encouragingly, "and what do you think it *is*, Dr. P.?"

"Not easy to say." He seemed perplexed. "It lacks the simple symmetry of the Platonic solids, although it may have a higher symmetry of its own... I think this could be an infloresence or flower."

"Could be?" I queried.... "Smell it," I suggested, and he again looked somewhat puzzled, as if I had asked him to smell a higher symmetry." (12)

The smell of the rose prompts Dr. P.'s recognition. In another powerful example, Sacks describes Dr. P.'s complete inability to recognize a glove. Dr. P. offers sophisticated geometrical descriptions of the glove, but utterly fails to recognize the "continuous surface infolded on itself with five outpouchings" as a glove.

Since perspectival identification in the case of visual cognition relies on a subject's visual space, disturbances of such perspectival identification amount to failures to articulate one's visual space. Such disturbances have been described for generations. (See, e.g., Holmes 1919.)

But the disturbances of perspectival identification may be subtler, pertaining predictably not so much to the subject's ability, so to speak, to construct a visual space as to the subject's ability to use it as a framework of identification. This kind of failure may mean, for example, difficulties in using the concepts *left* and *right*, difficulties in using one's own body as a reference point, difficulties in pointing (ostension), and in some rare cases, misplacing oneself in one's own visual space.

7. Implications for Neuroscience

All this provides strong cumulative evidence for the identity of the distinction between the "what" system and the "where" system, and the distinction between the two kinds of identification exemplified by the distinction between two kinds of quantifiers. And this identity is in turn significant in that it enables us to read off conclusions concerning the two cognitive systems from their logical representations. In other words, we are now ready to tackle the question as to how the conceptual results outlined here are related to the anatomical findings and other neuroscientific results discussed previously. Clearly, the cortical differentiation that corresponds to the functional difference between the two systems is not really open to serious criticism at this point. This correlation between the two functional systems and cortical differentiation is, by and large, very strong.

However, there is more to be said here. Conceptually speaking, the most remarkable feature of the analysis of the two modes of identification is that only one notion of knowledge is involved in the two modes. This is true in more than one sense. As has been shown, all the different constructions in terms of knowledge can be analyzed without evoking more than one sense of knowing—namely, knowing that. This can be considered a major accomplishment of Hintikka's epistemic logic, in combination with the two-modes-of-identification principle. Moreover, the distinction between the two kinds of identification does not turn on any distinction between different sentences S in the construction $K_a S$ except, of course, for the presence of different kinds of quantifiers. Here, an important interpretational point is seen directly from the use of appropriate notation. The distinction we have here is a distinction between two principles of identification, not between two kinds of knowledge or information. It is not even a distinction between two different constructions involving knowledge, such as the distinction between *de re* and *de dicto* knowledge. It is a distinction between two kinds of identificatory frameworks to which one's visual knowledge can be related.

A fortiori, the information provided by different neuronal pathways to different cortical areas need not be differentiated in order for two modes of identification to be applied. This result is completely consonant with Zeki's empirical objections to the two-pathways doctrine. What the univocity of knowledge suggests is that knowledge "where" and knowledge "what" are both extracted from the same, or at least overlapping, information. This is eminently compatible with Zeki's suggestion, according to which "perhaps a far better way to look at this system is to accept that each area will draw on any source to undertake its specialized task" (1993, 194)

If one acknowledges the fact that the same kind of knowledge or information is involved in the two distinct identificatory frameworks, one's research programs in neuroscience will have to be reconsidered. It must be expected, for example, that identificatory systems will draw on many different kinds of available clues, rather than being restricted to one particular source or kind of information. One would also abandon the idea that different aspects of the stimulus to the visual array should be such that they can be traced through distinct neural pathways in the brain. As we have seen, the two streams should probably not be construed as two largely separate informational routes running all the way through the visual system. Instead, different areas will call on different components of input processing most useful for the kinds of action being initiated. Later areas in the system are dedicated to solving specific sorts of problems (e.g., coordinating limb movements) and extracting information relevant to those respective tasks from relevant earlier processes.

8. Conclusion

The foregoing analysis has shown that conceptual investigations can potentially have a non-trivial role in neuroscience. In the case of the visual system, we have argued that the striking correspondence between two modes of identification, as distinguished in the semantical context, and two cognitive systems distinguished by neuroscientific investigation of the visual system (the "where" and "what" systems), is not coincidental, and that it can play a clarificatory role at the most fundamental levels of neuroscientific theory.

References

Bechtel, William, and Jennifer Mundale, 1999, "Multiple Realizability Revisited: Linking Cognitive and Neural States," *Philosophy of Science*, vol. 66, pp 175–207.
Bickle, John, 2001, "Understanding Neural Complexity: A Role for Reduction," *Minds and Machines*, vol. 11, pp. 467–481
Dretske, Fred, 1981, *Knowledge and the Flow of Information*, MIT Press, Cambridge.

De Yoe, Edgar, and David Van Essen, 1988, "Concurrent Processing Streams in Monkey Visual Cortex," *Trends in Neuroscience*, vol.11, pp. 219–26.

Fodor, Jerry, 1983, *The Modularity of Mind*, MIT Press, Cambridge.

Hintikka, Jaakko, [1969] 1975, "On the Logic of Perception," in Jaakko Hintikka, *Models for Modalities*, Reidel, Dordrecht, pp. 151–184.

Hintikka, Jaakko, 1972, "Individuation by Acquaintance," in David Pears, editor, *Bertrand Russell: Critical Essays*, Doubleday, Garden City, New York, pp. 52–79.

Hintikka, Jaakko, 1962, *Knowledge and Belief*, Cornell University Press, Ithaca, New York.

Holmes, Gordon Morgan, 1919, "Disturbances of Visual Space Perception," *British Medical Journal*, vol. 2, pp. 230–233.

Kosslyn, Stephen, and Richard Andersen, 1992, *Frontiers in Cognitive Neuroscience*, MIT Press, Cambridge.

Livingstone, Margaret S., and David H. Hubel, 1987, "Psychophysical Evidence for Separate Channels for the Perception of Form, Color, Movement, and Depth," *The Journal of Neuroscience*, vol. 7, pp. 3416–3468.

Marr, David, 1982, *Vision*, W.H. Freeman, San Francisco.

Maunsell, John, 1987, "Physiological Evidence for Two Visual Subsystems," in Lucia Vaina, editor, *Matters of Intelligence: Conceptual Structures in Cognitive Neuroscience*, D. Reidel, Dordrecht, pp. 59–87.

Milner, A. D., and Goodale, M. A., 1995, "The Visual Brain in Action," Oxford: Oxford University Press.

Mishkin, Mortimer, Leslie Ungeleider, and Kathleen Macko, 1983, "Object Vision and Spatial Vision: Two Cortical Pathways," *Trends in Neuroscience*, vol. 6, pp. 414–417.

Mountcastle, Vernon, 1980, *Medical Physiology*, 14th edition, C. V. Mosby, St. Louis.

Palmer, S. E., 1999, *Vision Science: Photons to Phenomenology*, Cambridge, MIT Press.

Pears, David, editor, 1972, *Bertrand Russell: Critical Essays*, Doubleday, Garden City, New York.

Sacks, Oliver, 1985, *The Man Who Mistook His Wife for a Hat*, Summit Books, New York.

Sayre, Kenneth, 1976, *Cybernetics and the Philosophy of Mind*, Routledge and Kegan Paul, London.

Schneider, Gerald, 1969, "Two Visual Systems: Brain Mechanisms for Localization and Discrimination Are Dissociated by Tectal and Cortical Lesions," *Science*, vol. 163, pp. 895–902.

Shannon, C. E., and Weaver, W., 1949, *The Mathematical Theory of Communication*, University of Illinois Press, Urbana.

Shepherd, Gordon, 1994, *Neurobiology*, third edition, Oxford University Press, Oxford.

Shipp, Stewart, and Semir Zeki, 1989, "The Organization of Connections between Areas V5 and V1 in Macaque Monkey Visual Cortex," *European Journal of Neuroscience*, vol. 1, pp. 309–332, 333–354.

Trevarthen, Colwyn, 1968, "Two Mechanisms of Vision in Primates," *Psychologische Forschung*, vol. 31, pp. 299–337.

Ungeleider, Leslie, and Mortimer Mishkin, 1982, "Two Cortical Visual Systems," in D. J. Ingle, M. A. Goodale, and R. J. W. Mansfield, editors, *Analysis of Visual Behavior*, MIT Press, Cambridge, pp. 549–586.

Vaina, Lucia, 1990, "'What" and "Where" in the Human Visual System: Two Hierarchies of Visual Modules," *Synthese*, vol. 83, pp. 49–91.

Van Essen, David, 1985, "Functional Organization of Primate Visual Cortex," in E. Jones, editor, *Cerebral Cortex*, vol. 3, Plenum Press, New York, pp. 259–329.

Van Essen, David, and John Maunsell, 1983,"Hierarchical Organization and Functional Streams in the Visual Cortex," *Trends in Neuroscience*, vol. 6, pp. 370–375.

Wade, Nicholas, and Michael Swanston, 1991, *Visual Perception: An Introduction*, Routledge and Kegan Paul, London.

Zeki, Semir, 1993, *A Vision of the Brain*, Blackwell Scientific, Oxford.

Zeki, Semir, and Stewart Shipp, 1988, "The Functional Logic of Cortical Connections," *Nature*, vol. 335, pp. 311–317.

7

Logical Explanations

1. Deduction as Explanation

We are all familiar with the expression used as the title of this chapter. It suggests that logic is the medium of choice for the purpose of explanation. But is this really the case? If we are to believe the majority of contemporary philosophers, whether or not they have acknowledged the point in so many words, the expression is little better than an oxymoron. These philosophers reject, in some sense or other, the idea codified in the proverbial phrase that the proper engine of explanation is logic. For instance, they reject the idea that to explain something is to deduce it logically from something that does not need explanation. A vestige of the "logical explanation" idea was built into Hempel's covering law theory of explanation. (Hempel 1965.) According to Hempel, roughly speaking, to explain a fact is to subsume it under some general law. Alas, many philosophers have criticized the covering-law theory, not to say poured scorn on it, typically by producing more or less clear-cut counterexamples to it. One of the best known rivals to the covering-law model is the view according to which to explain an event is to point out its cause. If so, pure logic has little to do with explanation, and the title of this chapter would therefore embody a misconception.

Now I am on most occasions suspicious of the "metaphysics of the stone age" (to borrow Quine's phrase) that is fossilized in our ordinary language. However, in the case of the problem of explanation, philosophers would have been well advised to take the suggestions of the commonplace locution figuring in the title of this chapter more seriously. This chapter is a part of a broader project calculated to show, notwithstanding many recent philosophers, but in keeping with the presuppositions of my title phrase, that logic does indeed play an important role in explanations and in explaining. The insight on which this campaign is based is that a little logic is a dangerous thing—in other words, that the earlier attempts to bringing logic to bear on the problem of explanation have used only very shallow concepts and results. This puts an onus on me to provide a better account backed up by sharper logical results.

Some aspects of this project have been discussed on earlier occasions, and hence can now be dealt with relatively briefly. (See Hintikka and Halonen 2005, Halonen and Hintikka 1999, Halonen 2001.) The most fundamental insight here is that ordinary logical deduction can already be thought of as a vehicle of explanation in a perfectly good sense. The paradigm case here is, of course, ordinary first-order deduction. Its explanatory powers nevertheless cannot be seen from any old system of so-called rules of inference. Such rules are only required to preserve truth, sometimes merely logical truth. Hence it should not be surprising that these rules do not automatically provide explanations of why (or how) logical consequence relations obtain. In order to uncover these explanations, we can resort to what logicians call "interpolation theorems." Such theorems can be discovered and proved by transforming first-order logical proofs to some especially perspicuous normal form. As such a normal form, we can use a simplified version of Beth's tableau technique. The simplifications presupposed here are two: (1) to transfer formulas between the left and the right side, and (2) all formulas are supposed to be in the negation normal form. Then the table construction can be thought of as an experimental attempt to describe a model in which the premise F is true but the conclusion G is false.

Even though I am trying to avoid technicalities in this chapter, it is in order to spell out the basic idea of the logic of logical explanations. Such an exposition has been given briefly in Halonen and Hintikka (1999), but not as explicitly as the topic deserves. It is reproduced here in a slightly revised form.

As was indicated, I will use a particularly simple variant of the tableau method. It is characterized by the fact that in it, no movement of formulas between the left and the right side of the tableau is allowed. The negation-free subset of the tableau rules can be formulated as follows, with λ as the list of formulas on the left side of some sub-tableau and μ similarly as the list of formulas on the right side:

(L.&) If $(S_1 \ \& \ S_2) \in \lambda$, add S_1 and S_2 to λ.

(L.$\vee$) If $(S_1 \vee S_2) \in \lambda$, start two sub-tableaux by adding S_1 or S_2, respectively, to λ.

(L.E) If $(\exists x)S[x] \in \lambda$, and if there is no formula of the form $S[b] \in \lambda$, add $S[d]$ to λ, where d is a new individual constant.

(L.A) If $(\forall x)S[x] \in \lambda$, for any individual constant b, add $S[b]$ to λ.

It suffices, in fact, to restrict this rule to cases in which b occurs in the same sub-tableau.

Right-hand rules (R.&), (R. $\vee$), (R.E), and (R.A) are duals (mirror images) of these rules. For instance:

(R.&) If $(S_1 \ \& \ S_2) \in \mu$, start two sub-tableaux by adding S_1 or S_2, respectively, to μ.

Negation can be handled by the following rewriting rule (RR): Rewrite $\sim\sim$S as S; $\sim(S_1 \vee S_2)$ as $(\sim S_1 \ \& \sim S_2)$; $\sim(S_1 \ \& \ S_2)$ as $(\sim S_1 \vee \sim S_2)$; $\sim(\exists x)$ as $(\forall x)\sim$; and $\sim(\forall x)$ as $(\exists x)\sim$. By means of this rewriting rule, each formula can effectively be brought to a negation normal form in which all negation signs are prefixed to atomic formulas or identities. We will abbreviate $\sim(a = b)$ by $(a \neq b)$.

As derived rules (construing $(S_1 \supset S_2)$ as a notational variant of $(\sim S_1 \vee S_2)$), we can also have:

(L. $\supset$)   If $(S_1 \supset S_2) \in \lambda$, add $\sim S_1$ or S_2 to λ, starting two sub-tableaux.

(R. $\supset$)   If $(S_1 \supset S_2) \in \mu$, add $\sim S_1$ or S_2 to μ.

For identity, the following rules can be used:

(L.self =)   If b occurs in the formulas on the left side, add $(b = b)$ to the left side.

(L. =)   If S[a] and $(a = b)$ occur on the left side, add S[b] to the left side.

Here, S[a] and S[b] are like each other except that some occurrences of a or b have been exchanged for the other one. The corresponding right-hand rules (R.self =) and (R. =) are like (L.self =) and (L. =) except that = has been replaced by its negation $\neq$ and vice versa.

As we stated, it can be shown that if $F \vdash G$ is provable in first-order logic, it is provable by means of the rules just listed. A proof means a tableau that is closed. A tableau is said to be closed if and only if the following condition is satisfied by it: There is a bridge from each open branch on the left to each open branch on the right. Here, a bridge means a shared formula (it can be assumed to be an atomic formula or identity). A branch is open if and only if it is not closed. A branch is closed if it contains a formula and its negation, or contains $(a \neq a)$ on the left or $(a = a)$ on the right.

The completeness of our set of rules can be proved in the usual way. (This completeness holds even if (L.A) and (R.E) are restricted as indicated above.) If $F \vdash G$ cannot be proved by our rules, there is a pair of possibly infinite branches on the left and on the right without a bridge to which no further applications of the rules are possible. The formulas on the left and the negations of the formulas form (after the obvious applications of (RR)) what has been called a "model set" or "Hintikka set." Then, F and $\sim$G are true in the same model, and G hence does not follow logically from G. This is enough to show that if G follows logically from F, then $F \vdash G$ is provable by our rules.

In the interpolation theorem, we are given a tableau proof of $F \vdash G$ by means of the rules listed here. It is assumed in the new interpolation theorem, just as in Craig's (1957) well-known theorem, that neither $\sim$F nor G is provable. It can be assumed that F and G are in the negation normal form. The crucial question is how an interpolation formula is found on the basis of this tableau. For this purpose, it may be noted that, because of the assumptions just made, there must be at least one branch open on the left and at least one on the right. Since the tableau is assumed to be closed, there must be a bridge connecting each such pair of open branches. It can also be assumed that all the formulas are in the negation normal form.

Then the new interpolation formula can be constructed as follows:

Step 1. For each open branch on the left, form the conjunction of all the formulas in it that are used as bridges to the right. They can be assumed to be atomic.

Step 2. Form the disjunction of all such conjunctions.

Step 3. Replace each constant introduced (i) by an application of (L.E), or (ii) by an application of (L.A) from the right side to the left, by a variable, say x, different for different rules and for different applications of the same rule.

Step 4. Moving from the end (bottom) of the tableau upwards step by step, prefix ($\exists$x) in case (i) to the formula so far obtained. In case (ii), prefix ($\forall$x) to the formula so far obtained.

It can easily be proved that the formula I_L obtained in this way is always an interpolation formula in the sense of Craig's theorem—that is, we have $F \vdash I_L$ and $I_L \vdash G$. A proof to this effect will not be given here, however. The resulting new interpolation theorem is specified much more closely than Craig's (1957), who only requires that the non-logical constants of the interpolation formula all occur both in F and in G. Instead of a detailed proof, which the reader can easily construct, we will illustrate the nature of the interpolation formula by means of a couple of examples.

Consider first the following closed tableau (Tableau 1) and the interpolation formula it yields:

TABLEAU I

(1) ($\forall$x)L(x,b) IP (6) L(b,b) from (1) by (L.A)	(2) ($\forall$y)(L(b,y) $\supset$ m = y) $\supset$ (m = b) UC (3) $\sim$($\forall$y)(L(b,y) $\supset$ m = y) from (2) by (R.$\supset$) (4) m = b from (2) by (R. $\supset$) (5) ($\exists$y)(L(b,y) & (m $\neq$ y)) from (3) by the rewrite rule (7) L(b,b) & (m $\neq$ b) from (5) by (R.E)

	(8) L(b,b) from (7) by (R.&) Bridge to (6)	(9) m $\neq$ b from (7) by (R.&) Closure by (4), (9)

The interpolation formula is trivially

$$L(b, b) \qquad\qquad (1.1)$$

This example may prompt a déjà vu experience in some readers. If one interprets L(x,y) as "x loves y," b as "my baby," and m as "me," we get a version of the old introductory logic book chestnut. The initial premise (IP) says:

Everybody loves my baby (1.2)

and the ultimate conclusion (UC) says

If my baby loves only me, then I am my baby. (1.3)

Textbook writers cherish this example, because it gives the impression of expressing a clever, non-trivial inference. In reality, their use of this example is cheating, trading on a mistranslation. In ordinary usage, (1.2) does not imply that my baby loves him/herself. Its correct translation is therefore

$$(\forall x)(x \neq b \supset L(x,b)) \qquad (1.4)$$

which does not any longer support the inference when used as the premise. Hence the inference from the initial premise to the ultimate conclusion turns entirely on the premise's implying L(b,b). This is, in an obvious sense, what explains the inference. This explanation of the consequence relation is strikingly reflected by the fact that L(b,b) is precisely the interpolation formula.

In order to see that the explanatory role of the interpolation formula in this example is no freak, consider another example of a closed tableau (Tableau 2) and its interpolation formula. To enhance an overview of the tableau argument, we have not indicated where the different steps come from. (This is easy for the reader to ascertain, anyway.)

TABLEAU 2

(1) $(\forall x)((A(x)$ & $C(x))\supset B(x))$ IP		(3) $(\forall x)(E(x) \supset (A(x) \supset B(x)))$ UC	
(2) $(\forall x)((D(x) \vee \sim D(x)) \supset C(x))$ IP		(4) $(E(\beta) \supset (A(\beta) \supset B(\beta)))$	
(9) $(A(\beta)$ & $C(\beta)) \supset B(\beta)$		(5) $\sim E(\beta)$	
(10) $\sim(A(\beta)$ & $C(\beta))$	(11) $B(\beta)$ Bridge	(6) $(A(\beta) \supset B(\beta))$	
(12) $\sim C(\beta)$	(13) $\sim A(\beta)$ Bridge	(7) $\sim A(\beta)$	
(14) $(D(\beta) \vee \sim D(\beta)) \supset C(\beta)$		(8) $B(\beta)$	
(15) $\sim(D(\beta) \vee \sim D(\beta))$	(16) $C(\beta)$ Closure		
(17) $\sim D(\beta)$			
(18) $\sim\sim D(\beta)$ Closure			

The interpolation formula is, as one can easily ascertain,

$$(\forall x)(\sim A(x) \vee B(x)) \qquad (1.5)$$

But does it in any sense provide an explanation as to why the conclusion holds? In this example, the first initial premise says that whatever is both C and A is also B. But the second initial premise entails the premise that everything is C anyway. Hence the cash value of the initial premises is that if anything is A, it is also B. The conclusion says that if any E is A, then it is B. But any A is B anyway, in virtue of the initial premises. Hence the crucial component of the premises that suffices to imply the conclusion is:

$$(\forall x)(A(x) \supset B(x)) \tag{1.6}$$

which is equivalent to the interpolation formula (5). Again, the interpolation formula expresses the reason ("explanation") why the logical consequence relation holds.

The new interpolation theorem applies more widely than Craig's interpolation theorem. The same construction as was used in the argument earlier can be used to find explanatory interpolation formulas even when the premise F and the conclusion G share all the same non-logical constants, in which case Craig's theorem becomes empty.

An example will illustrate this. Let

$$F = (\forall x)(L(c,x) \supset (\forall y)(L(x,y) \supset \sim L(y,x)))$$
$$G = \sim(\forall x)((\forall y)(L(x,y) \supset \sim L(y,x)) \supset L(c, x))$$

If $L(a,b)$ is read as "a loves b," then F says that c loves only people whose love is always unrequited, while G says that it is not the case that c loves all such unfortunate folks. A tableau (Tableau 3) for $F \vdash G$ might look like this

TABLEAU 3

(1) $(\forall x)(\sim L(c,x) \lor (\forall y)(\sim L(x,y) \lor \sim L(y,x)))$ IP	(2) $(\exists x)((\forall y)(\sim L(x,y) \lor \sim L(y,x))\&\sim L(c,x))$ UC
(3) $\sim L(c,c) \lor (\forall y)(\sim L(c,y) \lor \sim L(y,c))$ from (1)	(7) $(\forall y)(\sim L(c,y) \lor \sim L(y,c)) \& \sim L(c,c)$ from (2)
First branch:	First branch:
(4) $(\forall y)(\sim L(c,y) \lor \sim L(y,c))$ from (3)	(8) $\sim L(c,c)$ from (7) Bridge to (6)
(5) $\sim L(c,c) \lor \sim L(c,c)$ from (4)	Second branch:
	(9) $(\forall y)(\sim L(c,y) \lor \sim L(y,c))$ from (7)
(6) $\sim L(c,c)$ from (5)—merges with the second branch	(10) $\sim L(c,\beta) \lor \sim L(\beta,c)$ from (9)
(11) $\sim L(c,\beta) \lor \sim L(\beta,c)$ from (4)	(14) $\sim L(c,\beta)$ from (10)
(12) $\sim L(c,\beta)$ from (11) Bridge to (14) ǀ (13) $\sim L(\beta,c)$ from (11) Bridge to (15)	(15) $\sim L(\beta,c)$ from (10)

The interpolation formula is seen to be equivalent to

$$I = (\forall y)(L(c,y) \supset \sim L(y,c)) \ \& \sim L(c,c) \tag{1.7}$$

This makes sense as an explanation of $F \vdash G$. For what (1.7) says is that c itself is a counterexample to the claim that c loves all people whose love is never requited.

Such examples bring out vividly the fact that the interpolation theorem is already by itself a means of explanation. The precise sense in which this is the case will be discussed later in this chapter.

An interesting perspective opened up by these results is the possibility of measuring the difficulty of proving a consequence relation $F \vdash G$ by means of the complexity of the interpolation formula I, as constructed by our rule. An especially important component of this complexity is the number of quantifiers. It can be seen to equal the number of individuals one has to introduce to the configuration of individuals that is being built on the left side of a tableau in order to see that the consequence relation holds.

But these explanations (and these examples) tell only half of the story. Besides the interpolation formula I_L defined earlier, we can form another one. Indeed, the instructions for forming I_L (Steps 1–3 earlier) are not left-right symmetrical. Indeed, I_L depends almost exclusively on the left side of the tableau, the only exception being the steps where a constant that has not yet occurred on the left side is imported into it by an application of (L.A). Another interpolation formula I_R can be formed as follows:

Step 1* For each open branch on the right, form the disjunction of all the formulas in it that are used as bridges to the left. They can be assumed to be atomic.

Step 2* Form the conjunction of all such disjunctions.

Step 3* Replace each constant introduced (i) by an application of (R.A), or (ii) by an application of (R.E) from the left side to the right, by a variable, say x, different for different rules and for different applications of the same rule.

Step 4* Moving from the end (bottom) of the tableau upwards step by step, prefix $(\forall x)$ in case (i) to the formula so far obtained. In case (ii), prefix $(\exists x)$ to the formula so far obtained.

It can easily be shown that the formula I_R so obtained is an interpolation formula. It can also be shown that $I_L \vdash I_R$.

One can say even more here. Not only does the logical consequence relation hold in the case of our interpolation formulas. It is always a *trivial* or *analytic* consequence relation, sometimes called a "surface consequence" or "corollarial consequence." (See Chapter 8 of this volume.) Without attempting an explicit definition of this notion here, it can be characterized intuitively by saying that such a consequence relation can be seen to hold without considering configurations of individuals other than are already considered in I_L or in $\sim I_R$.

The following example (Tableau 4) illustrates the relationship between I_L and I_R:

TABLEAU 4

(1) $(\exists x)A(x)$ IP		(3) $(\forall x)B(x)$ UC	
(2) $(\forall z)(A(z) \supset (\forall y)L(z,y))$ IP		(4) $(\exists z)((\exists y)L(y,z) \, \& \sim B(z))$ UC	
(5) $A(\alpha)$ from (1)		$B(\beta)$ from (3)	
		(10) $(\exists y)L(y, \beta) \, \& \sim B(\beta)$ from (4)	
(6) $(A(\alpha) \supset (\forall y)L(\alpha,y))$ from (2)		(11) $\sim B(\beta)$ from (10) Closure from (9), (11)	(12) $(\exists y)L(y,\beta)$ from (10)
(7) $\sim A(\alpha)$ from (6) Closure from (5), (7)	(8) $(\forall y)L(\alpha,y)$ from (6)		(13) $L(\alpha, \beta)$ from (12) Bridge to (14)
	(14) $L(\alpha,\beta)$ Bridge to (13)		

Here, (2) can be taken to say that anyone who has the property A loves everybody. (1) says that such a person exists. The disjunction of (3) and (4) says that either everybody is B or else some non-B is loved by someone.

In this case we clearly have

$$I_L = (\exists x)(\forall y)L(x,y) \tag{1.8}$$

$$I_R = (\forall y)(\exists x)L(x,y) \tag{1.9}$$

$$I_L \vdash I_R, \text{ i.e. } (\exists x)(\forall y)L(x,y) \vdash (\forall u)(\exists z)L(z,u) \tag{1.10}$$

This is, again, most natural. For as soon as there is some A loving everybody, obviously there every non-B is loved by him or her—unless everybody is B. Hence (1.10) in a natural sense explains why the consequence relation in question holds.

Moreover, to see this we need to consider only the two individuals x,y to see that the consequence relation holds. This matches the tableau argument earlier, where precisely two individuals α and β need to be considered.

This example (Tableau 4) suggests a number of further things that can be said about the two interpolation formulas and their interrelation. It also suggests a proof that I_L and I_R are both interpolation formulas in Craig's sense.

First, $F \vdash I_L$ can be proved by applying to the right side the duals of the quantifier rules that were applied in the proof of $F \vdash G$ on the left, and that prompted the introduction of an individual to I_L.

Second, $I_R \vdash G$ can be proved dually. Hence, what remains to be proved is:

$$I_L \vdash I_R \tag{1.11}$$

A proof of (7) can in this example be obtained in effect as a part of the proof of $F \vdash G$. In general, an explicit argument to show the provability of (1.11) can be obtained by induction on the length of the tableau proof of $F \vdash G$. We will leave the details to the reader as an exercise.

Such as argument will show that (1.11) is a trivial consequence in more than one sense. Its tableau proof will be no longer than that of $F \vdash G$, from which it is easily obtained.

The corresponding conditional:

$$(I_L \supset I_R) \tag{1.12}$$

can be shown to be a surface tautology in the sense of Hintikka (1970). (See also Chapter 8, in this volume.) Moreover, the argument from I_L to I_R can be considered a "corollarial" in the sense of C. S. Peirce. (See Hintikka 1983). These observations illustrate the sense in which the consequence relation (1.11) can be said to be "trivial" or "analytic."

But in what sense does the interpolation formula I_L provide an explanation of why G follows from F—that is, why G must be true if F is? Let us assume, for simplicity, that no individual constants occur in F or in G, and that F and G are in the negation normal form. The atomic sentences in each alternative branch describe a part of a possible scenario in which F is true. This scenario involves a number of individuals. Where do they come from? A look at the situation (see the L-rules shown earlier) shows that there are two kinds of such individuals. Some of them are introduced by existential instantiation. They are individuals that exist in a scenario in which F is true. They typically depend on other such individuals. These dependencies are what the Skolem functions of F codify. The introduction of these individuals hence amounts to an analysis of the dependence relations among the individuals in models of F. In any case, the individuals said to exist by I_L must exist in the particular scenario corresponding to the branch in question.

The other individuals are introduced to the configuration of individuals in the scenario in question by applications of universal instantiation with respect to individuals that occur on the right side of the tableau. They are introduced into the right side by right-side applications of universal instantiation. What is the intuitive meaning of such individuals? They instantiate "arbitrary individuals" in the models of G, individuals whose identity is not known to us. There is a notion that is not usually employed in logical theory but that is familiar from routine mathematical thinking and routine mathematical jargon. They are the unknown individuals used in the proof. If G is false, they are the individuals calculated to serve as counterexamples vouchsafing its falsity. Hence, if G turns out to be true even for such test case values of universally quantified variables, G must be true in any case (if F is true). Naturally one does know which individuals they are. Applications of universal instantiation on the left in a tableau constructor mean that we are applying to such unknowns the general laws we know hold in the relevant model of F.

Thus a scenario that corresponds to a branch on the left side involves two kinds of individuals. On the one hand, there are the individuals that must exist in the scenario in question. On the other hand, there are the "unknowns" of which we need know that they have to conform to the general truths prescribed by F.

Thus the left interpolation formula I tells us everything about the structures in which F is true that is needed to understand the consequence relation from F to G. Likewise, the right interpolation formula I_R tells us everything about the models of G that is needed to see the consequence. Seeing that $I_L \vdash I_R$ then completes the explanation. We can speak of "seeing" here because the validity of $I_L \vdash I_R$ can be established without considering any individuals already considered in I_L or in I_r. In other words, the validity of $I_L \vdash I_R$ can be seen by using merely propositional reasoning, rather like what happens in the *apodeixis* part of a proposition in Euclid. We can, as it were, argue about and the same the configuration in question without having to take into account anything else. Such reasoning is "analytic" in the etymological sense: It suffices to analyze the "data" of the given configuration or figure, without carrying out any "auxiliary constructions."

If such a "seeing" does not qualify as an explanation of why G must be true if F is, it is hard to imagine what could so qualify. Now it is known (and can easily be proved) that any logical consequence relation in the usual first-order logic can be proved by means of the simplified tableau method used here. Thus we have proved the first main thesis of the chapter. Each first-order logical proof of G from F can be transformed into a form where it provides an explanation as to why G must be true if F is. Logical proofs yield (or can be transformed so as to yield) explanations as to why the consequence relation holds between them. "Logical explanations" can be rightly so called.

2. The Structure of Explanation

Needless to say, not all actual explanations are "logical explanations" in this simple sense. To think so would be to hold an extreme form of what might be called the "covering-law model" of explanation. According to such a view, to explain what happens is to subsume it under a general law. This is an oversimplified view. From a general law alone preciously little can be deduced. A more realistic account is provided by Hintikka and Halonen (2005). Even C. G. Hempel, who is usually credited with (or blamed for) the covering-law model, acknowledged that further premises are needed in explanation. These premises are not general laws but are *ad explanandum* in the sense that they specify certain features of the explanatory situation, perhaps initial conditions or boundary conditions. Discovering them is typically the crucial part of the process of explanation, and typically consists in finding them. Their status might repay further study. For instance, it may be asked whether they are in the last analysis needed because general theories are normally applied, not to the universe at large, but to some actual or possible "system" (to use a physicist's word) within it. The role of boundary conditions is then to identify the system in question.

If these *ad explanandum* premises are A, the underlying general theory T, and the explanandum E, then T and A must together entail E. If so, A will entail $(T \supset E)$. Then the interpolation formula between A and $(T \supset E)$ will provide the explanation in the sense diagnosed earlier in the case of purely deductive explanation.

At first sight, this simple schema perhaps does not seem to throw much light on the nature of explanation. A closer examination nevertheless reveals several interesting things, only two of which will be mentioned here. First, assume for the sake of example that *an explanandum* E is an atomic sentence of the form P(b), and assume that the particular individual a is not mentioned in T but is mentioned in $A = A[a]$. Then we have:

$$A[a] \vdash I[a] \tag{2.1}$$
$$I[a] \vdash (T \supset P(a)) \tag{2.2}$$

Hence also

$$T \vdash (I[a] \supset P(a)) \tag{2.3}$$

and therefore (since a does not occur in T),

$$T \vdash (\forall x)(I[x] \supset P(x)) \tag{2.4}$$

Thus, a byproduct of a successful explanation is in this case a covering law

$$(\forall x)(I[x] \supset P(x)) \tag{2.5}$$

implied by the background theory T.

Second, let us assume that there are no individual constants in T, and that its quantifiers are all universal. Then the explanatory interpolation formula I_L has two kinds of ingredients, besides the usual logical notions. A number of individuals are mentioned then that have to exist in the models of $(T \supset E)$, hence of $(\sim T \vee E)$. Now $\sim T$ does not introduce any individual constants that might affect I_L. Hence all the other steps in forming I_L are applications of the general laws holding in the models of F to the "unknowns" introduced by applications of right-hand universal instantiations.

These results throw an interesting light on the logical structure of explanation. The general theory of explanation will not be pursued much farther here, however. A couple of general comments on this theory are nevertheless in order.

First, in what sense does a successful explanation yield new information? It is quite striking that one looks in vain for an answer to this simple question in the literature. Admittedly, on the account of interrogative explanation given earlier in this essay an explanation involves finding the *ad explanandum* conditions A that means acquiring new information. But surely a deductive explanation also yields new information in some sense. The question is: In what sense? Here the distinction between depth information and surface information made in, among other places, Hintikka 1970 and Chapter 8 in this volume, serves us well. The depth of information of the interpolation formula that codifies an *explanans* cannot be greater than that of the premise F. However, the increase of depth (i.e., in effect the number of individuals considered in their interrelations to each other) typically increases when we look for the interpolation formula, which enables the elimination of inconsistent alternatives and thus increases surface information. In other words, the surface information of a non-trivial interpolation formula can be greater than that of the premise The new information yielded by explanation is surface information. Indeed, explanation may be the most prominent example of the role of surface information in epistemology.

This observation has a corollary concerning the discussions among philosophers dealing with explanation in the last several decades. It is doubtful whether one can find there a single example or argument that involves an increase of depth or involves sentences whose quantificational depth is greater than one (or, at most, two). This means that this entire discussion has been conducted by reference only to the very simplest and least informative types of explanation. (For this discussion, see Salmon 1984 and 1989 as well as Schurtz (1995).) No wonder that this discussion has often had the aura of triviality about it. This is part of what was meant earlier by saying that previous analysts have used only a rather shallow logic.

However, this does not mean that even simple explanatory interpolation formulas cannot be suggestive. Once I was looking for an example for my students and happened to think of that old chestnut, the "curious incident of the dog in the night-time" in Conan Doyle. There, are *ad explanandum* premises say (i) that there was a trained watchdog in the stable, in brief $(\exists x)D(x)$, and (ii) that no dog barked at the thief, in short $(\forall x) D(x) \supset \sim B(x,t)$). The general truths about the situation are (i) that the master of all the dogs in stable was the stable master, in short:

$$(\forall x)(\forall y)((D(x) \supset M(y,x)) \supset s = y) \tag{2.6}$$

and (ii) that the only person a watchdog does not bark at is its master, in short:

$$(\forall x)(\forall y)((D(x) \& \sim B(x,y)) \supset M(y,x)). \tag{2.7}$$

The conclusion is that the stable master was the thief, in other words (symbols) $s = t$. The tableau for $A \vdash (T \supset D)$ that I constructed looks somewhat like this Tableau 5:

TABLEAU 5

(1) (∃x)D(x) (2) (∀x)(D(x) ⊃ ~B(x,t))	(3) ((∀x)(∀y)((D(x) & M(y,x)) ⊃ s = y) & (∀x)(∀ y)((D(x) & ~B(x,y)) ⊃ M(y,x))) ⊃ s = t
(4) D(δ) from (1) (5) D(δ) ⊃ ~B(δ,t) from (2)	(8) s = t from (3) (9) (∃x)(∃y)(D(x) & M(y,x) & s ≠ y) ∨ (∃x)(∃y)(D(x) & ~B(x,y) & ~M(y,x)) from (3)

(6) ~D(δ) Closure	(7) ~B(δ,t) from (5) Bridge to (17) and (19)	(10) (∃x)(∃y)(D(x) & M(y,x) & s ≠ y) from (9) (11) (∃x)(∃y)(D(x) & ~B(x,y) & ~M(y,x)) from (9)

	(12) D(δ) & M(t,δ) & s ≠ t from (10) (13) D(δ) & ~B(δ,t) & ~M(t,δ) from (11)

	(14) D(δ) from (12) Bridge	(15) M(t,δ) from (12)	(16) s ≠ t from (12) Closure
	(17) D(δ) from (13) Bridge	(18) ~B(δ,t) from (13) Bridge	(19) ~M(t,δ) from (13) Closure

Here I managed to surprise myself pleasantly. The left-hand interpolation formula I_L (which in this case equals I_R) is

$$(\exists x)(D(x)\& \sim B(x,t) \tag{2.8}$$

In other words, the solution of the problem—the explanation of what happened—lies in the fact that there was a watch dog in the stables that did not bark—which is the very key to the solution Sherlock Holmes offers to the police inspector.

Another comment is that there are different—conceptually different—elements in an explanation, even if we restrict ourselves to *why*-explanations. Even in the deductive case, we have two interpolation formulas with different characteristic properties. The left-hand formula I_L tells what individuals there are in models of F and which laws characterizing those models apply to which unknowns that together make those models also models of G. The right-hand interpolation I_R tells what unknowns there are in the models of G and which individuals in the models of F serve to provide the existence of the individuals that together make models of G include the models of F. The explanation results from putting these two together, in other words, from the validity of the

consequence relation $I_L \vdash I_R$—or perhaps from the obviousness of this relation. This gives us a further insight into the structure of deductive explanation.

When we move to empirical explanation, the explanations so far considered are given to us through the interpolation formulas for the consequence
relation:

$$A \vdash (T \supset E) \tag{2.9}$$

Such explanations tells us what it is about A that necessitates (jointly with the
background theory T) that E. But we can apply our interpolation theorem
instead to

$$T \vdash (A \supset E) \tag{2.10}$$

Then we obtain an account of what it is about T that necessitates a configuration
of individuals instantiating A to instantiate also E. This "what it is about T" is
typically what might be called a local law L, which shows what the more general
law T amounts to in the explanatory situation. Producing the interpolation
formula for (2.10) will qualify as an explanation in a perfectly good sense,
although in a sense different from the one in which an interpolation formula
for (2.9) produces an explanation.

It could even be thought that the task of explanation involves finding, not
only A, but L. For in some scientific explanations, and in even more everyday
explanations, the ultimate general theory T is not known, or for some other
reason cannot operate as a starting point of an explanation.

This suggests a way of looking at covering-law theories of explanation. They
can be viewed as results of failing to distinguish the two senses of explanation.
In the latter sense related to (2.10), explaining can indeed amount to the search
of a law that accounts for the connection between A and E. But this law need
not be of the form of general implication, and most importantly it does not
spell out what it is about the initial conditions or boundary conditions that
necessitates the *explanandum*.

In the former sense, related to (2.9), explaining does not mean looking for a
covering law or any other kind of general law or theory. Rather, an explanation
amounts to seeing what it is about a configuration of individuals that is a model
of A that makes it also a model of E. Such an explanation is, as can be seen
from the analyses presented earlier, in effect a dependence analysis. Causal
explanations can be considered a special case of such dependence explanations.
The fact that successful explanations in this sense produce as a byproduct
covering laws in the form of general implications does not mean that they are
the tools of explanation.

These results help to answer a question that has been discussed by some
philosophers: Are there explanations in mathematics? The first part of the
answer is: Of course, in the same sense as any non-trivial ("theorematic")
deduction involves an explanation. However, explanations by means of additional information is possible in mathematics only in the second sense, starting

from (2.10) and yielding a "local law." Explanations of the first sense, starting from (2.9) and yielding a covering law, are not natural in mathematics. Mathematical theorems are not "explained" by reference to initial conditions, or even boundary conditions.

3. "How Possible" Explanations

What has been found so far shows the importance of the role of logic in explaining why something is or was the case of why something happens or happened. My purpose in the rest of this chapter is to extend this insight into the role of logic to a still further kind of explanation. The most prominent type of explanation is explaining why. Indeed, explanations of this type are often identified with answers to *why*-questions. Sometimes we also speak of explaining how something happened. This is the type of explanation so far examined in this chapter. However, there is yet another kind of task that can be identified by speaking of explaining. That is the task not of explaining *why* something happened, but *how* it was *possible* for it to have happened.

Such explanations have been discussed in the philosophical literature of the last several decades. An interesting example is found, for instance, in von Wright (1971). But these discussions have not led to any clear-cut analysis of the notion of "how possible" explanations or to any other simple conclusion.

The first philosopher to discuss "how possible" explanations at some length seems to have been William Dray (1957). His overall thesis was that historical explanations do not conform to the covering law model. I will not discuss his arguments here. As a separate topic, Dray argued in his Chapter VI that there is a separate class of explanations that do not conform to the covering law model, either, but that differ from *why*-explanations. These he identified as explanations as to how something is possible. They are the subject of the rest of this chapter.

What is the logical structure of "how possible" explanations? How is it related to the logical structure of attempted "why necessary" explanations? Dray claims that "[t]he two kinds, in spite of the parallel drawn between them are logically independent in the sense that they have different tasks to perform. They are answers to different kinds of questions." (Op. cit. pp. 161–162.) The second statement of Dray's is undoubtedly true, but only pleonistically so, and it does not imply the first one. There is a sense more illuminating than Dray's in which his statement is not only off the mark, but diametrically wrong. In an important sense, attempts to answer "how possible" and "why necessary" questions are not only not "logically independent" but proceed precisely the same way.

This point should in fact be obvious to anyone who has internalized the tableau method in logic that was briefly explained earlier. For what is going on in an application of this method? On the surface, one is trying to show why G is necessary, assuming that F. The way in which this attempt proceeds was explained in Section 1. Under the surface of the usual formalizations of logic, what happens is an investigation into whether G can possibly fail to be true given F. Indeed, this is investigated by the most straightforward manner— namely, by trying to describe a scenario (situation, model, "possible world") in which F is true but G not. In a most literal sense of the word, this is what the tableau method amounts to. It is in an attempt to see whether it is possible for G to be false when F is true. One can easily see how such an attempt can in some cases yield an explanation as to how it is possible.

The difference between "why necessary" and "how possible" explanations is a difference, not in the process of an attempted explanation, but in the outcome of the attempt. In order to see this, consider first the simplest case— that of propositional logic. In this case, a rule needs to be applied to any given formula only one. Hence a tableau construction comes to an end after a finite number of moves. Then it can simply be checked as to whether the tableau closes or not. If it does, the conclusion G cannot fail to be true if the premise F is true. As was described in Section 1 above, we can then extract an explanation from the closed tableau as to why this must be so.

If the tableau does not close, there is a pair of branches on the left and on the right, neither of which contains a contradiction and which do not have a bridge. Then the attempted counter-model construction (description) has succeeded, as fully as it can do so within the confines of propositional logic. If one takes the set of negated or unnegated atomic sentences in the left branch in the pair of open branches without a bridge, plus the negations of negated or unnegated sentences in the right branch, one has a description of a situation (scenario, course of events) in which the premise F is true but the putative conclusion G not. This description shows one in an obvious sense how G could possibly be false even though F is true. As a special case, leaving G out of the picture, we can in this way show how it is possible for F be true. Thus, in this simple case, one and the same double-edged process produces both "why necessary" and "how possible" explanations, depending on its outcome.

In practice, a logical "how possible" explanation may even be simpler than a "why necessary" one. In order to reach the former kind of explanation, we do not have to complete the entire tableau and to verify that it is closed. It suffices to construct one branch on the left and one branch on the right as far as they go, and then to ascertain that they are not connected by a bridge. This often involves much less work than completing the entire tableau.

A simple example is offered by the question of whether the following inference is valid or whether it is possible for it to fail:

God exists if God is omnipotent. God can do everything if God is omnipotent. If God can do everything, God can make a stone too heavy for God to lift. But if God can make a stone too heavy for God to lift, then it is not true that God can do everything. Therefore God does not exist.

A partial tableau might look like this (Tableau 6):

TABLEAU 6

(1) (O ⊃ G) IP	(5) ~G UC
(2) (O ⊃ E) IP	
(3) (E ⊃ H) IP	
(4) (H ⊃ ~E) IP	
(6) ~E from (4) and (3)	
(7) ~O from (2) and (1)	

Here, only one pair of branches is constructed. Neither one need be continued, and neither of them closes. Since there is no bridge to connect them, it can be concluded that the putative inference is invalid—that is ~G can be false while all the initial premises (1)–(4) are true. Yet the construction of the entire tableau may involve depending on the order of tableau rule applications up to sixteen branches. This illustrates the way in which "how possible" arguments can be simpler than "why necessary" arguments, even though the two proceed by means of the same rules.

In the countermodel obtained from the open tableau just constructed, the following sentences are true: ~O, ~E, G. This countermodel thus provides an explanation of how the initial premises can all be true but the putative ultimate conclusion false. The answer is: For God to exist but not be omnipotent.

The results concerning the propositional logic case can be generalized. The tableau method can be used in the entire first-order logic. And the relation to explanation is there the same as in propositional logic, *mutatis mutandis*. The most conspicuous *mutandis* is that in first-order logic, the tableau construction need not come to an end after a finite, predictable number of steps. Hence the tableau technique does not yield a decision method. But if some minimal case is exercised in applying the tableau construction rules, the story has the same moral for the theory of explanation as in prepositional logic. (Actually, it suffices to require that no opportunities of construction rule applications remain unused forever.) Again, if the tableau closes, we obtain a "why necessary" explanation. Again, if it does not close, we have a pair of branches whose negated or unnegated sentences describe a scenario that provides a "how possible" explanation by showing how G could fail to be true even though F is. The only novelty is that these branches may be infinite. Hence a "how possible" explanation can in this way be reached in some cases only in the limit. (This already marks an interesting difference between the two kinds of explanation.)

An example may illustrate the way in which a "how possible" tableau proof can in fact produce an explanation in the form of a counterexample. How is it possible for Adam to be the only person who loves Adam but not the only person who loves himself or herself? The following tableau (Tableau 7) yields an answer:

TABLEAU 7

(1) $(\forall x)(L(x,a) \supset x=a)$ Initial premise		(3) $(\forall x)(L(x,x) \supset x=a)$ Putative ultimate conclusion
(2) $L(a,a)$ Initial premise		
(7) $L(\varepsilon,a) \supset \varepsilon=a$ from (1)		(4) $L(\varepsilon,a) \supset \varepsilon=a$ from (3)
(8) $\sim L(\varepsilon,a)$	(9) $L(\varepsilon,a)$ Bridge to (6)	(5) $\sim L(\varepsilon,\varepsilon)$ from (3)
		(6) $\varepsilon=a$ from (3)

It was easy to see intuitively what happens here. The newly introduced individual ε—we may refer to her as Eve—is supposed to be the counterexample—that is, the other individual who loves himself or herself. The tableau construction has in fact produced a mini-model to answer the initial "how possible" question. In the model, there are two individuals, Adam and Eve, both of whom love themselves, while Eve does not love Adam. In other words, the following sentences in this model are true:

$$L(a,a), L(\varepsilon,\varepsilon), \sim L(\varepsilon,a).$$

Dray may very well be right in saying that "why necessary" and "how possible" explanations are answers to different questions. From this it does not follow that they are independent, however. On the contrary, in the situations so far considered, they are reached by the same procedure. As we can put it, we have found that there exists a clear-cut logic of "how possible" explanations. Indeed, it is the same usual first-order logic as is used in "why necessary" explanations. (Some of the minor qualifications that this statement needs are discussed later in this chapter.)

As a simple corollary, we obtain an explanation of why "how possible" explanations do not involve covering laws in any size, shape, or form. It was seen earlier in the chapter that such covering laws emerge as byproducts of explanations why. The interpolation formula that in a sense serves as "the" explanation serves as the antecedent of the covering law. But a "how possible" explanation is at hand only when the explanation tableau does not close—that is, when such an interpolation formula does not exist. Insofar as one can speak of an *explanans* in the case of "how possible" explanations, such an *explanans* is not constituted by an interpolation formula but by the description of a scenario that in its entirety provides the "how" of a "how possible" explanation. Hence, "how possible" explanations do not produce or otherwise involve covering laws. To this limited extent, Dray is right.

But this is not the end of the story. There are conceptual differences between the two kinds of explanations, but they are subtler than what is at first obvious. In order to see one of them, let us return to the simple case of explanations by means of propositional logic. Let us assume that one has found, by means of the tableau method, an explanation of how G can be false even though F is true. Can one stop one's explanatory enterprise there and then? In an interesting sense, one cannot necessarily do so. For what happens if one analyzes one's atomic sentences further? Maybe they are not logically independent of each other. Perhaps they have quantificational structures that will create dependencies between them. This is the problem of the independence of atomic sentences that haunted Wittgenstein, although for other reasons. Of course, a closed tableau cannot be opened by analyzing the atomic propositions involved in it. Consequently, consequence relations are not affected by such emergent interrelations between atomic propositions. Hence explanations are like true love: They are forever. But "how possible" explanations can be destroyed by a further analysis of the concepts they involve.

The interesting point here is not that "how possible" explanations are less reliable or more tentative than "why necessary" explanations. The subtle insight is that they have conceptual presuppositions that "why necessary" explanations do not have. They depend on a kind of tacit completeness assumption. They presuppose that the conceptual analysis that is codified in the language in which the explanations are codified has uncovered all the relevant logical connections between our atomic sentences. This is not a factual assumption in the usual sense. It is not expressible in the language in which the explanations themselves are couched. It is transcendental in the sense that it deals with the conditions of the possibility of "how possible" explanations—or at least the possibility of their conclusiveness.

All of this can be extended as a matter of course to explanations by means of first-order logic. There, an analysis of the primitive non-logical predicates and functions sometimes creates dependencies between sentences and other expressions that can destroy a "how possible" explanation. Obviously, "why necessary" explanations cannot be so affected.

Again, the conclusiveness of "how possible" explanations depends on the completeness of the conceptual analysis codified in the selection of the basic non-logical constants of the language used in the explanation. This conceptual presupposition is undoubtedly what has led some philosophers to consider them, if not *sui generis*, then at least different in kind from "logical" explanations, perhaps instantiating understanding rather than explanation. It is true that this conceptual element is not present in "why necessary," but that does not imply that a different kind of reasoning and argumentation is involved. As a matter of fact, "how possible" explanations are often involved in purely scientific contexts, as will be emphasized later.

Furthermore, the same insights can be extended to interrogative inquiry. This is not surprising in view of the fact that such an inquiry can be thought of as being conducted in a format closely related to the format of tableau construction in deductive logic. Not only can we use modified tableaux as our book-keeping device, these tableaux have the same interpretation as in a deductive context. Again, a tableau construction can be seen as an attempt to describe a scenario in which all the premises are true but the conclusion is false. The difference is that now these "premises" include answers to questions. These answers are inserted to the left side. The fact that answers may be tentatively disregarded ("bracketed") does not affect this interpretation.

It follows that empirical "how possible" explanations are predicated on the same presupposition of conceptual completeness as deductive "how possible" explanations discussed earlier. They, too, have a conceptual component. Over and above this, they rely on a related but different presupposition. In order for an interrogative "how possible" explanation to be conclusive, it has to be the case that further questions will not make a difference to the outcome of the inquiry. This presupposition can be highly significant, both in theory and in practice. A small example illustrates this. At one time during the Cold War, the treasurer of the Finnish Social Democratic party, arriving on a plane from Sweden, was stopped at the customs at the Helsinki airport and was found to be carrying large sums of cash—not an offense by itself if only he had declared the money. When asked why he was carrying such large sums of cash, he explained that he could not have sent the money through the bank because it was the weekend and the banks were closed. This excuse was not very successful, however. The cartoonist Kari Suomalainen envisaged Lieutenant Colombo asking the treasurer: "There is just one thing that still bothers me. If it was the weekend and the banks were closed, where did you get the money from?"

Here we can see one more interesting conceptual peculiarity of "how possible" explanations. This peculiarity is more sweeping and more important than the presupposition of conceptual completeness that interrogative "how possible" explanations share with deductive "how possible" ones. For what restricts the asking of questions in inquiry is the need to have already established their presuppositions. This might seem to make the range of relevant questions manageable. However, yes-or-no questions do not have any non-trivial presuppositions. Hence it is not easy to be sure that all relevant yes-or-no questions have been raised.

How can we know whether the presuppositions of completeness are satisfied? What kinds of assumptions could guarantee that they are satisfied? There does not seem to be any discussion found in the literature that addresses this question in so many words. Some considerations might nevertheless be relevant here. In some sufficiently broad sense, the evaluation of the basic concepts one is using is related to the problem of assigning prior probabilities to the different possibilities one's language can be used to specify. Hence the same considerations should be applicable in both cases.

More specifically, theorists of artificial intelligence have studied a type of reasoning that seems to be related to the completeness question raised here. It is known as "reasoning by circumscription." (For more on this, see McCarthy 1980, Lifschitz 1994.) One way of looking at it is to think of it as enthymemic reasoning from certain given premises. The additional tacit assumption characteristic of circumscription is that these premises are all that is relevant to the conclusion to be established. (Whether this is the best way of looking at circumscriptive reasoning need not be discussed here.) If so, the tacit enthymemic premises come very close to assuming that no further questions not prompted by the given premises will give the conclusion—in other words, amount to the kind of completeness assumption that one needs to back up "how possible" explanations.

How can this assumption be brought to bear on explanatory inquiry? Presumably we should study whatever results have been reached in the theory of circumscriptive reasoning. These results will not be discussed here. Instead, a conjecture might be of interest. The questions that are prompted by the explicit premises are presumably those whose presuppositions are sub-formulas of the given premises or substitution-instances of such sub-formulas. If so, a way of enforcing the interrogative completeness assumption might be to require that yes-or-no questions of the logical form "S or not S?" need be asked only when S is a sub-formula of one of the premises or a substitution-instance of one. This would, in effect, mean a ban on the use of the interrogative counterparts in non-cut-free deductive rules.

Whether this restriction captures in part the intentions of circumscriptive reasoners will not be examined here. It is clear in any case that such a restriction will discourage the splitting of tableau branches, and by so doing will make "how possible" explanations easier.

One important corollary to the methodological unity of "why necessary" and "how possible" questions is that the arguments used to answer them have to be evaluated by the same criteria. The difference between the two questions lies in the outcome of interrogative inquiry, including the principles of accepting or rejecting the outcome. However, the process of inquiry leading to the outcome must be assessed in the same way in both cases. The answers received by the inquirer have to be judged by the same criteria, including judgments concerning bracketing and strategic decisions as to what questions to ask next. This methodological unity implies furthermore that neither type of question is restricted to any particular subject matter.

A critical reader might object to what has so far been said about "how possible" explanations. What has been analyzed are "how possible" explanations in the sense of "how *conceivably* possible," not to say paradoxically "how possibly possible." In other words, what such an explanation provides is an account of how the *explanandum* might conceivably be true. Often, especially in explaining how a certain past event was possible, a "how possible" explanation is nevertheless expected to do more. It is expected to spell out how it was in fact possible that the event to be explained took place.

The search for such "how in fact possible" explanations does not require any new conceptual tools, however. In order to see this, compare two completed tableaux with each other. Let us assume that neither one is closed, and let us assume that in one of them there is only one pair of open branches on the left and on the right that do not have a bridge, whereas in the other one, there are several such unbridged pairs. As one can easily see, the unique pair provides an account of the only way in which the *explanandum* can have been possible. Assuming that the answers and the premises are true, the two branches provide an account of how the *explanandum* could in fact taken place. In order to find this unique pair of branches, we have, in principle, to complete the entire tableau. If the initial premises and the answers are true, but the conclusion false, then it follows in fact that the unique pair must describe what happened.

But there is much more to be said about the logic of "how possible" explanations. So far we have considered only logical proofs that are in the tableau form. They are not the only possible kinds of first-order proofs, however. They are characterized by the requirement that is usually called the "sub-formula property." Each new formula introduced in the tableau construction is a sub-formula of an earlier one, or a substitution instance of such a subformula. (See the rules given in Section 1.) The only reason why the tableau construction can nevertheless proceed to infinity is that ever new individual constants are introduced.

The rules that do not satisfy the sub-formula property are paradigmatically instantiated by a rule that allows the introduction of arbitrary disjunctions of the form $(S \vee \sim S)$ on the left side. Likewise this rule authorizes the introduction of conjunctions of the form $(S \& \sim S)$ anywhere on the right side. This rule will be called the "tautology introduction rule." It is obviously a truth-preserving rule, and hence is valid. It is obviously closely related to the principle of the excluded middle. The other valid rules that do not satisfy the sub-formula principle can be thought of as consequences of the tautology introduction rule. The most interesting of them is known as the "cut rule." It can do the same job as the tautology introduction rule.

It is known that whatever logical consequence relation can be proved by means of these rules can be proved without them, by means of the original tableau construction rules. Results to this effect are sometimes known as "cut elimination" results. For our subject matter, here such results mean that all "why necessary" explanations can be carried out without the cut rule or the rule of tautology introduction. But these rules can affect "how possible" questions, even when they do not introduce any new non-logical constants. The reason is that they can introduce new branches, including such pairs of open branches on the left and on the right without a bridge as serve as candidates for "how possible" explanations. Hence, efforts to find "how possible" explanations can be affected by the cut rule or the rule of tautology introduction, in that new potential explanations become possible. As a consequence, "how in fact possible" explanations become much more difficult to establish by means of tableau construction, for the number of possible explanations becomes larger.

An example of "how possible" explanations will illustrate what has been said. This example is fictional but nonetheless realistic. It is from C. P. Snow's novel *The New Men*, and the scene is an important and expensive nuclear experiment during World War . The experiment is going on, but slowly the scientific leaders of the team, Martin Eliot and Walter Luke, realize that it is failing. The expected reaction is not taking place in the nuclear pile.

As Martin and Luke looked at each other, no one around realized what the graph had told them. [It had told them that the entire experiment was a total failure. And they were directly responsible for this failure.]

Luke made no attempt at stoicism, less than most men. He assumed that he was the more wretched.... But [e]ven ... in his wretchedness, his powers were beginning to reassert themselves. It was frustration to him to feel those powers deprived, ... but underneath the misery and self-accusation his resolve was taking shape.

"It was just on the edge of being right," he said. "Why in God's name didn't I get it quite right? ...

> The heavy water is all right.
> The electronics are all right.
> The engineering is all right.

"I only hope the Germans are capable of making bloody fools of themselves like this. Or anyone else who gets as far. I tell you we've got as near as kiss your hand.

> *The engineering is all right.*
> *The heavy water is all right.*
> *The uranium is all right.*
> *The uranium is all right.*
> No, it blasted well can't be.

"*That must be it.* It must be the uranium—there's something left there stopping the neuts."

Martin, who had been sitting so still that he might not have heard Luke's outburst, suddenly broke in. From the beginning they had known that the uranium had to be pure to a degree that made them need a new metallurgy. After all, that still might not be pure enough. Was there an impurity, present in minute quantities, which happened to have great stopping power? I heard names strange to me. One Luke kept repeating (it was gadolinium, though on the spot my ear did not pick it up). "That's it," he cried.

> "There might be others," said Martin.
> "No," said Luke. "*That's it.*"
> "I'm not convinced," said Martin.

But he was. Even that night, Luke's authority had surged up again.

Later, other scientists said there was nothing wonderful about Luke's diagnosis; anyone would have reached it, given a cool head and a little time. What some of them did praise (even those who only passed compliments on those securely dead) was his recuperative power. (Snow, C.P., *The New Men*, pp. 107–112.)

What Luke was able to do there and then was to find a "how possible" explanation for the failure of the experiment. Needless to say, it had to be a "how in fact possible" explanation. It can also be noted that Martin and Luke first considered several "how conceivably possible" explanations in the guise of different elements that might have stopped the neutrons, out of which Luke eliminated all but one.

This example, though fictional, vividly shows also the importance of "how possible" explanations in science. Such explanations are not private reserve of historians.

"How possible" explanations are also common in detective stories and mystery stories. One prominent genre is a "locked room" mystery. Such mystery stories are not the best examples of explanatory reasoning, however, for typically the solution consists in inventing one particular gimmicky way of accounting for the puzzle without much of a chain of reasoning. A better example is something like Ian Rankin's story "Playback." In the story, there is overwhelming evidence against a suspect (John MacFarlane). Nonetheless, Inspector Rebus has his doubts, and in the end constructs a "how possible" explanation exonerating MacFarlane. In so doing, he uncovers the real perpetrator, Kenneth Thomson. In Ian Rankin's words:

It had been the perfect murder.

Well, almost. But Kenneth Thomsom had reckoned without Rebus's ability actually to believe someone innocent despite the evidence against him. The case against John MacFarlance had been overwhelming. Yet Rebus, feeling it to be wrong, had been forced to invent other scenarios, other motives, and other means to the fairly chilling end.

Here, Rebus's relevant ability clearly does not consist merely in being able to freely imagine alternative scenarios. Rebus has to carry out inquiries to back up his imputation of other motives and means to the different suspects. Rebus has to ask specific questions and usually to find answers to them in order to establish his "how possible" case. When did the victim die? About three A.M., the medical examiner tells Rebus. When was the phone call made that asked MacFarlane to come to the victim's flat? According to MacFarlane's machine, at 3:45 A.M. How come a phone call was apparently made by the victim to MacFarlane about forty-five minutes after her death? A click in the tape makes Rebus ask whether the call was perhaps a recording. The police laboratory confirms that it was a recording of a recording. Who besides MacFarlane could have made the recording in the first place? Her earlier, jilted lover Kenneth Thomson, of course. And so Rebus's line of reasoning goes. The alternative scenario he puts together is not merely "invented." It is a result of a careful series of questions and answers.

4. "How Possible" Explanations in Inquiry

"How possible" explanations are thus quite intriguing in their own right. However, their main interest is in their role in inquiry. In earlier publications of mine, partly collected in the fifth volume of my selected papers entitled *Inquiry as Inquiry* (Hintikka 1999), I have proposed modeling all knowledge-seeking as a questioning process. As the bookkeeping method for such interrogative inquiry we can use the tableau method explained earlier. Answers to the inquirer's questions are added to the relevant branch on the left-hand side. As was also indicated, the presupposition of a question must be present in the relevant branch on the left side before the question may be raised.

A major difference compared with deductive tableaux results from the fact that an answer may be false. The inquirer is therefore allowed to disregard—perhaps only tentatively, literally for the sake of argument—any given answer. A technical term, "bracketing," will be used. When a line in a tableau is bracketed, all other lines that depend on it must also be bracketed. Obviously, the inquirer must also be allowed to unbracket an answer in the light of other answers.

These are the only new definitory rules of the game of inquiry. The questions as to when to bracket and when to unbracket are strategic questions, and hence do not show up directly in the steps of the interrogative process. Yet some principles should be formulated as to what kinds of considerations should influence bracketing and unbracketing. The idea on which the interrogative model is based is that those considerations should involve further questioning ("inquiry as inquiry"), and questioning only. In earlier papers and books on the subject, relatively little has nevertheless been said as to what this further questioning might look like.

What has been found in this chapter provides an answer. Even though this answer does not tell the whole story of the strategy of bracketing, it is a major part of the answer. If an inquirer begins to suspect that an answer A that he, she (or it, if the inquirer is a computer) has received is not true, what can the inquirer do? An eminently natural thing to do is to inquire how A could possibly be false. Such an inquiry is also conducted as a (subordinate) interrogative inquiry. It can have two outcomes. If the tableau closes, showing (tentatively) that A cannot be false, the inquirer has strengthened the answer A by showing that it can be obtained in another way, too, as a conclusion of interrogative inquiry. This support can be shown to be the stronger the more the new argument for A differs from the original one.

If the subordinate inquiry produces a *prima facie* explanation of how A could be false, the inquirer has obtained some evidence supporting the bracketing of A. What can also be most important, the inquirer now knows one thing he, she, or it can do in order to support A: The inquirer might try to show that the countermodel just constructed is itself false. Having found this out, this countermodel thus yields useful indications where to direct one's further inquiry.

Among the concepts on which the results reached here throw new light is the notion of doubt. In Chapter 1 of this volume, it is argued that in epistemology and in decision theory, belief should be considered, not as a given state of mind of an agent, but always as being formed by some *rational* information-seeking process. Otherwise it makes little sense, for instance, to use belief as a determinant of rational decision making. Moreover, the inquiry prompting a belief can be conceptualized in the same way as an inquiry aiming at knowledge. The difference lies in the way the outcome of the inquiry is judged.

By a similar token, in a context of rational epistemology, doubt must not be construed as a mere psychological state. Doubt, too, must be backed by reasons, and ultimately by the inquiry that produced those reasons. But what kind of inquiry? An inquiry aiming at establishing ~A, where A is the proposition doubted, will produce belief in ~A, not doubt whether A. The obvious way of making the distinction between the two is to separate arguments calculated to show that ~A from arguments calculated to show how A could be false. An interrogative inquiry of the latter kind will be the same as an inquiry calculated to show, not ~A, but A, but of course with a different outcome. This is what constitutes the difference between reasons to believe that ~A and reasons to doubt that A. This agrees with the role of doubt ("reasonable doubt") in our actual epistemological life. For instance, when defense counsel in a jury trial wants to establish reasonable doubt about the guilt of the defendant, it is not enough to point out weaknesses in the prosecutor's line of thought. The defense counsel will have to show by argument how some specific claim of the prosecution could be false.

Speaking more generally, what happens in a jury trial is not merely that each of the opposing counsels constructs an argument for one of the two opposite conclusions. Such arguments are, of course, supposed to be "why necessary" arguments. Each of the counsels also tries to produce "how possibly false" arguments to criticize the opposing counsel's reasoning. Indeed, it suffices for the defense counsel to produce strong enough "how possibly false" arguments to throw reasonable doubt on the prosecutor's conclusions. Hence, the argumentative tasks of the two opposing counsels are not symmetrical. An acquittal does not mean that the innocence of defendant has been proved, only that his or her guilt has not been proved beyond reasonable doubt.

Thus, in epistemology, we have to think of knowledge, belief, and doubt as all being acquired by the same kind of procedure—namely, interrogative inquiry. The differences between the three lie partly in the different possible outcomes of the process and partly in different ways of evaluating the outcome. This shows the unexpected unity that prevails in appropriately developed epistemology. The same conclusion also illustrates the fact that the central subject matter of a realistic epistemology is not the definition of knowledge but the nature of interrogative inquiry.

From the requirement that doubt must be formed by the same process as belief and knowledge, it follows that if an inquirer fails in his or her attempt to motivate a doubt—say, the doubt whether A—by trying to show how ~A could be possible, the upshot is an argument for A, possibly a telling one. This is the rationale of the strategy of philosophers such as Descartes who adopt a skeptical stance for the purpose of refuting it and thereby reaching constructive conclusions.

"How possible" explanations can also serve as stepping stones to "why necessary" explanations. This argumentative tactic is illustrated by examples of the kind offered in Section 3, especially the one borrowed from C. P. Snow. In order to see how such a transition can take place, suppose that the inquirer has constructed, first, a tableau showing how it is conceivably possible that A, and then developed the argument (and hence the tableau) further so as to show that how it is in fact possible that A. This means that in the improved pair of tableaux, there is only one pair of open branches on the left and on the right without a bridge. Now, it may happen that this is the only pair of open branches on the left and on the right. Then it can be shown that the tableau can be transformed into another one that provides an argument to prove, not that A, but that ∼A. This illustrates an interesting argumentative tactic.

What this shows is that a "how possible" explanation can be a step in reaching a "why necessary" explanation. Suppose that an inquirer has constructed an interrogative tableau argument to show how it is possible that F. If the inquirer then manages through further argument to pare down the tableau in question in such a way that there is only one open branch in it on each side, then the inquirer is in a position to show why it is necessary that F.

From a purely logical viewpoint, this kind of transformation is possible only in special cases. However, examples suggest that such special cases are not so rare in practice, and perhaps even typical. For when a scientist is confronted by a phenomenon that calls for an explanation, surely his or her first thought is to ascertain how such an event is possible in the first place, and not a mere fluke. It is hoped that such an inquiry will lead to an account of how precisely the *explanandum* came about. And what has been seen is that such a full account of how the *explanandum* came about can be converted into an account of why it happened. Perhaps this possibility of building a bridge from "how possible" explanations to "why necessary" explanations is why the distinction between the two kinds of explanation has not received much attention from earlier methodologists.

Recognizing the role of "how possible" explanations thus helps us to understand the dynamics of inquiry in general.

References

Beth, E. W., 1955, "Semantic Entailment and Formal Derivability," *Mededelingen van de Koninklijke Nederlandske Akademie van Weterschappen, Afd. Letterkunde, N. R.* vol. 18, no 13, pp. 309–342.

Craig, William, 1957, "Three Uses of the Herbrand-Gentzen Theorem in Relating Model Theory and Proof Theory," *Journal of Symbolic Logic*, vol. 22, pp. 269–285.

Dray, William, 1957, *Laws and Explanation in History*, Oxford University Press, New York.

Halonen, Ilpo, 2001, "Interrogative Model of Explanation and Covering Laws" (dissertation), Department of Philosophy, University of Helsinki.

Halonen, Ilpo, and Jaakko Hintikka, 1999, "Interpolation as Explanation," *Philosophy of Science*, vol. 66, pp. 414–423.

Hempel, C. G., 1965, *Aspects of Scientific Explanation and Other Essays*, Free Press, New York.

Hintikka, Jaakko, 1999, *Inquiry as Inquiry: A Logic of Scientific Discovery* (*Selected Papers*, vol. 5), Kluwer Academic, Dordrecht.

Hintikka, Jaakko, 1983, "C. S. Peirce's 'First Real Discovery' and Its Contemporary Significance," in E. Freeman, editor, *The Relevance of Charles Peirce*, The Hegeler Institute, La Salle, Illinois, pp. 107–118.

Hintikka, Jaakko, 1970, "Surface Information and Depth Information," in J. Hintikka and P. Suppes, editors, *Information and Inference*, Reidel, Dordrecht, pp. 263–297.

Hintikka, Jaakko, and Ilpo Halonen, 2005, "Toward a Theory of the Process of Explanation," *Synthese*, vol. 143, pp 5–61.

Lifschitz, Vladimir, 1994, "Circumscription," in Dov Gabbay, C. Hogger, and J. Robinson, editors, *Handbook of Logic in Artificial Intelligence and Logic Programming*, vol. 3, Oxford University Press, New York, pp. 297–352.

McCarthy, John, 1980, "Circumscription—a New Form of Nonmonotonic Reasoning," *Artificial Intelligence*, vol. 13, pp. 27–39.

Salmon, Wesley C., 1984, *Scientific Explanation and the Causal Structure of the World*, Princeton University Press, Princeton, NJ.

Salmon, Wesley C., 1989, "Four Decades of Scientific Explanation," in P. Kitcher and W. C. Salmon, editors, *Scientific Explanation: Minnesota Studies in the Philosophy of Science*, vol. XIII, University of Minnesota Press, Minneapolis, pp. 3–219.

Schurz, Gerhard, 1995, "Scientific Explanation: A Critical Survey," *Foundations of Science*, vol. 3, pp. 429–465.

Snow, C. P., 1954, *The New Men*, Charles Scribner's Sons, New York.

von Wright, G. H., 1971, *Explanation and Understanding*, Cornell University Press, Ithaca, NY.

8

Who Has Kidnapped the Notion of Information?

In this day and age, the notion of information should be everybody's concern. Ours is supposed to be the information age, and we all share, in different degrees, the problem of coping with a deluge of information flooding over us. Our life is increasingly dominated by computers, which are nothing but machines for processing information. Information can even serve as a commodity (utility) in economics and decision theory. Hence it is important for each of us to master this concept intellectually and to have ways of gaining an overview over the different kinds of information we receive.

To exaggerate but a little, almost everybody has in fact gotten into the act of discussing what they call "information," except for philosophers. There are communication theorists à la Claude Shannon (Shannon 1948; Shannon and Weaver, 1949; Hartley 1928) and there are logico-linguistic theorists of semantic information like Yehoshua Bar-Hillel (1964). There are uses of the concept of information in science (see, e.g., Brillouin 1956) and in psychology (see, e.g., Attneave 1959), not to mention the role of genetic information in biology. Last but not least, there are computer scientists who are trying to use the tools of their trade to deal with what they call information and what they relate closely to computational complexity. They include prominently Kolmogorov and Chaitin, whose works are listed in the references. Computer scientists' notion of information looms especially large here because it may be expected to spell out the sense of information prevalent in the "information age." It has even been claimed that this notion of information can be put to use to illuminate such important matters in logic as Gödel's incompleteness theorem (e.g., Chaitin 1974, 1982(b)). At the same time, the notion of information has been evoked in different parts of science, most conspicuously, perhaps, in the form of genetic information. It is far from clear, however, what (if anything) is meant by these different "informations" and whether they are the same notion—or whether they are related to each other at all. These questions seem to mark a most urgent challenge to philosophical analysis.

189

The notion of information should also be part of the professional business of logically oriented philosophers. In Chapter 1 of this volume, I argue that information, rather than knowledge or belief, should be the most basic concept of epistemology. In another direction, a *prima facie* plausible view identifies logical inferences with such argument steps that do not introduce any new information into an argument or line of reasoning. ("New" information here means, of course, new to the argument in question, not to the arguer or to the arguer's audience.) This idea is sometimes expressed by saying that logical inferences and logical truths are analytic. However, this term is historically speaking a misnomer, and it does not contribute anything to the understanding of the problem. It is better to speak of a distinction between conceptual and factual information, with conceptual information being devoid of the factual one.

The assumption that purely logically inferences are informationally empty (in the sense of factual information) is not merely a pet idea of some individual philosophers, either. It is the cornerstone of some of the most important methods that we have for reaching an overview of complex facts pertaining to some subject area. The first and foremost technique of this kind is the axiomatic method. In it, the overview is reached by compressing all the factual information concerning some subject matter—for instance, a scientific theory—into a body of axioms. Once that has been done, the subject matter in question can be studied by deriving theorems from the axioms by purely logical means. When this procedure succeeds, the payoff can be spectacular. What it means, in slightly exaggerated terms, is being able to replace experimentation and observation by deduction. This should delight all economy-minded participants in the business of science, be they Congressional committees or followers of Ernst Mach. Buying computer time is much cheaper than building accelerators or satellites.

What has not been emphasized enough is that such axiomatization presupposes that purely logical inferences are tautological in the sense of not contributing any new information. Otherwise axiomatization would not provide an overview of the whole field, for then new information could be introduced in any old (or new) derivation of theorems from axioms. It is no accident that the best theorists and practitioners of the axiomatic method—in the first place, the great David Hilbert—have realized completely clearly that the usefulness of the axiomatic method is predicated on the uninformativeness of logical inference. (See Majer 2001.) This is what is illustrated by Hilbert's quip to the effect that in the derivation of geometrical theorems from axioms, we might as well speak of tables, chairs, and beer mugs instead of points, lines, and circles. But since in philosophy, no good insight goes unpunished, Hilbert was branded a "formalist," even though his early axiomatic and model-oriented position came very close to being diametrically opposed to formalism. Even in his famous list of unsolved mathematical problems, Hilbert was pleading the cause of purely logical axiomatization in science, as his Problem no. 6 shows.

More generally speaking, if logical inference is not tautological, logical systematization does not make any sense as a scientific or philosophical method.

In view of this background, a survey of the philosophy of the last half century reveals a shocking truth. Not only have philosophers failed to provide us with a clear understanding of the different uses of information and of their interrelations, but they have shot themselves in the foot. They have denied the analytic (tautological) nature of logical inference and logical truth, and thereby deprived themselves of the resources of axiomatization and other methods of studying purely logical relationships between the different items of our knowledge. A result is a series of inane appeals to what is called "intuition." In an earlier work (Hintikka 1999), I deconstructed the notion of intuition that analytic philosophers are fond of appealing to. In a nutshell, what happened was that, blinded by what was perceived as the success of Chomsky's generative grammar, philosophers began to imitate what they thought of as Chomsky's intuitionistic methodology. This was a double mistake. Even if they had been right about Chomsky, contemporary philosophers would not have had the excuse that Chomsky the Cartesian linguist would have for his appeals to intuition.

But perhaps I am being unfair in blaming this disaster on the philosophical community at large. In this case, the criticism can be squarely directed at one philosopher. He is W. V. Quine, who denied that logical truths are tautological (analytic), and who more generally wanted to reject the entire analytic–synthetic distinction that more appropriately should be called "conceptual versus factual contrast." Later in this chapter, I will show that Quine's rejection was prompted by a couple of perceptive insights that he nevertheless tried to implement in a disastrously mistaken way.

One can, in fact, pinpoint the philosopher's mistake. On one occasion (Quine 1970, pp. 3–5), he discusses the notion of information, and correctly connects it with the classes of excluded and admitted possibilities. The more alternative possibilities a proposition excludes, the more narrowly can we restrict our attention, which is the manifestation of having more information. Quine is on the right track in relating the notion of information to the range of excluded possibilities. But he is unrealistic as to how this insight is to be implemented. Quine says that such a use of the notion of information would be feasible only if we could specify all the different possible states of the physical world. This claim is doubly mistaken. First, a physical theory is typically applied, not to the entire huge universe as a whole, but to what physicists call "a system"—that is, a part (real or imaginary) of the world sufficiently isolated to be considered as a model of the theory in its own right. Now, the different possible states of such a system can often be specified without any trouble, thus allowing the application of informational concepts to the system in question. For instance, a toss of a dice can result in six possible states.

Here, the connection between the notions of information and probability serves us well. For we do not apply our probability theory only to the states of the entire universe—in fact, we practically never do so—and hence there is absolutely no reason to think that the notion of information can only be used in such a global manner.

Second, we do not always have to investigate the world in order to see what the different relevant possibilities are. For a logical theory of information and for many of its applications, it suffices to rely on the distinctions between different possibilities that are made by the very language we are using. These distinctions give us a useful starting point for further analysis. Even though there may be a price to pay for this reliance on language, it enables us to get over Quine's objections once and for all.

These possibilities are easiest to distinguish from each other in the case of propositional language, conceived of as truth-function theory or Boolean algebra. There, the finest partition of the possibilities concerning the world are expressed by what have been dubbed "constituents." For instance, if there are only two atomic propositions in our language, A and B, then the constituents are:

$$(A \ \& \ B)$$
$$(A \ \& \ \neg B)$$
$$(\neg A \ \& \ B)$$
$$(\neg A \ \& \ \neg B) \tag{1}$$

Any proposition of our truth-functional mini-language can be represented as a disjunction of some of these constituents. This representation is called "distributive normal form." This form displays the logical status of the proposition in question, and the respective normal forms of two propositions display their logical relationships. When the normal form of S_1 is a part of that of S_2, S_1 logically entails S_2. As extreme cases, we have propositions whose normal form is a disjunction of all constituents. Such a proposition is logically true but does not convey any information. It is literally empty, or nugatory. Wittgenstein proposed calling such propositions "tautologies," and the name has stuck. Such tautologies are entailed by all propositions. More generally, when S_1 logically entails S_2, the latter does not add anything to the information of the former, because it does not rule out any possibilities that the former doesn't already exclude. In this sense, purely logical inferences are tautological.

At the other end of the spectrum there are propositions that exclude all possibilities. They are contradictory propositions, and they entail all the other propositions.

More generally speaking, other things being equal, the longer the normal form of a sentence S is, the more probable it is, and the less information it carries. The reason is that the longer the normal form of S is, the more possibilities it admits. One might even try to use the relative number of constituents in the normal form of S as the logical probability of P(S) of S, and the relative number of constituents excluded by S as a measure of the informativeness of S. Clearly,

$I(S) = 1 - P(S)$. A differently calibrated measure of information inf(S) can be defined as $-\log P(S)$.

In an applied propositional language, these measures are appropriate only on the assumption that all the constituents are equiprobable, which means that there are no probabilistic connections between the atomic sentences. Otherwise, different constituents will have to be weighted differently. This would mean that measures of probability and information are not determined purely logically. Likewise, the status of logical truths as tautologies is predicated on the absences of any logical connections between the atomic sentences in the sense that all the constituents must be logically possible.

Subject to such qualifications, propositional languages constitute an information-theorist's paradise. The notion of information admits of a sharp definition, and it is related to the logical relations between propositions in a clear-cut and natural way.

Wittgenstein believed initially that all logic could be considered truth-functional logic. Then the paradisical situation just described would hold in general. Unfortunately, such a belief is unrealistic, and was in fact given up by Wittgenstein himself. The question now becomes as to whether, and if so how, the treatment of the concept of information can be extended from propositional languages to others. As a representative case of such "other" languages, we can consider languages whose logic is the usual first-order logic (aka quantification theory).

Logical positivists tried in effect to implement a generalization by giving up the specific idea of defining notions such as tautologicity and information in terms of admitted and excluded possibilities, and trying instead to rely on the idea of truths based only on the meanings of our language. This approach has been justly criticized. (See, e.g., Dreben and Floyd 1991.) Perhaps the worst thing about it is that how such a determination by meanings alone is supposed to work has never been spelled out in realistic detail.

Somewhat surprisingly—and perhaps also embarrassingly—it turns out that means of generalizing the treatment of information from propositional languages to all first-order languages have been available to philosophers for a long time, indeed almost precisely for a half century. This generalization is accomplished by extending the theory of distributive normal forms to the entire first-order logic. (See Hintikka 1953 and 1965.) Given a supply of non-logical predicates (properties and relations), we can again define the constituents that at a given quantificational depth do specify the basic possibilities concerning the world. It is even possible to describe in intuitive terms what such constituents are. They are ramified lists of all the different kinds of sequences of d individuals that exist in a world in which the constituent in question is true. By "ramified" I mean, of course, lists in which we keep track of which sequences share an initial segment of a length shorter than d members.

If we restrict our attention to propositions of a given depth d and to consistent constituents, the situation can be said to be precisely the same as in truth-functional propositional logic. With this qualification, it is thus the case that we can use at least a comparative (qualitative) notion of information in all first-order languages. I will call this notion of information "depth information." We can also identify the truths of first-order logic with tautologies in the sense of propositions that do not convey any depth information. (We might call them "depth tautologies.") Valid logical inferences do not increase the depth information of our propositions. If we could restrict our attention to consistent constituents only, the situation would be precisely the same as in truth-functional logic.

But we cannot do so without further ado. What has been said so far, unfortunately or fortunately, is not the end of the story. The rest of it has so far been covered by the innocent-looking phrase "consistent constituent," which I used in introducing the extension of the idea of information from truth-function theory to first-order languages. The notion of constituent is a syntactical (formal) one. The distributive normal form of a sentence as a disjunction of constituents can be thought of as being reached by a purely formal rule-governed transformation. Only the excessive length of most constituents prevents us from writing out the distributive normal form of any one sentence. But some of such purely formally defined constituents are inconsistent. And we cannot simply look away from such inconsistent constituents, for there is no mechanical (recursive) method of recognizing inconsistent constituents. Indeed, such a recursive method of recognizing inconsistent constituents would yield a decision method for first-order logic.

Now a partial method of weeding out inconsistent constituents is implicit in the very meaning of a constituent. As was indicated, a constituent is a list of all the kinds of individuals that exist in the world. These kinds of individuals are defined by lists of all individuals that exist in relation to them, and so on. In other words, a constituent C is a ramified list of all the different sequences of d individuals (down to the depth d of the constituent in question) that one can "draw" from a world in which C is true. After i draws, $i < d$, and there still are further individuals to be "drawn" from the world. Those different lists of individuals must all match. If they do not, the constituent in question is inconsistent. Such a constituent is called "trivially inconsistent." In other words, a trivially inconsistent constituent is one whose several parts do not match.

The striking fact here is that there are inconsistent constituents that are not trivially inconsistent. They look on the surface like consistent constituents—all their different parts cohere with one another. The inconsistence of one of them, say C, will emerge only when one transforms C into disjunctions of increasingly deeper constituents. If C is inconsistent, then at some greater depth d, all those deeper constituents will turn out to be trivially inconsistent. (This illustrates the importance of the parameter that is here being called "depth.") However, there is no recursive function that tells us how deep we have to go in order for such a hidden inconsistency to surface. This is the ultimate logico-mathematical reason why we cannot simply dismiss inconsistent constituents. We do not always know in practice which ones we would have to dismiss.

In order to convey to the reader a sense in which a constituent can be inconsistent, I can perhaps offer some informal explanation. A constituent is like a jigsaw puzzle or a domino set. It does not give one a picture of the world; it merely presents one with a supply of pieces out of which one has to assemble a picture. One is given a finite number of inexhaustible boxes of pieces of different kinds. The constituent states that at least one piece from each box must be used and that the puzzle can be completed. Thus, a constituent may imply the existence of an individual that cannot exist, or imply the existence of two different possible individuals that cannot exist in the same world. For instance, a constituent might imply the existence of a person who loves all and only those people whose love is never requited. (We might call such a person the universal consoler.") Or a constituent might assert the existence of both someone who hates everyone and the existence of someone whom nobody hates. (I waive, for the sake of illustration here, the question of whether these peculiarities necessarily mean that the constituent in question is not trivially inconsistent.) In the second example, we have, according to traditional terminology, two possible individuals that are not compossible.

Hence we have also to countenance constituents that are not trivially inconsistent when we are dealing with the notion of information. These constituents must be thought of as specifying alternative possibilities that language users (and logic users) have to keep an eye on. The result is a new concept of information that we might call "surface information." In a perfectly natural sense, it is surface information rather than depth information that our propositions can be used to codify in the first place. It is the kind of information that we human beings in fact convey, receive, and apply.

Surface information corresponds to a kind of probability (which we might call "surface probability") in the same way in which depth information corresponds to the usual (depth) probability. By the same token as in the case of information, the notion of subjective probability with which we actually traffic in real life is surface probability. Indeed, the great theorist of subjective (personal) probability, L. J. Savage (1967), is on record as maintaining that the appropriate notion of subjective probability must behave (to use the terminology of this chapter rather than Savage's) like surface probability.

Surface information behaves in some ways like depth information, and in some other ways unlike it. The most striking difference is that purely logical inference can enhance one's surface information. By the same token, not all logical truths are surface tautologies. Likewise, as Savage already pointed out in effect, surface probability is not invariant with respect of logical equivalence.

It is important to realize that surface information is, Savage notwithstanding, an objective notion. Or, strictly speaking, we have to say that it is as objective as the language that is being used, for at least qualitatively speaking, the notion of surface information is determined by that language.

A fascinating insight here is that in the most practical terms imaginable, surface information can be fully as valuable as depth information, and can even be said in a sense to be about reality. The reason is that before I have actually eliminated an inconsistent constituent, so to speak, from the normal form of the totality of my knowledge, I have to be prepared for its truth, just as much as in the case of a consistent constituent. In terms of the light-hearted example just given, as long as I do not know that a universal consoler, in the sense explained earlier cannot exist, I have to be prepared to meet such a person and possibly make preparations for such an encounter. What if he tries to seduce my unhappy niece? When I come to know the inconsistency, I will of course be relieved of the need of such precautions. But this relief is not automatic, and will involve some deductive labor whose amount cannot be mechanically predicted. It does not make any difference to my preparations, or my failure to take such preparations, whether the elimination of the offending constituent takes place deductively on the basis of factual evidence. More generally, there is no way of making the distinction between depth information and surface information on the basis of the informed person's reactive behavior.

On the logical level, the inseparability of surface information and depth information shows up in the fact that there is no computable method of telling, in general, whether we have eliminated enough inconsistent constituents to tell that a given first-order consequence relation holds or does not hold. (This "fact" is, of course, but another alias of the unsolvability of the decision problem for first-order logic.)

This inseparability (in a sense) of conceptual and factual information seems to have been Quine's insight. As such, it is a most astute idea. There is a sense in which Quine is right, on the surface of things. In a sense, factual and conceptual (logical) truths are inseparable and have a similar effect on a language user's behavior. But it is not feasible, even from a behavioristic point of view, to try to deny a distinction altogether. For it can sometimes be ascertained behavioristically whether a given agent is rejecting a certain proposition—for instance, a certain constituent—for factual or conceptual reasons. For these two types of reasons come from an agent's previous exploratory or deductive enterprises. And these two types of activity are obviously distinguishable behavioristically. But, behaviorism aside, what we obviously need here is a finer distinction than the crude analytic versus synthetic distinction that was, in effect, a distinction between no factual information and some factual information. We need a sense of information that is factual in the sense of helping one to cope with the world but that can be increased by purely logical means. It seems unlikely that we can even understand how computers can contribute to our intellectual and material well-being without some such concept of surface information. For, unlike telescopes or microscopes, computers do not help us in enhancing our store of factual information in the sense of depth information.

This concept of surface information is an idea whose time has come. It can be seen to play a crucial role in important human activities. For instance, what happens when we explain something? The explanation does not add any factual information to the *explanandum*. An answer is provided by the recent theory of explanation that I have developed with Ilpo Halonen. (See Hintikka and Halonen 2005.) The gist of the theory is the use of suitable logical interpolation results. Suppose that a first-order proposition G is a logical consequence of F. In order to see that this consequence relation holds, it must be seen that those constituents that are in the normal form of F but not in that of G are all inconsistent. Eliminating them does not add to the depth information of F, just because they are inconsistent, but it increases the surface information of F.

When suitably normalized, the interpolation formula I shows how the two kinds of reasons why a constituent can be inconsistent play out in the particular case at hand. It spells out what individuals there exist in a model of F that help to make it a model of G, too, and how the individuals in a model of G must be related to those in the models of F. This obviously amounts to a kind of account or explanation of why G logically follows from F. For instance, if one wants to bring about G by making F true, the interpolation formula I tells one what kinds of individuals one must create or introduce for the purpose and how they must be related to all the other individuals in the purported model (or system, in physics-speak). If this does not amount to an explanation of how (and why) the truth of F makes the truth of G necessary, it is hard to see what could be.

This shows, in fact, a remarkable feature of logical proofs. Suitably normalized, they not only show *that* the consequence G follows from the premise(s) F, they also show in a perfectly good sense *why* the consequence relation holds. This goes a long way toward explaining the usefulness of logical inference in applications.

Empirical explanations can be thought of as showing that the *explanandum* E follows from the antecedent condition A on the basis of a background theory T. "The" explanation will then be the interpolation formula for the logical consequence.

$$A \vdash (T \supset E) \tag{2}$$

Such an explanation shows what it is about the antecedent conditions A that enables the explainer to subsume E under the general theory T. It explains why E is necessitated by A, given the background theory T. Such explanations do not add to the depth information of A or to that of (T $\supset$ E), but they typically add to their surface information.

In brief, explanation is a matter of enhanced surface information, illustrating the function of this concept.

So far, I have not discussed how we can—if we can—assign numerical measures to information, either depth or surface information. Before discussing this problem, it is relevant to point out that it does not affect the special case of zero information. This is the case in which all the relevant constituents occur in the distributive normal form of a proposition. Take, for instance, a depth tautology. All consistent constituents of a given depth occur in its normal form. It does not exclude any actually realizable possibilities and hence does not convey any depth information. The only possible course of action is to assign to it zero (depth) information.

This incontrovertible conclusion has a considerable philosophical interest. It means that in first-order languages, logical truths are depth tautologies, and vice versa. The philosophical interest of this result lies in part in its being a refutation of Quine's claim that logical truths can be considered as analytic in his sense—that is, purely conceptual. We can now see that that claim is simply and plainly wrong.

This conclusion is not belied, either, by there being alternative "non-classical" logics. Their existence carries little conviction until their precise nature, prominently including their semantics, has been spelled out. Briefly, as far as I can judge the situation, neither constructivistic nor intuitionistic logics qualifies as counterexamples. Constructivistic logics ensue from classical logics by imposing stricter conditions on the Skolem functions that produce the "witness individuals" that show the truth of a quantificational proposition. Intuitionistic logics ought to be considered as variants of epistemic logics, and not alternatives to first-order logic. And as far as the new independence-friendly logic is concerned, Jouko Väänänen (2002) has shown that distributive normal forms exist also in it, even though they are no longer unique. But what about languages that are not semantically complete—in other words, whose logic has no complete formal proof method? The simplest such logics include IF first-order logic. In such languages, one cannot characterize depth information by inference from the totality of deductive consequences one can draw from it.

An answer to this question is that a semantical definition of depth information is still possible. And one can "almost" implement it in an IF first-order language. For in such a language, there exists a complete disproof procedure, and hence a complete deductive method of weeding out inconsistent constituents. Hence, everything that has been said remains applicable except that the resulting notion of information is the one that goes naturally with no-counterexample information.

But how can we, in general, assign measures of depth information and depth probability to first-order propositions? Here, the groundwork has been done for us by Carnap and other inductive logicians. Admittedly, they have considered mostly only special cases, especially monadic first-order languages. But their results are informative enough to show what the overall situation is.

In his early work on inductive logic, Carnap tried to develop a purely logical measure of probability for monadic first-order languages. The general situation in such languages is that we have a contingency table of N cells into which we can classify observed individuals. The logical probabilities are the prior probabilities of different distributions of individuals into the cells. Observations of individuals falling into the different cells yields the information we have to base our probability judgment on.

One of the simple but basic insights into this situation is that the prior probabilities determine, and are determined by, how rapidly an inductive logician allows evidence to influence his or her (or its, if we are doing artificial intelligence) probabilities on evidence. This idea can be expressed explicitly by considering what is known as the "characteristic function" of the probability measure. It is the function that expresses the probability that, given a specified body of evidence, the next randomly chosen individual belongs to the cell No. i ($1 \leq i \leq N$). The requirement of randomness is implemented by stipulating that our probability distribution is exchangeable.

This requirement is a kind of symmetry assumption. Carnap initially made use of other strong symmetry assumptions, too. He assumed that the characteristic function f depends only on the number n_i, of observed individuals in the cell No. i, on the total number of observed individuals n, and on the number N of the cells. He established the remarkable result that even these strong assumptions do not determine uniquely the characteristic function nor *a fortiori* the prior probabilities. These are determined only up to a freely chosen parameter λ. More explicitly the characteristic function has the form

$$\frac{n_i + \dfrac{\lambda}{N}}{n + \lambda} \tag{3}$$

This is a fascinating expression. It can be considered as a kind of weighted average between the observed relative frequency n_i/n and the purely symmetrical factor $1/N$. The greater λ is, the more heavily the second factor is weighted. What this means is that the greater λ is, the more slowly an inductive reasoner is letting experience affect his or her posterior probabilities—that is to say, to move them closer to the observed relative frequencies and away from the *a priori* factor $1/N$. In other words, λ is an index of caution.

Now, the optimal choice of such an index of caution cannot be made on logical principles alone. The optimal choice of λ depends on how orderly one's universe of discourse is. In fact, it has been shown that the optimal choice of λ is a monotonic function of the amount of order in the universe as measured by its entropy. (See Kurt Walk's paper in Hintikka and Suppes 1966.)

These innocent-looking technical results and others like it have extremely important philosophical implications. Even if we make the strong symmetry assumptions that Carnap uses in his sample case, our measures of probability and information depend on factual assumptions concerning the world, roughly speaking on the regularity (orderliness) of the world. In the simplest case, this dependence is mediated by the index of caution λ. The uneliminability of this index means that all use of the concepts of probability and information rests on tacit assumptions concerning the orderliness of the world.

This is a remarkable result. It has something of a déjà vu ring about it, in that any historian of philosophy knows that assumptions concerning the regularity of the world have played a major role as a proposed foundation of inductive inference. Perhaps we can also understand how such assumptions steal into one's approach so easily. Many philosophers have not realized that the mere use of probabilistic concepts in dealing with induction presupposes an assumption concerning the degree of orderliness of the universe. (It is an indication of the critical acumen of David Hume that he did not fall into this trap. He saw that the use of probabilities in induction does not solve the philosophical problem.)

But the situation is in fact even more complicated. (For more on the following discussion, see the articles in Hintikka and Suppes 1966 and 1970.) The notion of orderliness is systematically ambiguous. There are different kinds of order and disorder in the world. For instance, even in the simple situation studied by Carnap, one kind of orderliness is manifested by some of the cells' being totally empty. That means that certain general laws hold in the world. Carnap's symmetry assumptions do not allow us to cope with that kind of eventuality in realistic terms. However, if we simply allow the characteristic function to depend also on the number of cells left empty by the evidence, we obtain a more flexible treatment that enables us to deal with inductive generalizations. (See Hintikka and Niiniluoto 1980.)

As one might have expected, it turns out that the characteristic function will then depend on other parameters, which can be interpreted as indices of caution of different sorts and whose optimal choice depends on the different kinds of order in our universe of discourse. When relations are admitted, even further kinds of orderliness and further kinds of correlated indices of caution make their appearance.

The upshot of the work of Carnap and others is that any measure of *a priori* probability, and hence any measure of information that we might want to use, will tacitly embody multiple assumptions concerning different kinds of orderliness in the world. As we might put it, there is no purely logical quantitative notion of information, even though there exists a comparative notion of information for the typical languages (first-order languages) with which we have been dealing.

This result is diametrically opposite to what Carnap undoubtedly hoped to establish. It is of interest to note that already during Carnap's sojourn at the IAS in 1952–54 John von Neumann objected to Carnap's idea and claimed that all information is at bottom physical in nature. (See Köhler 2001.) A further examination would be needed to understand von Neumann's reasons for his essentially correct claim. One thing we can be certain about, however: John von Neumann's claim was not, and should not be, backed up by a rejection of the analytic–synthetic distinction, as has been claimed. This distinction concerns the case of zero information, which was seen to be unaffected by the vagaries of assigning numerical measures of probability and information to propositions.

These results concern both depth information and surface information. Since any measure of the order in the world obviously depends on the language used, this impossibility of a purely logical notion of information can be considered the price we must pay for being able to use any reasonable notion of information. These results also show in what sense the notion of information is and is not objective. The choice of one's measure of information is not determined purely logically. Such a choice amounts to a guess concerning objective reality, and it is in principle affected by what one knows about the reality.

Our results have also implications for the philosophical appraisal of the Bayesian approach to scientific inference. What they show is that there is no presuppositionless Bayesian inference. Such an inference relies on a prior probability distinction that inevitably embodies assumptions concerning the world. The dependence does not invalidate practical applications of Bayesian methods. Indeed, statisticians such as L. J. Savage have turned the dependence into a resource in that they propose to use it on purpose to codify background information. (Savage 1962 and 1972.) However, this kind of use of Bayesian methods is not what philosophers typically have in mind. In order to reach a theoretically satisfactory overview, the straightforward Bayesian inference ought to be complemented by a theory as to how our prior probabilities should be modified in the tests of evidence.

Moreover, if the only application of our probabilistic concepts is the confirmation of hypotheses and theories, it can be argued—and has been argued—that in the limit, Bayesian methods yield the right result as long as no possible hypothesis is assigned a zero prior probability. But this is not the only use of probabilities. In particular, it does not help to understand how the notion of information can be used in the best way. As far as this notion is concerned, Keynes was right: In the long evidential run, one's favorite measure of information might very well turn out to be dead wrong. Hence, what is badly needed is a theory of how to change one's priors in the light of evidence. The priority of prior probabilities should not be understood as temporal priority, as far as actual inquiry is concerned.

It seems to me that such a theory would make a substantial difference to many people's ways of thinking about probabilistic reasoning. It will be suggested in Chapter 9 that one victim of such a theory will be the currently fashionable theory of so-called cognitive fallacies originally developed by Tversky and Kahneman. The most conspicuous indication of its fashionableness is that Tversky and Kahneman received the 2002 Nobel prize in economics for their theory. (See Kahneman et al., 1982; Moser 1990; Piatelli-Palmorini 1994; Tversky and Kahneman 1983.)

Our results have also implications for the evaluation of Quine's philosophy. It is often said that his main insight is that factual meaning and conceptual assumptions cannot be disentangled from each other. In one perspective, what has been found might look like a vindication of Quine's position. For what we have seen is that in trying to measure factual information, we cannot eliminate the influence of *a priori* assumptions. I am in fact prepared to give Quine credit for having perceived this unavoidable role of prior assumptions in our factual judgments. But at the same time we have to realize that, if so, Quine has both misidentified the nature of the prior assumptions in question and misjudged the way in which his insight is to be implemented. As to the first point, what has been seen shows that the prior assumptions in question are factual rather than linguistic or otherwise conceptual. They are naturally coded by means of the choice of one's conceptual base, in that they typically appear in the form of symmetry assumptions, as in the classical λ-formula (3). But this does not make these assumptions themselves conceptual.

As to the question of to how the inextricability of conceptual and factual information is to be dealt with, Quine's recommendation to simply give up the distinction between factual and conceptual is a counsel of theoretical despair. Even the true nature of the very fact of inextricability cannot be adequately understood without a theoretical apparatus that involves even finer distinctions than the one Quine proposes to abolish. Even though Quine's ideas seem to be motivated by a valid insight, the way he has sought to implement it has been injurious to the course of analytic philosophy. We need a far sharper logical analysis of the problem situation than Quine was capable of.

How, then, can we define measures of surface information? In principle, we can try to work along the same lines as in the case of depth information—in other words, to use the weighted number of constituents ruled out as a guideline. It is not easy, however, to find simple theoretically motivated measures of this kind. One complicating factor is the relativity of such measures to one's conceptual basis. As an illustration, consider a derivation of G from F. This can increase one's surface information, and that increase is measured by the sum of the weights of the constituents we have to eliminate to demonstrate the consequence relation. But constituents with what basis? Those involving all the non-logical constants occurring both in F and in G? But such measures may be changed by adding redundant parts to F or to G. It turns out that it suffices to consider constituents whose non-logical vocabulary is shared by F and G. But that basis can then be different from that of the normal forms of both F and G. Moreover, suitable interpolation theorems can bring out those constituents that have to be eliminated from the reduct of the normal form of F to the common vocabulary in order to see the consequence relation, and similarly for G. Thus we have many interesting conceptual possibilities here, but no simple measures of surface information.

In such circumstances, it is tempting to take an altogether different tack. Instead of trying to measure the surface information of a proposition in terms of the "impossible possibilities" it rules out, one can try to use the complexity of the elimination process of these possibilities as the measure of their surface information. In other words, the weight of an eliminable possibility depends on the amount of work (which one can, for instance, think of as *Kopfarbeit*, or as computer time) that it takes it to rule it out.

In order to weight inconsistent constituents in a theoretically (and practically) interesting way, we would have to have some insight into the structural reasons for their inconsistency. In particular, it might be relevant to anticipate how the addition to the number of individuals we are considering together—which means adding to the depth of a constituent—affects the situation. But at this moment, neither logical nor computational theory seems to offer any real insights into the behavior of constituents. The only crude parameter of interest here seems to be the depth at which an inconsistent constituent turns out to be trivially inconsistent.

At this point, the reader is supposed to have another déjà vu experience. What was just recommended as a possible measure of surface information is, roughly speaking, the same notion of information as is used by complexity theorists. What we have thus reached is a vantage point from which this third main type of information can be seen to occupy a legitimate conceptual niche. We might call this kind of notion of information "computational."

At the same time, we can see that such "information" is quite different from our usual ideas of information and should be kept strictly apart from them for the sake of clarity. For one thing, it is related only to surface information, not depth information. It behaves in many ways differently from both these senses of information. For instance, if an inconsistent constituent is deep, it represents a narrow possibility, and hence its elimination does not in some non-computational sense add much to our surface information. Because of its depth, it may nevertheless be cumbersome computationally to eliminate, and hence it will be assigned a large measure of computational information.

Another anomaly is that computational information does not depend only on the proposition to which the concept is applied. It depends also on the method of logical proof. This dependence can be neutralized in some cases by choosing a suitable normalized proof method. But when there is no theoretically privileged proof method, this dependence may lead—and has led—to nonsensical results. As an example, we can consider Raatikainen's (1998(a) and 1998(b)) analysis of Chaitin's measures of information in formalized elementary number theory. There, the information of a proposition (coded in its Gödel number) does not depend, only or even roughly, on the proposition itself. It depends crucially on the way in which Turing machines are coded into the elementary arithmetic in question. By changing this code, a given proposition can be assigned any arbitrarily chosen value. Obviously, in such contexts, the term "information" is used, to put the point charitably, in a Pickwickian sense.

Suitably defined measures of computational information can nevertheless be used in logical theorizing, if handled properly. For instance, in a formal system, the computational information of a formula F (as a function $d(g(F))$ of the Gödel number $g(F)$ of F) can be characterized as the depth to which one has to go in order to prove its inconsistency (if it is inconsistent). Such a notion of computational information offers a way to discuss the decision problem of the system in question. For instance, the unsolvability of the decision problem for the system in question means that for any recursive function $r(x)$ we have $d(g(y)) > r(y)$ from some y_0 ($y > y_0$) on.

Applied to a given system of elementary number theory, since any method of computation in it corresponds to a recursive function, from some point y_0 we can no longer calculate the computational information of sentences with a Gödel number $> y_0$. This result is a restatement of Chaitin's well-known Limiting Theorem. It sounds like a surprising and deep result, but in reality it is only a trivial (and misleading) restatement of the unsolvability of the decision problem for the system in question.

Writers such as Chaitin are misleading their readers by using the term information as if it were meant in something like our everyday sense, when in reality it means in his results and his colleagues results—something entirely different. As a result, their approach to problems such as those prompted by Gödel's incompleteness results have led only to obfuscation of the issues. I am appalled that philosophers have given up their critical mission so completely as not to have pointed out this shady practice.

Instead of such misleading popularization, students of computational information might have been well advised to have a closer look at what their sense of information depends on in those applications in which it is possible to compare it with other senses of information. Here I can only point out one important distinction. An attempt to prove that G follows logically from F in first-order logic can be thought of as an experimental attempt to construct a countermodel in which F is true and G false. This attempt is guided by the sets of formulas A so far reached that are intended to be true in the hypothetical countermodel. Apart from propositional rules, there are essentially two kinds of applications of rules of inference that contribute to the complexity of the proof. There are (i) existential instantiations that introduce new individuals to the attempted countermodel and (ii) applications of the rule of universal instantiation to formulas in A with respect to all the permutations of names of individuals already in the approximation to a countermodel so far reached. The number of new formulas that can be added at any stage by (i) is at most the number of existentially quantified formulas in A, while the number of new formulas that can be introduced by (ii) can be of the order of n^a—where a is the number of all the different universal qantifiers in A and n is the number of names that have not yet been substituted for universally quantified variables. Thus, universal instantiation is likely to introduce many more new formulas and in this way increase the computational complexity of the theorem-proving process more quickly than existential instantiation.

For instance, suppose we have reached the following three potential premises:

$$(\forall x)(\forall y)(\forall z)((Rxy \ \& \ Ryz) \supset Rxz) \tag{4}$$

$$Rab \tag{5}$$

$$(\forall x)(\forall y)(Rxy \supset Ryx) \tag{6}$$

and the potential conclusion

$$Raa \tag{7}$$

Here, there are no ways of applying (i). In contrast, a $= 5$ and n $= 2$, and hence there are $2^5 = 32$ ways of introducing new formulas by universal instantiation.

As this simple example shows, in an attempted proof it is the universal instantiations that on the face of things complicate the process so much that it soon becomes impossible for any real-time computers to carry out. (If a concrete example is needed, the party problems in Ramsey theory can serve the purpose.) Yet, often, only a fraction of the universal instantiations is needed for the actual proof. For instance, in our mini-example it suffices to introduce only one instantiation (instead of all of the 32 ones)—namely, the following:

$$(\text{Rab } \& \text{ Rba}) \supset \text{Raa (from(4))} \qquad (8)$$

$$\text{Rab} \supset \text{Rba (from(6))} \qquad (9)$$

Here, (5) and (8)–(9) imply (7) in virtue of propositional logic.

Students of mechanical theorem-proving have accordingly sought means of keeping the instantiations (ii) minimal—for instance, by postponing them (for instance, through a use of dummy symbols)—until it is easier to see which ones are really needed. This is in fact what much of the theory of mechanical theory-proving amounts to.

However, in a general theoretical perspective, the crucial steps are (i) and not (ii)—that is, introduction of new individuals by existential instantiation rather than application of already established or assumed general laws to known individuals. This is because the impossibility of a countermodel can be seen only by considering approximations of a certain minimal size, measured by the number of individuals in it. In an attempted proof, this number is increased only by existential instantiations (i).

Of course, the choice between different possible existential instantiations makes a difference. Hence, what is really needed in the theory of mechanical theorem-proving is a set of guidelines for choosing the optimal existential instantiations. This problem is not new. In the traditional axiomatic geometry, it was known as the problem of carrying out the optimal auxiliary constructions. Leibniz complained that "we still do not have a method of always determining the best constructions." (*Nouveaux Essais*, Book IV, ch. 3, sec. 6.) My main point here is a generalization of Leibniz's. We still do not have a good theoretical overview in the theory of theorem-proving on how the new individuals that are needed in our logical thinking are best introduced.

In any case, the minimal number of such auxiliary individuals that are needed to bring out the hidden inconsistency is an interesting parameter. It indicates the minimal complexity of the configurations of individuals that have to be considered in order to bring hidden inconsistencies to daylight. It seems to yield much better measures of surface information than the mere length of the deductive (computational) argument needed to prove the inconsistency. Perhaps computer scientists could use such a measure of information instead of, or in addition to, the simple-minded notion of the length of a deductive argument. For one thing, suitable non-elementary deductive methods can, in effect, allow the virtual introduction of several auxiliary individuals in one fell, inferential step, which confuses the conceptual situation.

But to measure surface information by means of the complexity of the configurations needed for the proof amounts essentially to the same thing as the use of the depth at which the inconsistency of a constituent becomes apparent in the form of trivial inconsistency. And if this were the recommended way of measuring surface information, then we would be returning to the idea of measuring surface information in the same way as depth information, with the help of a system of weighting inconsistent constituents in a suitable manner. Perhaps the critics are right and the idea of the "amount of work" needed to rule out merely apparent possibilities is too crude to allow any interesting philosophical or other general theoretical conclusions. The close connection between surface information and depth information argues for developing their respective theories in the same way.

The same conclusion is suggested by other considerations. One of them is the fact just pointed out that in a purely deductive (computational) sense, the introduction of several new individuals can in a certain sense be compressed into one deductive step. This is what happens with rules that do not satisfy the sub-formula principle (in the framework of countermodel construction). Such rules are known among proof theorists as rules that are not cut-free. It is highly suggestive that the interpolation formulas that serve explanatory and other theoretically interesting purposes can be obtained only from cut-free proofs, such as tree method proofs or tableau proofs, not from proofs using cut rule or unlimited *modus ponens*.

We have thus seen how Quine has tried to destroy the notion of information and how complexity theorists have twisted it out of recognition for their special purposes. But we have also reached several constructive suggestions concerning this notion. In particular, studying the varieties of the concept of information throws an interesting light on the role of logic in the total structure of our knowledge, both on the way logical consequence relations can be established and on how they serve our wider theoretical purposes.

References

Attneave, Fred, 1959, *Applications of Information Theory to Psychology*, Holt, Rinehart and Winston, New York.

Bar-Hillel, Yehoshua, 1964, *Language and Information: Selected Essays on Their Theory and Application*, Addison-Wesley, Reading, MA, and Jerusalem Academic Press, Jerusalem.

Bar-Hillel, Yehoshua, 1955, "An Examination of Information Theory," *Philosophy of Science*, vol. 22, pp. 86–105. Reprinted in Bar-Hillel (1964), ch. 16.

Bar-Hillel, Yehoshua, 1952, "Semantic Information and Its Measures," *Transactions of the Tenth Conference on Cybernetics*, Josiah Macy Jr. Foundation, New York, pp. 33–48. Reprinted in Bar-Hillel (1964), ch. 17.

Bennett, Charles H., 1982, "The Thermodynamics of Computation – A Review," *International Journal of Theoretical Physics*, vol. 12, pp. 905–940.

Boolos, George S., and Richard C. Jeffrey, 1989, *Computability and Logic*, third edition, Cambridge University Press, Cambridge.

Brillouin, Leon, 1956, *Science and Information Theory*, Academic Press, New York.

Calude, Christian, 1994, *Information and Randomness*, Springer-Verlag, Berlin.

Carnap, Rudolf, 1952, *The Continuum of Inductive Methods*, University of Chicago Press, Chicago.

Carnap, Rudolf and Yehoshua Bar-Hillel, 1952, "An Outline of a Theory of Semantic Information." Technical Report No. 247, M.I.T. Research Laboratory in Electronics. Reprinted in Bar-Hillel (1964), ch. 15.

Chaitin, Gregory J., 1987, *Algorithmic Information Theory*, Cambridge University Press, Cambridge.

Chaitin, Gregory J., 1982(a), "Algorithmic Information Theory," *Encyclopedia of Statistical Sciences*, vol. 1, John Wiley, New York, pp. 38–41.

Chaitin, Gregory J., 1982(b), "Gödel's Theorem and Information," *International Journal of Theoretical Physics*, vol. 22, pp. 941–954.

Chaitin, Gregory J., 1974, "Information-Theoretic Limitations of Formal Systems," *Journal of the ACM*, vol. 21, pp. 403–424.

Cherry, Colin, 1957, *On Human Communication*, M.I.T. Press, Cambridge, MA.

Cherry, Colin, 1952, "The Communication of Information," *American Scientist*, vol. 40, pp. 640–664.

Cover, Thomas M., Peter Gacs and Robert Gray, 1989, "Kolmogorov's Contributions to Information Theory and Algorithmic Complexity," *The Annals of Probability*, vol. 17, no. 3, pp. 840–865.

Davis, Martin, editor, 1965, *The Undecidable*, Raven Press, New York.

Davis, Martin, 1973, "Hilbert's Tenth Problem Is Unsolvable," *The American Mathematical Monthly*, vol. 80, no. 3, pp. 233–269.

Davis, Martin, 1978, "What Is a Computation?" in L. A. Stern, editor, *Mathematics Today*, Springer-Verlag, Berlin, pp. 241–267.

Dreben, Burton, and Juliet Floyd, 1991, "Tautology: How Not to Use the Word," *Synthese*, vol. 87, pp. 23–49.

Dretske, Fred, 1981, *Knowledge and the Flow of Information*, Blackwell, Oxford.

Feinstein, A., 1958, *Foundations of Information Theory*, McGraw-Hill, New York.

Ford, Joseph, 1989, "What Is Chaos and Should We Be Mindful of It?" in *The New Physics*, P. Davies, editor, Cambridge University Press, Cambridge, pp. 348–371.

Gödel, Kurt, 1931, "Über formal unentscheidbare Sätze der Principia Mathematica und verwandter Systeme I," *Monatshefte für Mathematik Physik*, vol. 38, pp. 173–198. Reprinted in English translation in K. Gödel: *Collected Works, vol. I: Publications 1929–1936*, edited by S. Feferman et al., Oxford University Press, New York and Oxford, pp. 144–195.

Hartley, R. V. L., 1928, "Transmission of Information," *Bell Technical Journal*, vol. 7, pp. 535–563.

Hintikka, Jaakko, 2004, "A Fallacious Fallacy?" *Synthese*, vol. 140, pp. 25–35. And as Chapter 9 in this volume.

Hintikka, Jaakko, 2002, "A Distinction Too Few or Too Many: A Vindication of the Analytic vs. Synthetic Distinction," in *Constructivism and Practice: Toward a*

Historical Epistemology, Carol C. Gould, editor, Rowman and Littlefield, Lanham, Maryland, pp. 47–74.

Hintikka, Jaakko, 1999, "The Emperor's New Intuitions," *Journal of Philosophy*, vol. 96, pp. 127–147.

Hintikka, Jaakko, 1993, "On Proper (Popper?) and Improper Uses of Information in Epistemology," *Theoria*, vol. 59, pp. 158–165.

Hintikka, Jaakko, 1970(a), "On Semantic Information," in *Information and Inference*, Jaakko Hintikka and Patrick Suppes, editors, D. Reidel, Dordrecht, pp. 3–27.

Hintikka, Jaakko, 1970(b), "Surface Information and Depth Information," in *Information and Inference*, Jaakko Hintikka and Patrick Suppes, editors, Reidel, Dordrecht, pp. 263–297.

Hintikka, Jaakko, 1968, "The Varieties of Information and Scientific Explanation," in *Logic, Methodology, and Philosophy of Science III*, B. van Rootselaar and J. F. Staal, editors, North-Holland, Amsterdam, 311–331.

Hintikka, Jaakko, 1965, "Distributive Normal Forms in First-Order Logic," in *Formal Systems and Recursive Functions*, J. N. Crossley and Michael Dummett, editors, North-Holland, Amsterdam, pp. 47–90.

Hintikka, Jaakko, 1953, *Distributive Normal Forms in the Calculus of Predicates (Acta Philosophica Fennica*, vol. 6) Societas Philosophica Fennica, Helsinki.

Hintikka, Jaakko, and Ilpo Halonen, 2005, "Toward a Theory of the Process of Explanation," *Synthese*, vol. 143, pp. 5–61.

Hintikka, Jaakko, and Ilkka Niiniluoto, 1980, "An Axiomatic Foundation for the Logic of Inductive Generalization," in *Studies in Inductive Logic and Probability*, vol. 2, Richard C. Jeffrey, editor, University of California Press, Berkeley and Los Angeles, pp. 157–181.

Hintikka, Jaakko, and Patrick Suppes, editors, 1970, *Information and Inference*, Reidel, Dordrecht.

Hintikka, Jaakko, and Patrick Suppes, editors, 1966, *Aspects of Inductive Logic*, North-Holland, Amsterdam.

Kahneman, D., P. Slovic, and A. Tversky, editors, 1982, *Judgment under Uncertainty: Heuristics and Biases*, Cambridge University Press, Cambridge.

Köhler, Eckehart, 2001, "Why von Neumann Rejected Carnap's Dualism of Information Concepts," in *John von Neumann and the Foundations of Quantum Physics*, Miklòs Redei and Michael Stöltzner, editors, Kluwer Academic, Dordrecht, 2001, pp. 97–134.

Kolmogorov, Andrei N., 1970/1983, "Combinatorial Foundations of Information Theory and the Calculus of Probabilities," *Russian Mathematical Surveys*, vol. 38, no. 4, pp. 29–40. (Text written in 1970.)

Kolmogorov, Andrei N., 1968, "Logical Basis for Information Theory and Probability Theory," *IEEE Transactions on Information Theory, IT-14*, pp. 662–664.

Kolmogorov, Andrei N., 1965, "Three Approaches for Defining the Concept of Information Quantity," *Problems of Information Transmission*, vol. 1, no.1, pp. 1–7.

Leibniz, Gottfried Wilhelm, Freiherr von, 1982, *Nouveaux essays sur l'entendement humain: New Essays on Human Understanding*, translated and edited by Peter Remnant and Jonathan Bennett, Cambridge University Press, New York.

Li, Ming, and Paul Vitányi, 1993, *An Introduction to Kolmogorov Complexity and Its Applications*, Springer-Verlag, New York.

Loewer, Barry, 1987, "From Information to Intentionality," *Synthese*, vol. 70, pp. 287–317.

Loewer, Barry, 1982, "Review of Dretske," *Philosophy of Science*, vol. 49, pp. 297–300.

Majer, Ulrich, 2001, "The Axiomatic Method and the Foundations of Science: Historical Roots of Mathematical Physics in Göttingen (1900–1930), in *John von Neumann and the Foundations of Quantum Physics*, Miklós Redei and Michael Stölzner, editors, Kluwer Academic, Dordrecht, 2001, pp. 11–33.

Matiyasevich, Yuri V., 1993, *Hilbert's Tenth Problem*, MIT Press, Cambridge, Mass.

Moser, P. K., editor, 1990, *Rationality in Action*, Cambridge University Press, Cambridge.

Nauta, Doede, Jr., 1972, *The Meaning of Information*, Mouton, The Hague.

Odifreddi, P., 1987, *Classical Recursion Theory*, North-Holland, Amsterdam.

Paris, Jeff and Leo Harrington, 1977, "A Mathematical Incompleteness in Peano Arithmetic," in J. Barwise, editor, *Handbook of Mathematical Logic*, North-Holland, Amsterdam, pp. 1133–1142.

Piatelli-Palmarini, Massimo, 1994, *Inevitable Illusions*, John Wiley, New York.

Quine, W. V., 1987, "Gödel's Theorem," in W. V. Quine: *Quiddities*, The Belknap Press of Harvard University Press, Cambridge, MA, ch. 19, pp. 376–388.

Quine, W. V., 1970, *Philosophy of Logic*, Prentice Hall, Englewood Cliffs, NJ.

Raatikainen, Panu, 1998(a), *Complexity, Information, and Incompleteness: Reports from the Department of Philosophy*, University of Helsinki.

Raatikainen, Panu, 1998(b), "On Interpreting Chaitin's Incompleteness Theorem," *Journal of Philosophical Logic*, vol. 27, pp. 569–586.

Raatikainen, Panu, 1998(c), "Algorithmic Information Theory and Undecidability," *Human and Artificial Information Processing – Proceedings of SteP'98, Publications of the Finnish Artificial Intelligence Society*, Jyväskylä, 1998, pp. 1–10.

Raatikainen, Panu, 1997, "The Problem of the Simplest Diophantine Representation," *Nordic Journal of Philosophical Logic*, vol. 2, pp. 47–54.

Redei, Miklós, and Michael Stöltzner, editors, 2001, *John von Neumann and the Foundations of Quantum Physics*, Kluwer Academic, Dordrecht.

Rogers, Hartley, Jr., 1958, "Gödel Numbering of Partial Recursive Functions," *Journal of Symbolic Logic*, vol. 23, pp. 331–341.

Rogers, Hartley, Jr., 1967, *Theory of Recursive Functions and Effective Computability*, McGraw-Hill, New York.

Savage, L. J., 1972, *The Foundations of Statistics*, second edition, Dover, New York.

Savage, L. J., 1967, "Difficulties in the Theory of Personal Probability," *Philosophy of Science*, vol. 34, pp. 305–310.

Savage, L. J., et al., 1962, *The Foundations of Statistical Inference*, Methuen, London.

Schumacher, J. M., 1993, "Information and Entropy," *CWI Quarterly*, vol. 6, no. 2, pp. 97–120.

Shannon, Claude, 1948, "A Mathematical Theory of Communication," *Bell System Technical Journal*, vol. 27, pp. 379–423, 623–656.

Shannon, Claude, and Warren Weaver, 1949, *The Mathematical Theory of Communication*, University of Illinois Press, Urbana, IL.

Shuster, H. G., 1988, *Deterministic Chaos: An Introduction*, second revised edition, VCH Publishers, New York.

Solomonoff, Ray J., 1964, "A formal theory of inductive inference," *Information and Control*, vol. 7, pp. 1–22, 224–254.

Svozil, Karl, 1993, *Randomness and Undecidability in Physics*, World Scientific, Singapore.

Turing, Alan M. (1936–7), "On Computable Numbers, with an Application to the Entscheidungsproblem," *Proceedings of the London Mathematical Society* (2), vol. 42, pp. 230–265; correction, ibid, 43, pp. 544–546.

Tversky, A., and D. Kahneman, 1983, "Extensional Versus Intuitive Reasoning: The Conjunctive Fallacy in Probability Judgment," *Psychological Review*, vol. 90, pp. 293–315.

Väänänen, Jouko, 2002, "On the Semantics of Information and Independence," *Logic Journal of the Interest Group in Pure and Applied Logic*, vol. 10, pp. 337–350.

van Lambalgen, Michiel, 1987, "Random Sequences," PhD dissertation, University of Amsterdam.

Walk, Kurt, 1966, "Simplicity, Entropy, and Inductive Logic," in *Aspects of Inductive Logic*, Jaakko Hintikka and Patrick Suppes, editors, North-Holland, Amsterdam, 1966, pp. 66–80.

Wicken, Jeffrey S., 1987, "*Entropy and Information: Suggestions for Common Language*," *Philosophy of Science*, vol. 54, pp. 176–193.

Zurek, W. H., editor, 1990, *Complexity, Entropy, and the Physics of Information*, SFI Studies in the Sciences of Complexity, vol. VIII, Addison-Wesley.

Zvonkin, A. K., and L. A. Levin, 1970, "The Complexity of Finite Objects and the Development of the Concepts of Information and Randomness by Means of the Theory of Algorithms," *Russian Mathematical Surveys*, vol. 25, pp. 83–124.

9

A Fallacious Fallacy?

One of the major current developments in cognitive psychology is what is usually referred to as the "theory of cognitive fallacies," originated by Amos Tversky and Daniel Kahneman. The purported repercussions of their theory extend beyond psychology, however. A flavor of how seriously the fad of cognitive fallacies has been taken is perhaps conveyed by a quote from Piatelli-Palmerini (1994, xiii), who predicted "that sooner or later, Amos Tversky and Daniel Kahneman will win the Nobel Prize for economics." His prediction was fulfilled in 2002.

The theory of cognitive fallacies is not merely a matter of bare facts of psychology. The phenomena (certain kinds of spontaneous cognitive judgments) that are the evidential basis of the theory derive their theoretical interests mainly from the fact that they are interpreted as representing fallacious—that is, irrational judgments on the part of the subject in question. Such an interpretation presupposes that we can independently establish what it means for a probability judgment to be rational. In the case of typical cognitive fallacies studied in the recent literature, this rationality is supposed to have been established by our usual probability calculus in its Bayesian use.

The fame of the cognitive fallacies notwithstanding, I will show in this chapter that at least one of them has been misdiagnosed by the theorists of cognitive fallacies. In reality, there need not be anything fallacious or otherwise irrational about the judgments that are supposed to exhibit this "fallacy." I will also comment on how this alleged fallacy throws light on the way probabilistic concepts should and should not be applied to human knowledge-seeking (truth-seeking) activities.

The so-called fallacy that I will discuss is known as the "conjunctive fallacy" or the "conjunction effect." It is best introduced by means of an example. Here, I follow the formulation of Piatelli-Palmerini (1974, 65–67, abbreviated).

211

Consider the following information that one is supposed to have received:

Linda is 31 years old, single, outspoken, and very bright. She majored in philosophy. As a student she was deeply concerned with issues of discrimination and social justice, and also participated in antinuclear demonstrations.

In the experiments of Tversky and Kahneman, the subjects are asked to rank a number of statements as to what Linda's profession is for their probability. Among them, there are the following:

(T)　Linda is a bank teller
(T & F)　Linda is a bank teller and is active in the feminist movement

If the reader finds on the basis of his or her intuitive judgment that (T & F) is more probable (credible) than (T), that reader is in a large company. In a typical experiment, between 83 percent and 92 percent of subjects agree with this ranking. Yet there is something strange going on here. Speaking of such a probability ranking, Piatelli-Palmerini (1994, 65–66) writes:

That is what almost all of us do, though again this is a pure cognitive illusion. In fact, the likelihood that *two* of these characteristics should be simultaneously true (that there is what scientists call a "conjunction") is *always* and *necessarily* inferior to the probability of anyone of these two characteristics taken alone. If you think for a moment, you will be obliged to admit that it *must* ... be more likely that Linda is a bank teller and takes part in some movement or other (case T, in fact, specifies nothing more than that) than it is that Linda is both a bank teller and is an active feminist.

Moreover, this alleged fallacy has little to do with the subjects' defective knowledge of the laws of probability.

What is really surprising is that there is no great difference in the average responses from the "uninformed" subject (that is, one who has no real notion of the laws of probability) and those of statistical experts. (Piatelli-Palmerini, 1994, 66.)

Such evidence has persuaded many psychologists that there is an inevitable "built-in" tendency in the human mind to commit the conjunction fallacy.

I believe that this way of looking at the experimental results of Tversky and Kahneman (among others) is misguided. There need not be anything fallacious about the conjunction effect. At the same time, I do not see any reason here to doubt the usual laws of probability calculus, rightly understood.

The first main idea of my argument to this effect is exceedingly simple. It is admittedly true that the probability *simpliciter* of a conjunction cannot be higher than that of one of its conjuncts. But in the conjunction phenomenon, we are not dealing with prior probabilities; we are dealing with probabilities on evidence (conditional probabilities). Then the probability $P_1((T \& F)/E_1)$ of (T & F) on certain evidence E_1 is unproblematically smaller than (or at most equal to) the probability $P_2 (T/E_2)$ of T on certain evidence E_2 only if the prior probability distributions P_1 and P_2 are the same and if the relevant evidence E_1 or E_2 is the same in both cases. Both of these assumptions are obviously made by the likes of Piatelli-Palmerini who believe that subjects' probability estimates are irrational.

But neither of the two assumptions can always be made in the critical situations. First, the total available evidence is not completely the same in the two cases. Everything else is, of course, identical evidence-wise in the two cases, except for one thing. In the situations in which the fallacy arises, the two items of information T and (T & F) are thought of as being conveyed to the subject by two different informants. Moreover, the two differ in that the information they convey is different.

But this seems to be a distinction without difference. For the main distinguishing factor is merely that a different person is relaying the information to the probability appraiser. This should not make any difference, it seems. Neither of the two messages T and (T & F) brings in new facts into the background evidence with respect to which probabilities are being estimated. For instance, no causal connection is known or presumed to obtain between, on the one hand, the fact that T or that (T & F) and, on the other hand, the fact that these propositions are conveyed to the appraiser by this or that person. Moreover, the appraiser has by definition no independent knowledge about the two sources of information. The two informants might as well be two different databases. Hence their being different does not seem to make any difference to the evidence with respect to which the Bayesian conditionalization is being carried out. And in a very real sense, I can grant that $E_1 = E_2$.

There seems to be no doubt that the irrelevance of the source for the objective evidence has greatly encouraged the idea that the conjunction effect is somehow fallacious.

However, this is not the end of the story. What are often forgotten are the presuppositions of strict Bayesian inference—in particular, the role of "prior" probabilities. Here we are led to examine some of the most fundamental questions of probability evaluation.

How are the degrees of credibility supposed to be changed by new information? The simplest approach in fact forms the historical background of the theory of cognitive fallacies. Even though the term is not completely accurate historically. I will call it the "Bayesian approach." According to it, an inquiry starts from an assignment of prior probabilities to the propositions of the language used in the inquiry. The influence of new evidence is taken care of by conditionalization. The probability of an event H on the evidence E is simply the conditional probability $P(H/E)$. When new evidence E^* is added, the resulting probability (degree of credibility) will be $P(H/E \& E^*)$.

This is a simple and attractive model. It has serious problems, however. For philosophical purposes, it cannot be considered a presuppositionless general model. For a closer analysis quickly shows that the choice of the priors amounts to non-trivial assumptions concerning the world. These assumptions cannot be known to be correct *a priori*, and therefore we may in principle be forced to change them in the teeth of the evidence.

This point is not new, and it should be obvious. Indeed, L.J. Savage (1962) defended Bayesian methods precisely because the prior probability distribution is (according to him) a handy way of codifying background information relevant to some given decision problem. Along different lines, the same point is testified to by Carnap's attempt to build a purely logically based prior probability distribution. This probability distribution is restrained by strong symmetry assumptions. However, it turns out that even Carnapian assumptions leave open a parameter λ, which can be thought of as an index of the order in the Carnapian universe in question. This is a substantial assumption that can be verified only by one's knowledge of the whole universe. Accordingly, any estimate of λ may always in principle be subject to change in the light of future experience. And the same result will in principle hold in other cases, too. We cannot exclude the possibility that experience may force us to change our "prior" probability distribution. Of course, being "prior" then does not any longer mean antecedent to the entire cognitive enterprise, but only antecedent to one particular probability evaluation.

Hence, even if we start by following the Bayesian approach we sooner or later face the task of re-evaluating of our prior ("a priori") probabilities. How are we to do so? There is a branch of studies called "probability dynamics" that addresses this very problem. I am not proposing here to offer any criticisms of the fine print of these studies. However, they do not incorporate one of the most important ways in which we in fact reevaluate those probability distributions on which our rational judgments of credibility rest. The evidence (information) that is the basis of our knowledge of prior probabilities does not come to us as a gift from a Platonic heaven or from some inscrutable oracle. It comes from different sources, which in a rational inquiry are known to the inquirer.

But how does this analysis apply to the conjunction effect? What we have to realize is that what in a Bayesian approach are the priors is the probability distribution on the informational input the evaluator receives from different sources. And one of the most common ways of evaluating these probabilities (degrees of credibility) is by considering the source of the different items of input. This is, of course, the first and foremost question we raise concerning the testimony of human witnesses. Is the witness likely to be reliable or not? And such reliability is not an *a priori* matter but has to be evaluated by reference to other evidence plus, of course, some *a priori* knowledge. For instance, we may look at the other answers by the same witness to see whether he or she is in a position to provide information or compare the witness's answers with facts that we know (or assume to be known). In a simple case, if a witness's testimony contradicts known facts, or other testimony by the same witness, we know that he or she is lying. Conversely, if the witness's answers conform to what we are entitled to expect on the basis of known facts, or confirms with the witness's other testimony, our estimation of that witness's reliability is enhanced.

There is nothing magical about such *a posteriori* judgments of reliability, either. Whenever enough background information is available, they can, in principle, be made in accordance with the usual laws of probability calculus. For a simple example, let us assume that it is initially known that there are two possibilities concerning a given source of information, both equally likely— namely, that it always yields a true answer and that it yields a true answer with the constant probability 1/10. Then, if we receive an answer that is known to be true, the probability that that source of information always tells the truth is raised from 0.5 to 0.8333....

Now we come to the crux of the conjunction "fallacy." The fact that answers like T or (T & F) come from a different source of information does not change the objective evidence E on the basis of which their credibility has to be judged. But in the light of what has been said, it may affect the prior probability distribution. For the sources of the information may affect the prior probabilities $P_1(T)$ and $P_2(T \text{ & } F)$ that are the basis of the conditionalized probabilities $P_1(T/E)$ and $P_2((T \text{ & } F)/E)$. Even though the former are known technically as "prior" probabilities, according to what was found they can be affected by evidence, though not by conditionalization. And part of that evidence is the two different messages that the two sources provide the evaluator with. For when we are evaluating an answer A from a source of information with an unknown but presumably constant propensity to give true answers, that particular answer A itself constitutes part of the data on the basis of which the reliability of its source, and hence its own reliability, must be judged. Hence the probabilities assigned in the course of an actual inquiry to two answers (messages) A, B from two different sources of information may have to be judged by reference to different "prior" probability distributions.

In particular, even when on any fixed evidence E and any one probability distribution P, the two answers $P(A/E) > P(B/E)$, the answer B may so much increase the credibility of the second source of information by comparison with the source of the first answer that after the answers have actually been given, the credibility of B is greater than that of A. This can be the case even though the rest of the available evidence is the same in the two cases.

In practice, it is hard to put numerical values to the probabilities in question, but simple qualitative examples are easy to give. Indeed, Linda the bank teller example can serve as a case in point.

Speaking more explicitly (and more generally), when the two messages A and B come from different sources, they must be judged by reference to different "prior" probability distributions P_a and P_b. Then it may very well be the case that the following are all true:

$$P_a(A/E) > P_a(B/E)$$
$$P_b(A/E) > P_b(B/E)$$
$$P_a(A/E) < P_b(B/E)$$

There is nothing strange about the use of two different "prior" probability distributions in the case of the two different sources of information. It is merely an extension of the strategy recommended by Savage of building background information that cannot be naturally expressed as specific evidence E into what in Bayesian scheme are the priors.

These observations provide a basis for a solution to the conjunction paradox. What happens in the Linda case is that the two propositions T and (T & F) are thought of as answers by two different sources of information to the question: What is Linda doing now? The background information does not tell us much about whether T is likely to be true or not. If anything, the story about Linda makes it unlikely that she should be a bank teller, of all things. In contrast, the information that F (i.e., that Linda is active in the feminist movement) is made likely by the background information. Hence it enhances the credibility of the second witness, for the reasons adumbrated earlier. For this reason, the answer (T & F) coming from a different source of information might have to be assigned rationally a higher degree of credibility than the answer T, coming from a different witness. There need not be anything fallacious or otherwise irrational, such as the conjunction effect.

This diagnosis of the conjunction effect has a number of implications. For instance, the conjunction effect takes place only if the added conjunct is apt to enhance the credibility of the source of information in question. If F were the statement "Linda is a stamp collector," the conjunction effect would be distinctly weakened. Furthermore, the conjunction effect becomes smaller when it is not natural to think of the two statements as being made by two different speakers with different degrees of reliability and/or access to relevant information.

Nothing in the line of thought I have followed turns on using a notion of probability different from the normal epistemic probability. Hence the solution proposed here is different from a suggestion by Gerd Gigerenzer (1991). He attributes the alleged paradox to a confusion between epistemic and statistical probability. However, there is a connection. When the statistical character of probability judgments is made explicit, it becomes unlikely that the propositions whose probabilities are at issue are expressed by statements made by two different witnesses. Hence it is not surprising that changing Linda-type examples into ones in which the statistical character of the probability judgments in question is emphasized can appreciably reduce the conjunction effect, as Gigerenzer has shown.

For instance, Tversky and Kahneman pointed out as early as in 1983 that the situation is quite different if one changes the operative question in the Linda case to the following:

There are 100 persons who fit the description above (i.e., Linda's). How many of them are

(a)   bank tellers
(b)   bank tellers and active in the feminist movement

This drastically reduces the conjunction effect. Gigerenzer interprets this to mean that the conjunction effect results from the use of a single-case epistemic probability concept rather than a frequency concept. The diagnosis proposed in this chapter suggests a less drastic explanation. If we put the question in frequentist terms, we destroy the tacitly accepted scenario in which (a) and (b) are answers by two different witness-like sources of information. As was seen, this should be enough to greatly reduce the conjunction effect, which is what Tversky and Kahneman found.

Apart from this indirect influence, nothing in the arguments presented here turn on a contrast between different kinds of probability—for example, between single-case probabilities and probabilities that can be interpreted as frequencies.

It is also worth reiterating that my diagnosis does not depend on any assumptions concerning whatever connections there might be between the two witnesses and the subject matter of T and (T & F). What is at issue is merely the different testimonies, which by definition have only informational and not, for example, causal connections with the facts of the case.

In a nutshell, I might sum up my diagnosis of the conjunctive fallacy by saying that given suitable collateral evidence, certain messages are self-confirming in that they tend to increase our confidence in their source. There is nothing paradoxical in this kind of self-confirming effect. What makes the Linda case unusual is that the extra information that makes (T & F) more probable is introduced by the very assertion of this proposition by the second presumed witness. This assertion is therefore, in a certain sense and to some degree, self-certifying. Such a self-certification might at first sight seem paradoxical and maybe even impossible. The line of thought sketched here nevertheless shows that such a self-certifying effect is possible without any fallacy whatsoever.

I am not aware of any recent discussions of such a self-certifying effect. It nevertheless seems to have been noted by some earlier analysts of human reasoning. One of them is Aristotle. In his *Rhetoric* (I, 2, 1356a, 5–20), he notes that a speaker's persuasive power depends on his "character" (*ethos*). This sounds natural enough. A man who is known to be honest is more believable than a known liar. But then Aristotle goes on to say, speaking of the confidence the rhetor is trying to bring about in the audience:

But this confidence must be due to the speech itself, not to any preconceived idea of the speaker's character.

Moreover, Aristotle is already on the record as saying that rhetorical persuasion is of the same kind as dialectical one. (See *Rhetoric* I, 1, 1357a, 1–10.) Hence Aristotle's recommendation seems blatantly circular. How can a speaker demonstrate that his arguments are reliable by means of those very same arguments? It is to be noted that *ethos* is clearly a property of the speaker, and it is one of the factors that is supposed to enhance the credibility of what he says. How, then, can what he says serve to establish that *ethos* without circularity? An answer lies in what has been said. A rhetor can establish his reliability by offering arguments that cohere with each other and that are in keeping with what his audience knows about his subject matter.

Another example is offered by Newton's famous description of his experimental method toward the end of his *Opticks* (1952, pp. 404–405). (See also Hintikka 1992.) There, Newton describes how his method consists in establishing partial generalizations by means of experiments and observations. These partial generalizations are then extended to further values, and combined with each other. This process Newton calls "induction." It is not a step from particular cases to a generalization but the quantitative counterpart to Aristotle's *epagoge*, which also consisted in combining several partial generalizations under a single comprehensive one. Then Newton (1952, p. 404) goes on to say:

And although the arguing from Experiments and Observations by Induction be no demonstration of general Conclusions; yet it is the best way of arguing which the Nature of Things admits of, and *may be looked upon as so much the stronger, by how much the Induction is more general.* (emphasis added)

What this obviously means is that if a scientist can find a general law that embraces more of the partial generalizations that have been established as special cases, he or she should trust it more than a generalization that covers fewer such partial generalizations. This seems to fly to the face of the laws of probability in the same way as the conjunction effect. For a generalization covering more ground makes, *ceteris paribus*, a stronger claim than one covering fewer partial generalizations, and ought to be less probable rather than more so. Is Newton being irrational? I do not think so. In any case, it is not hard to see what Newton has in mind. All we have to do is to think of the different (wider or narrower) partial generalizations as having been proposed by different sources of scientific truths. The source whose generalization covers more sub-cases than that of another one is more trustworthy because its very own answer shows that it can provide more insights into nature's laws than the other "oracle's" answers. In this sense, Newton is merely treating nature's testimony in the same way as we all would treat the testimony of a human witness.

In order to align the Newtonian case with the conjunction effect, we should note that an extended generalization's being more general in Newton's sense means that it agrees with more partial generalizations—that is, agrees better with collateral information in the same sense in which (T & F) agrees better with what we know of Linda on the basis of the background information than T alone.

Most of the argumentation presented in this chapter could have been presented in the framework of the interrogative model of inquiry that I have developed in collaboration with my associates. (For this discussion, see Hintikka, Halonen, and Mutanen, 1999.) I have nevertheless wanted to keep my conceptual apparatus in this chapter as simple as possible.

For a more systematic discussion of the conjunction effect and of other alleged cognitive fallacies, however, the interrogative approach to inquiry is nevertheless likely to be helpful. Some of the general theoretical conclusions concerning the conjunction effect may nevertheless be anticipated here. The conjunction effect is not only not a fallacy, there is nothing merely heuristic or intuitive about it either. Admittedly it is not easy in practice to give numerical values to the probabilities involved in my diagnosis, such as the probability of some particular witness's telling the truth. But such practical difficulties do not affect the conceptual structure of the problem.

In particular, the three steps in my line of thought in this chapter have a clear-cut objective import as soon as we begin to consider inquiry as a question-answer sequence (interspersed by logical inferences). They are: (i) the need to sometimes modify the priors in the light of new evidence; (ii) the fact that such a modification often amounts to a reevaluation of the degrees of reliability ascribed to different sources of information; and (iii) the fact that the evidence conveyed by an answer may affect the very priors in relation to which the probability of the answer is to be judged.

A few general remarks are still in order. First, even apart from the line of thought presented here, I find the Tversky-Kahneman discussion of the conjunction effect less than satisfying. They claim that certain human judgments are fallacious. Such a claim is only the first word on the subject, not the last one. For if it were true, it would pose the even more intriguing question: How come? How can it be that humans, including trained specialists, commit such elementary howlers? What is the psychological mechanism that creates them? In spite of the bulk of the relevant literature, I have not found a theoretically satisfactory explanation in it. In contrast, it seems to me that something like an account along the lines adumbrated here is likely to be acknowledged as being fairly commonsensical when it is explained to people. Hence the gist of what I am arguing here is that if this is how the conjunction effect comes about, there is nothing fallacious about it.

There is one more interesting general feature of the conjunction effect that deserves attention. In the psychological experiments concerning the conjunction fallacy, subjects are asked to make a spontaneous "intuitive" judgment about certain probabilities. In contrast, I have described a moderately complex line of discursive reasoning that leads to the same judgment as the "conjunction effect." Am I talking about the same thing as the experimentalists?

Yes, I am, as one will realize as soon as one sees that what masquerades as a spontaneous "intuitive" judgment is often only the tip of a discursive iceberg. There is no more contradiction in my analysis of the apparently spontaneous conjunction affect in terms of changes of prior probabilities than there is in Sherlock Holmes's calling his acknowledgment of Dr. Watson's recent sojourn in Afghanistan an "intuition" even though it is accompanied by an explicit description of the discursive reasoning that led him to that conclusion.

I have discussed how so-called intuitions often hide unconscious reasoning processes in Hintikka 2000. It might very well be a wiser approach to the cognitive "fallacies" to try to analyze what actually goes into them rather than to attribute them to hardwired human biases.

References

Aristotle, 1991, *On Rhetoric*, newly translated by George A. Kennedy, Oxford University Press, New York.

Bell, D. E., H. Raiffa, and A. Tversky, editors, 1988, *Decision Making: Descriptive, Normative, and Prescriptive Interactions*, Cambridge University Press, Cambridge.

Carnap, Rudolf, 1952, *The Continuum of Inductive Methods*, University of Chicago Press, Chicago.

Gigerenzer, Gerd, 1991, 'How to Make Cognitive Illusions Disappear: Beyond "Heuristic Biases,"' in W. Stroebe and M. Hewstone, editors, *European Review of Social Psychology*, vol. 2, John Wiley, New York, pp. 83–115.

Hintikka, Jaakko, 2000, "The Theory-Ladenness of Intuitions," in F. Beets and E. Gillet, editors, *Logique en Perspective*, Ouisia, Bruxelles, pp. 259–287.

Hintikka, Jaakko, 1995, "On Proper (Popper?) and Improper Uses of Information in Epistemology," *Theoria*, vol. 59, pp. 158–165 (for 1993, appeared 1995).

Hintikka, Jaakko, 1993, "Socratic Questioning, Logic, and Rhetoric," *Revue Internationale de Philosophie*, vol. 47, pp. 5–30.

Hintikka, Jaakko, 1992, "The Concept of Induction in the Light of the Interrogative Approach to Inquiry," in John Earman, editor, *Inference, Explanation, and Other Frustrations: Essays in the Philosophy of Science*, University of California Press, Berkeley, pp. 23–43.

Hintikka, Jaakko, I. Halonen, and A. Mutanen, 1999, "Interrogative Logic as a General Theory of Reasoning," in R. Johnson and J. Woods, editors, *Handbook of Applied Logic*, Kluwer Academic, Dordrecht, pp. 295–337.

Kahneman, D., P. Slovic, and A. Tversky, editors, 1982, *Judgment under Uncertainty: Heuristics and Biases*, Cambridge University Press, Cambridge.

Moser, P. K., editor, 1990, *Rationality in Action: Contemporary Approaches*, Cambridge University Press, Cambridge.

Newton, Isaac, 1952, *Opticks*, Dover, New York.

Piatelli-Palmerini, Massimo, 1994, *Inevitable Illusions*, John Wiley, New York.

Savage, L. J., et al., 1962, *The Foundations of Statistical Inference*, John Wiley, New York.

Tversky, A., and D. Kahneman, 1983, "Extensional Versus Intuitive Reasoning: The Conjunction Fallacy in Probability Judgment," *Psychological Review*, vol. 90, pp. 293–315.

10

Omitting Data—Ethical or Strategic Problem?

In discussions of the ethics of science, the practice of omitting data, also referred to often as "data selection," has played a significant role as an interesting test case of real or alleged scientific fraud. Babbage's classic taxonomy of scientific frauds distinguishes three kinds of such fraud—to wit, "forging," "cooking," and "trimming" of data. The meaning of these terms is obvious, with omitting data as a clear-cut case of cooking. In the literature dealing with dishonesty in science, several prominent scientists have been accused of omitting data, among them no lesser a figure than Isaac Newton, who has been charged with maintaining the impossibility of an achromatic lens while in possession of evidence suggesting the possibility of such a lens. (See Bechler 1975; Kohn 1988, 36–39.) The most thoroughly analyzed case is undoubtedly Robert A. Millikan's famous oil drop experiment, which helped him to earn a Nobel Prize. (See Franklin 1981 and 1986, ch. and 229–232; Holton 1978; Broad and Wade 1982, 34–36.) As is well known, Millikan's experiments aimed principally at measuring the electric charge, e. They "depended on introducing droplets of liquid into the electric field and noting the strength of the field necessary to keep them suspended." (Broad and Wade 1982, 34.) Contrary to his public pronouncements, Millikan excluded as many as 49 observations out of a total of 140. Because of this, one author concludes that "Millikan's selective reporting of his results . . . [does] not conform with the norms and ethics of science, and . . . [is to] be branded as misconduct." (Kohn 1988, 62.)

In this chapter, I will argue that the entire matter of data omission is a much more complicated matter epistemologically than has been realized, which makes both ethical and methodological judgments much more difficult than most writers assume.

But where do we find the tools needed for an adequate analysis of the problem of data omission? The traditional approaches to scientific method do not help us very much. By and large, they encourage a judgmental attitude to the practice of omitting data, in that a typical picture of scientific inference depicts

221

a step from particular data to a generalization or law. In such a perspective, omitting data looks suspicious indeed.

A more useful approach is to conceptualize knowledge-seeking in general, and scientific inquiry in particular, as a series of questions put to a source of answers, which in the case of empirical science is nature. Indeed, the idea of thinking of scientific experiments as questions put to nature goes back to Bacon and Kant. However, it has been made precise only recently when an explicit logic of questions and answers has been developed. I have been advocating this approach for a while (see, e.g., Hintikka 1999) and I have referred to it as the "interrogative model of inquiry." It has among other things led to interesting insights into the role of mathematical and other conceptual knowledge in experimental science (Chapter 5 in this volume). The greatest merit of the interrogative model is, nevertheless, that it enables us to consider scientific inquiry as a process, so that we can, for instance, apply to it strategic concepts and distinguish between different types of questioning processes. These features of the interrogative model turn out to be helpful in discussing the data omission problem.

One obvious distinction we have to make is between what might be called "definitory rules" of the process and its "strategic rules." The distinction can in fact be made in all strategic games studied—for instance, in game theory. On the one hand, there are the rules that specify which moves the players are allowed to make and what counts as winning and losing, and more generally what the payoffs are. On the other hand, there are the strategic rules that tell a player how to play the game successfully. The distinction is obvious in games such as chess, but it can also be made in "games" such as theorem-proving in logic and in the "game" of interrogative inquiry. It is important to realize that strategic rules need not be merely heuristic. They can in principle (albeit usually not in applications) be as sharp and explicit as the definitory rules.

Interestingly, it turns out that the so-called rules of inference in logic are definitory rather than strategic. They do not say anything about which inferences a logician ought to make in a given situation—that is, given a number of potential premises. They only specify which inferences a logician may draw without committing a fallacy.

The basic features of a game of inquiry are clear. A play of the game begins with a number of initial premises. Whenever the presupposition of a question has been established, the inquirer may ask it. If an answer is forthcoming, it is added to the list of available premises. (This presupposes, of course, an analysis of the question–answer relation and a specification as to which answers are available in the particular game in question.) Such interrogative moves can be interspersed by logical inference moves. In the case of scientific inquiry, typical answers are outcomes of observations and experiments.

This model is not only simple, it is also safe, in that it does not involve much idealization. It might at first sight be doubted whether it can throw much light on issues in the philosophy of science. Yet, perhaps surprisingly, even merely considering its gross features it puts problems such as data omission in a new light even though the description of interrogative inquiry just given obviously needs further elaboration.

In a typical application of interrogative inquiry—for instance in the cross-examination of a witness in a court of law—the inquirer cannot simply accept all answers at their face value. They can be false. Hence we must have rules allowing the rejection or, as I will call it, the "bracketing of an answer," and rules governing such bracketing.

But this seems totally unrealistic. How can we possibly hope to formulate realistic rules for the rejection or acceptance of any answers—any data—that an inquirer might ever receive? I reply with a question: rules of what kind? Strategic rules will obviously be difficult to formulate, but that is simply the difficulty in question in the problem of finding the right research strategies. That is a problem we can hope to study but not to solve in one fell swoop. But what I was looking for are only definitory rules of scientific inquiry—that is, rules that merely tell what an inquirer may do. And for the bracketing of answers, all that is enough is merely to allow bracketing and naturally, also allow unbracketing at some later stage of inquiry. What is involved here is merely the perfectly commonplace idea that the answers that an inquirer receives can be tested—and often must be tested—for their veracity by means of further questions and answers. A witness's testimony in a court of law is tested by comparing it with other kinds of testimony and with the "answers" that take the form of physical evidence. The same holds, of course, for scientific inquiry: The "answer" (result) yielded by one experiment is tested by repeating the same experiment or by performing a collateral one.

Thus we have already reached an interesting insight. From the point of view of the interrogative model—and there does not seem to be a more realistic general methodological theory available—a decision to omit (or not to omit) data is a strategic decision, not a matter of what a scientist must or must not do. This does not mean that omitting data is not often fraudulent in purpose. It means that what is involved can be, as Talleyrand said, worse than a crime—to wit, a mistake. Certainly a blanket injunction never to omit data cannot be part of any realistic methodology or any ethics of science. This suggests strongly that the entire issue of data omission has to be reconsidered, for omitting data is generally considered to be automatically forbidden. This issue is much more complicated. I will argue that this implication of the interrogative model agrees well with scientific practice.

So how are we to look at actual cases of scientific investigation? For instance, what is there to be said of Millikan's procedure? First, everybody agrees that if a scientist has reasons to think that something has gone wrong in an experiment or observation, he or she has every right to disregard the result. This can be thought of as a part of the definitory rules of scientific procedure, which already for this reason must allow certain types of data omission. In Millikan's case, the 140 observations were all supposed to have been made after he had convinced himself that he had worked the earlier bugs out of his experimental apparatus. Yet in 2 cases, the apparatus malfunctioned, and 5 were omitted because of observational problems. And 12 were excluded for reasons to do with the calculation of the value of e from observations. None of these decisions to omit is objectionable methodologically or ethically. In 22 experiments, Millikan did not calculate e, and accordingly these played no part in his argument—they did not produce any data to be omitted. And 2 were dropped for no obvious reason.

That leaves 6 interesting cases. In 5 of them, "Millikan not only calculated a value of e but compared it with an expected value.... His only evident reason for rejecting these five events is that their values did not agree with his expectations.... This is a clear case of trimming." (Franklin 1986, p. 230.) Here we have in fact a beautiful case of the strategic nature of data omission. What was the strategic situation that Millikan was in? Apparently he had strong theoretical reasons to think that the value of e was a constant. Even if this were not unequivocally the case historically, let us assume for the sake of argument that it was the case. He also had a body of data that suggested an approximate value of e. Now he makes an observation that gives a value distinctly different from that approximate value. What is he to do? In view of his theoretical background, the fact that the result differs from the others is *ipso facto* a danger sign. It suggests that there might be something wrong with the exceptional observation. This is a perfectly rational suggestion. It illustrates a phenomenon that has not received sufficient attention on the part of philosophers of science but that is studied in Chapter 9. It is brought out beautifully by the interrogative model. This model, unlike typical Bayesian ones, is not predicated on fixed *a priori* probabilities. Indeed, all that bracketing means is changing the prior probabilities that the inquirer associates with the different answers. The intriguing phenomenon here is that an answer can affect its own probability—for instance, by cohering or not cohering with the other answers the inquirer has already obtained.

This is precisely what is going on in the case of Millikan's 5 rejected droplets. The very fact that the values they yield differ significantly from the other ones is a rational ground for being suspicious of them. Omitting (bracketing) such data is therefore a strategic decision that can be fully justified. Such an omission can in fact improve the estimated value obtained from the different experiments and observations. In Millikan's case, it did not change his overall result very much. (See Franklin 1986, 230). There are, in this case, absolutely no reasons to criticize Millikan methodologically or ethically.

This does not close the ethical issue, however. Here, the strategic viewpoint again suggests an interesting insight. In the philosophy of science, a distinction is often made between contexts of discovery and contexts of justification. Different criteria are supposed to be in operation in the two kinds of contexts. In the actual practice of science, the same process usually serves both the making of a discovery and the justification of it. Now we know from game theory, that utilities can in general be assigned, absolutely speaking, only to entire strategies, not to individual moves. Hence the same process must serve both purposes, and the optimal strategies must likewise serve both discovery and justification. If I open an experimental paper in a scientific journal, I expect to find both some results and some reasons to think that they are reliable. Now, omitting data can be amply justified if the inquirer's only purpose is to find the truth. However, the same omission may make the task of judging the level of justification more difficult or even be positively misleading. This is what happened in Millikan's case. Omitting data did not lead him essentially further from truth, even though it did not in this case help him either. However, it did lead him to claim an appreciably smaller statistical error than he was entitled to. Thus, Millikan did not violate the canons of truth-seeking, but he did violate the canons of caution. The peculiar twist in this kind of situation is that one and the same strategy must satisfy both canons. This is one of a number of things that make the judging of data omission difficult. Presumably what Millikan ought to have done is omit the 5 cases but report the omission in estimating his statistical error. However, this is not the kind of procedure that an author of a scientific paper is supposed to follow. Maybe we should in fact rethink the format in which experimental results are being reported.

Even more interesting is the one remaining omission of data. Franklin considers it even more serious. "That event . . . was among Millikan's very best observations. . . . Millikan liked it: 'Publish. Fine for showing two methods. . . .' When Millikan calculated e for the event, he found a value some 40 per cent lower than his other values. He dismissed the event with the comment 'Won't work' and did not publish it." This looks like a barefaced case of cooking the data.

However, once again the situation is more complicated than first appears. Here we in fact come to an interesting further strategic question. If an experiment is a question put to nature, we have to ask: What was the question that Millikan was putting to nature? There are two possible questions that are not exclusive:

(a) What is the value of e?
(b) Does electric charge always come in multiples of one and the same charge?

I have been assuming so far that (a) is the question. If so, Millikan had good reasons to be suspicious of the odd observation. In order to see this, we might indulge in virtual history and imagine that one of Millikan's oil drops had yielded a value of e that is about twice his other results. Should he have included it among his other data in his calculations? Obviously not. He would undoubtedly have concluded that the droplet in question had two electrons in place of one. He would even be justified in adding a value half of the observed one to his data.

Somewhat in the same way, in the case of the observed fractional value of *e*, Millikan could simply have said something like: "Maybe in some cases, electric charge comes in some unknown fraction of *e*. Maybe I have observed such a case. But such observations are irrelevant to my purpose of measuring *e*." There is no actual evidence that this is how Millikan thought about the situation. But he would have been entitled to reason that way, and hence entitled to bracket the anomalous observation, even though he thought that it was correctly made. And, if so, we cannot convict Millikan of a violation of the ethics of science.

In this direction, we nevertheless run into another problem complex. It is the problem as to what to do with *prima facie* counterexamples to a theory, sometimes known as anomalies. For instance, should we bracket them, at least temporarily, should we try to explain them in terms of the old theory by means of supplementary inquiry, or should we try to find a better theory to account for them? These questions are strategic ones, and hence do not affect the ethics of science, my overall topic here.

However, if Millikan's overall "principal question" included (b), and if he were trying to prove that electric charge is quantized in the sense of assuming only values that are multiples of *e*, the situation would be different. Then the odd fractional observation could have been a potential counterexample, and it would have been serious cooking of the data to omit that observation.

It is indeed known that some sub-atomic particles do have fractional charges such as 1/3 *e* or 2/3 *e*. Furthermore, the question has been raised as to whether Millikan might have in fact observed such a fractional charge. Even though it is very unlikely that that would have in fact happened (Franklin 1986, 157–164), that judgement is wisdom by hindsight, and does not change Millikan's methodological situation. In particular, it does not change the judgment that if Millikan had been trying to prove the quantization of electric charge, he would have been guilty of cooking his data.

From the strategic point of view, this is all a straightforward consequence of the interrogative approach. The strategies of a player depend on his or her payoffs—in plain English, on what the player is trying to achieve. The evaluation of Millikan's procedure thus depends crucially on what overall question he was putting to nature—not that he was necessarily clear on the matter himself.

Thus the evaluation of data omission is both ethically and strategically a much more complicated matter than has generally been assumed. In particular, such omission is not always forbidden, but on the contrary can be called for by sound strategic principles. The way all this follows from, and is put in an interesting framework by, the interrogative model helps one to appreciate the power of this model to illuminate the actual methodology of science in a realistic manner.

References

Babbage, C., 1830, *Reflections on the Decline of Science in England and on Some of Its Causes*, B. Fellowes, London.

Bechler, Z., 1975, "'A Less Agreeable Matter': The Disagreeable Case of Newton and Achromatic Refraction," *British Journal for the History of Science*, vol. 8, pp. 101–126.

Broad, W. and Wade, N., 1982, *Betrayers of the Truth: Fraud and Deceit in the Halls of Science*, Simon & Schuster, New York.

Franklin, A., 1981, "Millikan's Published and Unpublished Data on Oil Drops," *Historical Studies in the Physical Sciences*, vol. 11, pp. 185–201.

Franklin, A., 1986, *The Neglect of Experiment*, Cambridge University Press, Cambridge.

Hintikka, J., 2004, "A Fallacious Fallacy?" *Synthese*, vol. 140, pp. 25–35. And as Chapter 9 in this volume.

Hintikka, J., 1999, *Inquiry as Inquiry (Selected Papers,)* Vol. 5, Kluwer Academic, Dordrecht.

Holton, G., 1978, "Subelectrons, Presuppositions, and the Millikan–Ehrenhaft dispute," *Historical Studies in the Physical Sciences*, vol. 9, pp. 166–224.

Kohn, A., 1988, *False Prophets: Fraud and Error in Science and Medicine*, revised edition, Barnes and Noble, New York.

Index